Being a University

W0007232

There is no single idea of the university. Ever since its medieval origin, the concept of the university has continued to change. The metaphysical university gave way successively to the scientific university, and then to the corporate and the entrepreneurial university. But what might lie ahead?

Being a University charts and critiques this conceptual development and examines the future possibilities for the idea of the university. Ronald Barnett pursues this quest through an exploration of pairs of contending concepts that speak to the idea of the university – such as space and time; being and becoming; and culture and anarchy. On this foundation is developed an imaginative exposition of possible ideas of the university, including *the liquid university* and *the authentic university*.

In the course of this inquiry, it is argued that:

- Any thought that the idea of the entrepreneurial university represents the endpoint of the evolution of the idea of the university has to be abandoned. The entrepreneurial university is excessively parochial and ill-matched to the challenges facing the university.
- A responsibility of the university is precisely that of working out an imaginative conception of its future possibilities. The boldest and largest thinking is urgently required.
- The fullest expression of the university's possibilities lies in the reclamation of the universal aspirations that lay in earlier ideas of the university. *The ecological university* represents just such a universal aspiration, suited to the unfolding demands of the future.

Being a University should be essential reading for all professionals and academics in Higher Education, as well as those with an interest in educational policy and politics, and the philosophy, sociology and theory of education.

Ronald Barnett is recognised as one of the world's leading scholars of higher education and the university. He is Emeritus Professor of Higher Education at the Institute of Education, University of London, UK, and is a writer, speaker and consultant on higher education matters.

Foundations and Futures of Education

Series Editors:

Peter Aggleton *School of Education and Social Work, University of Sussex, UK*
Sally Power *Cardiff University, UK*
Michael Reiss *Institute of Education, University of London, UK*

Foundations and Futures of Education focuses on key emerging issues in education as well as continuing debates within the field. The series is inter-disciplinary, and includes historical, philosophical, sociological, psychological and comparative perspectives on three major themes: the purposes and nature of education; increasing interdisciplinarity within the subject; and the theory-practice divide.

Previous titles include:

Language, Learning, Context
Wolff-Michael Roth

Learning, Context and the Role of Technology
Rosemary Luckin

Education and the Family
Passing success across the generations
Leon Feinstein, Kathryn Duckworth and Ricardo Sabates

Education, Philosophy and the Ethical Environment
Graham Haydon

Educational Activity and the Psychology of Learning
Judith Ireson

Schooling, Society and Curriculum
Alex Moore

Gender, Schooling and Global Social Justice
Elaine Unterhalter

Education – An 'Impossible Profession'?
Tamara Bibby

School and Schooling in the Digital Age
Neil Selwyn

Forthcoming titles include:

Irregular Schooling
Roger Slee

School Trouble
Deborah Youdell

The Struggle for the History of Education
Gary McCulloch

Being a University

Ronald Barnett

Routledge
Taylor & Francis Group

LONDON AND NEW YORK

First edition published 2011
by Routledge
2 Park Square, Milton Park, Abingdon, Oxon, OX14 4RN

Simultaneously published in the USA and Canada
by Routledge
711 Third Avenue, New York, NY 10017

Routledge is an imprint of the Taylor & Francis Group, an informa business

© 2011 Ronald Barnett

Typeset in Garamond by Swales & Willis Ltd, Exeter, Devon

British Library Cataloguing in Publication Data
A catalogue record for this book is available from the British Library

Library of Congress Cataloging-in-Publication Data
Barnett, Ronald, 1947–
    Being a university / Ronald Barnett.
    p. cm.
    Includes bibliographical references and index.
    1. Education, Higher—Aims and objectives. 2. Universities and colleges—Philosophy.
    3. Postmodernism and education. I. Title.
    LB2322.2.B36 2011
    378.001—dc22
    2010020494

ISBN13: 978–0–415–59266–6 (hbk)
ISBN13: 978–0–415–59268–0 (pbk)
ISBN13: 978–0–203–84248–5 (ebk)

To the memory of my mother,
Mildred Barnett (1910–2009)

Being is still waiting for the time when it will become thought-provoking to man.

(Martin Heidegger, 'Letter on Humanism', in *Basic Writings*, 2007: 227)

Does anything remain upon which an integrating self-understanding of universities could be founded?

(Jürgen Habermas, 'The Idea of the University:
Learning Processes', 1987: 3–22)

Humanity is in crisis, how many academics actually talk about the crisis of humanity, what are the causes of this crisis? How many academics see themselves as part of the crisis of humanity?

(Roy Bhaskar, *From Science to Emancipation,* 2002: 65)

The universality of the contemporary disaster necessarily implies immediate radical reform of the University.

(Paul Virilio, *The University of Disaster,* 2010: 117)

Rare are those who dare even to dream utopian dreams about possible alternatives.

(Slavoj Žižek, *First as Tragedy, Then as Farce,* 2009: 77)

Contents

Acknowledgements

Writing a book always owes much to many individuals beyond the writer. It is a pleasure to record my warm thanks and appreciation in a number of ways.

First, my thanks go to the academic editors of the Routledge series in which this book appears, namely Peter Aggleton, Sally Powers and Michael Reiss, who first invited me to submit a proposal and then saw in my proposal a possible book that might do justice to their Foundations and Futures of Education series. I am especially appreciative of the care and helpfulness with which Michael and Peter – in taking responsibility for this particular volume – have worked through my manuscript, offering me detailed suggestions and encouragement.

I want also to thank Denise Batchelor, Glynis Cousin, Joelle Fanghanel, Carolin Kreber, and Jon Nixon, who kindly took up my enquiry to them to read and comment on the manuscript. Their efforts and their advice have been offered to me with such generosity. I just hope that they will forgive me for not doing full justice to their many ideas, which I continue to dwell on in a spirit of friendly dialogue.

A project of this magnitude is stimulated and sustained also by conversations over several years, some of which bear directly on the text and some of which are more indirect, offering encouragement in all manner of ways. Friends and colleagues whose conversations have been helpful here include Bahram Bekhradnia, Roy Bhaskar, Bob Burgess, John Brennan, Roger Brown, Bob Cowen, Rob Cuthbert, Gloria Dall'Alba, Eric Garcia, Neil Garrod, Claudius Gellert, Beena Giridharan, Lesley Gourlay, Lucy Green, Mary Henkel, Yvonne Hillier, Ana Hoyos Gonzalez, Peter Jarvis, Gunther Kress, Donna Lamping, Sue Law, Richard Lewis, Ingrid Lunt, Bruce Macfarlane, Nick Maxwell, Rajani Naidoo, Gareth Parry, Michael Peters, Alison Phipps, Stephen Rowland, Paul Standish, Marilyn Strathern, Peter Scott, Bill Taylor, Ted Tapper, Paul Temple, Simeon Underwood, David Watson, Gareth Williams, Geoff Whitty, Gina Wisker, Michael Worton, and John Wyatt.

I should also like to express my appreciation of the assistance that I have received from Iris Cheung, especially in helping me and never losing patience with my bibliographic queries and also for her own comments on the manuscript.

I am also very happy to record my thanks for the following permissions:

As the basis for Chapter 3, R. Barnett (2005) 'Convergence in Higher Education: The Strange Case of "Entrepreneurialism"', *Higher Education Management and Policy*, 17(3), Paris: OECD Publishing, www.oecd.org/edu/imhe/journal.

As the basis for a section in Chapter 6, three paragraphs from my introduction to R. Barnett (ed.) (2005) *Reshaping the University: New Relationships between Research, Scholarship and Teaching*, Maidenhead: McGraw-Hill/Open University Press, pp. 7–8.

I would want, also, to express my warm appreciation to Anna Clarkson, Senior Publisher at Routledge and who oversees the series in which this book appears. Probably without realising it, Anna has been very helpful to me in quietly encouraging my efforts.

Lastly, through her interest in this book, our many conversations and unflagging cheerfulness, a big thank you to Elisabeth Wigley, who has both ensured that my own energies for this project have never faltered and has stimulated many of the ideas here.

I remain, of course, entirely responsible for the errors and omissions that must surely still be present.

Ronald Barnett

Introduction
Being possible

Being a university

What is it to *be* a university? What might such an institution become? Are there forms of 'university' that are emerging and which should attract our concern? Are there kinds of 'university' that we can barely glimpse and that we might favour, that we might even encourage?

This, then, is the territory of this book; nothing other than the *being of the university*. Why put the matter in this rather formal way? Why not speak of 'the idea of the university' or 'the purposes of the university' or even 'the functions of the university'? I put it in this way because I want to indicate that the university has possibilities in front of it. It could be other than it is. Universities could be other than *they* are.[1]

These suggestions may seem awkward. There is here perhaps an uneasy juxtaposition of the university as an idea and universities as real social institutions. However, this juxtaposition – of idea and reality – will be an abiding feature of the explorations in this book. For I want precisely to confront the reality of universities as they have been, are now and are becoming with ideas as to how they could *go forward*. We cannot make judgements on how matters are in the world unless we have to hand ideas that can serve as a basis for critical standards. Here, then, is the first feature of this inquiry, a juxtaposition of ideas about the university and an understanding of how universities have been and are developing in actual fact.

Another feature of this inquiry is also to hand. For over a hundred and fifty years, it has been acceptable to talk of 'the idea of the university'. Now, that phrasing, with its implication that there is or could be simply a single idea of the university, is problematic. It is not only that, with the arrival of mass higher education systems around the world, we are witnessing many different kinds of institutions bearing the name 'university'. More pertinent still is a point about ideas as such. It is that, given the complexity of modern society, there will be many ideas as to what it is to be a university. The point is crucial for these explorations, for it implies that there are different ideas of the university that may claim attention. In turn, it is unlikely that any single institution can be a pure instantiation of any one idea of the university; different ideas of the university are likely to reside in the one institution. But, still, we can identify different ideas of the university and engage with them one by one.

A third feature of this inquiry follows on and picks up on the idea of being. 'Being' was perhaps the central category for Heidegger. For Heidegger, 'being' was always 'being possible' (Heidegger, [1927] 1998: 183).[2] Being was replete with potentiality. Here is a further reason why we can speak of the being of the university. For that phrase suggests the 'being possible' of the university; the possibilities that lie ahead of the university. What *are* the options before universities? What range of ideas might helpfully come into view as we survey the potentialities that lie within universities? What is their being in this sense? And so our inquiry is here, in the here-and-now, but it is also in the future, the *possible-future*. It is also in the past since we cannot understand universities unless we have some understanding of their origin and distant past. Even new universities are likely to be influenced by continuing sediments of the idea of the university. So, this inquiry must have time horizons to it, as it surveys the past, present and emerging forms that the university has acquired *and may acquire in the future*.

That consideration leads us to a final feature of this inquiry. For being, understood as being-possible, opens up the idea of *becoming*. Being cannot be understood without a sense of its unfolding, of its becoming. And so it is with universities. To comprehend their being implies a sense of their becoming, their possibilities and their movement over time towards their possibilities. But becoming is not a neutral concept: it is value-laden; value-saturated indeed. Becoming implies *fully* becoming. To speak, therefore, of a university's becoming implies a full realisation of *its* potentialities. So in front of us must lie a search for what it might be for universities – albeit in a broad-brush sense – to realise their possibilities. What, in short, might it be for a university fully to *be* a university? The past and the present can inform; but the idea of the university has continually to be revisited and re-imagined.

These, then, are the ingredients of this inquiry: first, a juxtaposition of the idea of the university with observations on universities as they are; second, an understanding that the idea of the university is a problematic idea and that any meta-idea of the university may be a mirage; third, a search for ideas of the university that may be realised and which we may want to endorse; and finally, an inquiry into the fullest forms of realising the university in the world, if their being and their becoming are to attain their full potential.

Ideas of the university

This book is a continuation of a journey on which I embarked in 1990, with my first book, *The Idea of Higher Education*. In several books since, I have characterised my work as social philosophy. In trying to understand universities and higher education, I start from a recognition that they are social institutions, concretely existing in the world. So there is an onus on any speculative inquiry to try to understand something as to how universities and higher education actually are. In turn, it becomes a not unimportant matter to be clear about the distinction between concepts and institutions.[3]

The terms 'university' and 'higher education' are often run together (in the UK at least), with little, if any, distinction being made between them. In this conflation, the term 'higher education' is often asked to do duty for both 'university' and 'higher education'. But this is to do injury to both concepts. 'Higher education' is an educational process that may or may not be found in universities: it is a *critical* concept that provides standards such that educational processes in universities (or institutions of higher education for that matter) can be assessed as to the extent to which they fulfil the criteria implied in the idea of higher education. We may judge that institutions of higher education, including universities, do not always provide a 'higher education' to their students, whatever this idea is taken to be.

But to conflate 'university' and 'higher education' is to do injury also to the nature of universities as institutions. For a university is a complex entity which is far from exhausted by talk of 'higher education'. Many other academic and developmental activities, other than higher education, are to be found within it. And this complexity grows. To teaching and learning in the university have been successively added over the centuries scholarship, research, consultancy, knowledge transfer and public engagement, and several other functions as well. Hence the emergence in the 1960s and 1970s of terms such as 'the multiversity' (Kerr, [1963] 1995) and 'the mega-university'.[4] The university is not to be confused, therefore, with higher education,[5] and the idea of the university, accordingly, deserves our conceptual and speculative attentions no less than does the idea of higher education.

It is the actual character of universities, therefore, that sets the scene for these reflections. The more philosophical, the more speculative, inquiry works in that context. It has to work in that context in order that any possibilities that are envisaged have a degree of feasibility to them. Unless this criterion of feasibility is satisfied, two dangers loom. First, and self-evidently, forthcoming proposals may not be feasible. They may have a castles-in-the-air quality. They just never could be realised, being mere fanciful dreams, unlinked to reality. Second, they may be ideological, serving narrow interests. So by being tested against reality, against the ways in which universities and their practices actually are, our ideas for their future development may have some possibility of being ideologically light, even if they can never be ideologically free.[6]

At the heart of my previous work has been an effort to argue for and to show that our ideas about and our practices in higher education could be other than they are. To that end, I have tried to explore, develop and even create concepts that may provide resources for going forward in a better way.[7] Whether it is quality arrangements, curricula, the forms of learning encouraged among students, teaching approaches, the kinds of knowledge that are sought, or management practices and conceptions of leadership: all these and other aspects of universities, I have sought to show, could be construed and conducted in different ways; and better ways.

In finding inspiration for the ideas that I have developed, I have drawn especially on philosophy and social theory.[8] As a result, the ideas for which I have contended could have been purely abstract, with the reader left to fathom what, if any, application to the real world of universities and higher education there might be. Here lies another reason for trying to show the cash value of my thinking. I have long held the belief, especially in regard to a social institution such as education, that intellectuals have a responsibility to indicate the implications of their ideas – if any – for our actual practices.

Feasible utopias

There is a further and even more compelling reason for my trying to bring my reflections into close company with actual practices in universities. My work has been a search for what might be termed *feasible utopias*.[9] By 'feasible utopias' I mean this. Our lives and our institutions are played out amid structures of various kinds – social, cultural, international, ideological – but they are not entirely determined: we have options before us. My work, therefore, constitutes an attempt both to set out the general character of the structures in which universities and higher education are placed and, more importantly, to identify *positive options* that are available in that context.

The options for which I have argued in my books are utopian, in that they are precisely not the present situation, and probably are unlikely ever to be fully realised, given the structures of power and ideology at work. However, I have tried to show that these utopias are not entirely fanciful for the depictions that I have conjured can already be glimpsed in our daily practices in universities and higher education. They are, therefore, *feasible* utopias. In the best of all *possible* worlds, they could just be realised even if it is unlikely that they will be.[10]

My work, therefore, has been primarily speculative in searching out for more humane ways of conceiving of and of taking forward universities and their major practices. I have sought, through an exploration and development of key concepts, to set out a picture of how things might be in the best of all *possible* worlds, so far as universities and higher education are concerned.

This project has also been inescapably *critical*. In arguing for certain kinds of ideas of the university and its associated academic practices, I have both implicitly and often explicitly confronted current conceptions and practices. I have tried to point up the pernicious nature of the ideologies that bear in on universities at present.[11] This critical dimension has, in turn, helped to open the terrain for the more positive and creative conceptions that I have put forward.

Towards the ecological university

Despite the exigencies of markets, entrepreneurialism, bureaucracy and globalisation and shifting knowledge structures and identity structures that characterise universities, they still have options before them. There are spaces into which they can move. So there is an ethical space in which universities have their being, whether they acknowledge this or not. Each university is responsible in part for its own form and character. Universities have, therefore, *responsibilities*. Those responsibilities derive partly from a sense as to what it means to be a university in the modern era. The idea of the university lives on.

The modern university lives amid multiple networks.[12] This 'networked university' forms ever more networks. But to what end should the university be developing its relationships? What are its responsibilities in the matter? Is the university simply to concentrate, say, on developing links with the business and industrial sectors and on developing its position in the academic marketplace, or are there other possibilities for its networking? And what values might inform this networking? It should do this – I shall argue – as part of its potential role not merely in engaging with the public sphere but in *enhancing* the public sphere.

A helpful metaphor for exploring these matters may be that of ecology. 'Ecology' points to systems of relationships between organisms and their environment. The term has also come to have positive value attached to it, in the wake of environmental degradation. Accordingly, the *ecological university* is one that takes seriously its relationships with its total environment and it does what it can to further the wellbeing of that total environment. The ecological university cares about its environment. And since the environment of universities is global (as well as regional and local), the ecological university has a care towards the whole world.[13] The ecological university does what it can, within its compass, to be a good for the world.[14]

Tone

Any book has a certain tone but describing that tone poses difficulty, not least for the author. But in a field – such as educational studies – where tone is to some extent an open matter, the reader is perhaps entitled to some sense of the character of the journey ahead. I would suggest the following of this book. It has a philosophical pitch since, after all, it is grappling with the most fundamental issues concerning the purposes of the university and its future possibilities. But the book is, I hope the reader will find, full of practical examples – and even a little empirical evidence – to support the argument being made. The argument itself is also carried forward with a certain determination. I hope, nevertheless, that readers will feel that the argument is measured, for I bring forward and weigh possible nuances and even counter-views. But I am pressing an argument of my own through to the final chapter.

Occasionally, I suggest possible weaknesses in the viewpoints of other scholars but I am not primarily here engaging in critical exegesis. Partly, this reticence is a matter of personal taste: I am not keen to criticise the efforts of other scholars and writers, all of whose work I admire in some ways. Partly, this is a matter of wanting to press on and developing the argument. I believe that the matters I am engaging with here require urgent attention and the matters in question are so important and the forces against which I contend so formidable that any counter-argument, if it is to be effective, has itself to be pressed with some degree of determination. Partly, I want to offer the reader an uncluttered text which strikes out boldly for a particular viewpoint. (Readers who want to go more deeply into the issues are invited to delve into the notes and the links there to the bibliography.)

But there is another dimension to the tone. My argument here accords a large space to the imagination for it is part of the argument here that we desperately need more imagination to be brought to bear in identifying new ideas for the development of the university. Accordingly, I have wanted to give myself some space in which – doubtless rather inadequately – I stretch my own imagination in conjuring possibilities for the university. There is, admittedly, therefore a personal tone to the journey here. It may be felt, too, that there is some passion but hopefully it will also be sensed as controlled passion as ideas are brought forward and evaluated.

In a book of this kind, too, there are always difficulties of language. I hope that the way I use language will become apparent. This is primarily an exploration of possibilities for the university. If, therefore, I use a formulation such as 'The university is a space for imagining', this is to be understood as an expression of an idea and of a feasible possibility and not as an empirical statement. This book is also a bringing forward of ideas of the university, future possible ideas indeed, and placing them in the context of the history of and the present nature of universities; in other words, it is a critical juxtaposition of the way universities are with the way that they might be. Consequently, sentences may contain the expressions 'universities' and 'the university' and even 'a university'. I hope that the way the argument runs will indicate just how the different terms are to be interpreted.

It is perhaps worth mentioning here, too, that in using the phrase 'the university', I am not wanting to tie myself to any sense of there being an essence of the university or any one large idea of the university. It is part of the argument here, indeed, that there are *many* ideas of the university both currently and emerging (and reflected even in a single university), even if I also go on to argue for a certain cluster of ideas – of understanding, learning and inquiry – as vital to our understanding of the unfolding university.

Lastly, on the gendered inflexions in the language: the English language is such that it is often difficult to find gender-neutral expressions, without doing injury to the language itself. In previous books, where I have focused on pedagogical matters, in wanting to speak of a hypothetical student, I have often drawn on the personal pronoun 'she', there being no gender-neutral pronoun. Here, though, with my canvas being the university in the whole world, I find myself having to use an expression such as 'humanity'. While sensitive to the occasional gendered character of the text, I do believe in clarity of argument and I hope that the reader will feel able to go with the grain of the text as it flows.

The course of this inquiry

This book is divided into three parts. In *Part I*, I identify and evaluate different forms of being that have characterised the university up to this point. This first part, therefore, is both historical and contemporaneous, and develops the proposition that the idea of the university itself has undergone changes and *continues* to unfold.

In *Chapter 1*, I introduce the idea of *the metaphysical university*. The metaphysical university took its bearings from assumed connections between knowing and an ascent into worlds of pure being. Its forms of knowing offered personal salvation. The question then arises: is the notion of the 'metaphysical university' entirely passé or might it still have meaning for us today? The metaphysical university, I shall suggest in *Chapter 2*, has been succeeded by *the scientific university,* a university that has taken its bearings from a systematic pursuit of knowledge under an interest of control, although the forms of that pursuit are changing. The scientific university is now being overtaken (as the dominant idea of the university) by *the entrepreneurial university*, the subject of *Chapter 3*. This university takes its bearings from a belief that the use value of knowledge should be maximised. Here, 'impact' is a key consideration. In the wake of these developments can be discerned *the bureaucratic university*, the topic of *Chapter 4*. This is a university that takes its bearings from a sense of the university as a corporation, severed from culture, *and* which is coming to rely on strongly managed forms of organisation.

Having identified and critiqued dominant forms of being assumed by the university historically and currently, *Part II* turns to locate and explore key concepts that are embedded within the university's historical forms. This part of the book is a search for large ideas that might help towards an understanding of the wider possibilities in front of universities, beyond those of the contemporary self-understandings of universities. In this way, we may develop resources to build ideas for a fuller development of the university. Each of the four chapters in Part II takes the form of an exploration of the relationships between a pair of concepts that speak to each other and even contend *with* each other: *being* and *becoming*; *space* and *time*; *culture* and *anarchy*; and *authenticity* and *responsibility*.

Building on the conceptual resources opened by the explorations of Part II, I turn, in *Part III*, to identifying possible claimants for the university's proper becoming in the medium to long term. I examine four possible *feasible utopias*: *the liquid university*; *the therapeutic university* (this conception has its critics but I shall advance a defence of a version of it); *the authentic university*; and finally, *the ecological university*. I shall give increasing credence to these conceptions of the university as the chapters proceed. It follows that my greatest allegiance will be to 'the ecological university', a university that is sensitive to its global responsibilities and the possibilities that present for global engagement. It also has room for the most optimistic interpretations of the other three feasible utopias without their limitations.

I conclude with a Coda on 'the spirit of the university'. The ecological university does not just have a spirit of its own but is full of spirit. Spirit will not be confined but leaps out, into the realms of the universal and the infinite. The metaphysical university cannot be resuscitated but, yet, there may still be strains in the idea of the metaphysical that can help the university recover its possibilities. The entrepreneurial university is not the end-point of the unfolding of the university. There are choices before it. However, those choices are not immediately present and so much work lies ahead for the imagination.

Part I

Critiquing being

1 The metaphysical university

Introduction

For two thousand years or more, we were in the presence of the metaphysical university. This was a university that was informed by large ideas as to the relationship between – successively – man and God, man and the universe, man and the State, and man and Spirit. In the West, from the Greeks onwards, but in other traditions of higher learning as well (in Persia, India and China), a full encounter with knowledge was felt to open up new forms of human being. Typically, pure knowing was felt to free one from ignorance and illusion so that one could see the world as it really was. Plato's metaphor of the cave offered a stark image of such a view: being confined within a cave, one had no way of knowing that one's perceptions of the world were but a flickering shadow, without substance, of the world as it was. But with knowledge, one could come into the light. The university came to be understood as an institution through which individuals could come to stand in a new and surer relationship with the world.

Over time, as stated, an encounter with knowledge was variously held to open up a relationship with God, or the universe, or the State or even being itself. The university was the institutional and pedagogic embodiment of such ideas: the university offered salvation in one or other of these forms. These are large and abstract ideas. They are, indeed, metaphysical ideas: they conjure images of entirely new relationships with the supra-sensible order of things. Intellectual activities promised a displacement from the immediate world into a different world, not ordinarily even glimpsed. One might even be tempted to speak of the grand narratives of the university. Here are the big ideas that supplied a legitimacy to what, in largely illiterate societies, were arcane sets of activities.

But what, if anything, might such ideas hold for us today? Can 'the metaphysical university' be helpful to us in the twenty-first century? Surely, such a way of thinking of the university should be abandoned? After all, that whole way of understanding the university was in large part the clerkly class legitimising itself and its activities. Strangely, perhaps, it is just possible that that way of thinking about the university does not have to be abandoned entirely.

Metaphysical or transcendent?

Connected to the idea of the metaphysical is the idea of the transcendent. It could even be suggested that, strictly speaking, instead of 'the metaphysical university', we should rather speak of 'the transcendent university'. 'The metaphysical university' and 'the transcendent university' are overlapping ideas but each has some relevant nuances.

In 'the transcendent university', through his own cognitive efforts, the scholar not only can glimpse an entirely new mode of being above and beyond the immediate world in a non-physical universe but also, through his own cognitive efforts,[1] can embark on a journey into such an ethereal world. The scholar can transcend this rather base world, with its impurities and corruption, and ascend into a pure untainted world of 'scholastic reason' (Bourdieu, 2000); and a world that is ethically superior at that.[2] 'The major philosophical goal of the medieval university . . . was "the pursuit of [divine] truth and learning"' (Scott, 2006: 6–7).[3]

To speak of 'the metaphysical university' can *also* conjure this sense of transcending human experience. However, metaphysics is a broader idea than transcendence. In one of its many meanings, it denotes an 'investigation of the nature, constitution and structure of reality' (Audi, 1999: 563). So the idea of the metaphysical is less value-laden than the idea of the transcendent; it does not presuppose an elevated state of mind although it allows for that to emerge as one possibility. In this sense, metaphysics is a narrower term than transcendence. But it is also a larger term than transcendence in that it conveys a sense of a relationship being opened out with the world as a whole, or at least very large entities in the world. Here, the very term 'metaphysical *university*' gains weight from its affinity with '*universe*', in implying the aim of gaining a cognitive state that is in unity and harmony with the whole universe. The unity of the metaphysical university corresponds to the unity of the universe, for this kind of university is a space for inquiry into every aspect of the universe.

The term 'the metaphysical university' is more helpful, therefore, than 'the transcendent university'. 'Transcendent' presumes the outcome of the (metaphysical) inquiry before it starts, namely that it will offer an elevation into a purer state of mind. On the other hand, the term 'metaphysical' conveys a sense that the non-physical realm to which the university was going to grant access was all-encompassing and is less value-laden than 'transcendent'. I shall, therefore, continue to speak of the metaphysical university.

Where is the mystery?

Why is it that writers have struggled for two centuries or more to elucidate the idea of the university? Even the nature of the task is not clear: is it an exercise in institutional history, in philosophy of education, in sociology, in value judgements, in personal wishful thinking or even perhaps in a poetic prose? What it is to engage in reflection on the idea of the university is an enigmatic matter, at once bewitching and elusive. The very idea *of* the idea of the university has become problematic (Rothblatt, 1997).

One reason for the problematic nature of reflection on the idea of the university is that the nature of the university is partly mysterious. Wherever universities are to be found, the idea of the university speaks to large, even if unspoken and unformulated, ideas as to the nature of man, of being, and of man's relationships with the universe. Furthermore, these ideas may clash. The idea that gaining knowledge and understanding leads to insight into pure forms of being stands in stark contrast to a belief that gaining knowledge and understanding enables man to intervene in the world so as to control it to his own ends. It is, accordingly, impossible to give a full and unambiguous description of the entity that is a university. Hence, the philosopher, Gilbert Ryle, in his giving an allegedly non-explicit response, when asked by an overseas visitor in Oxford 'Where is the University of Oxford?' A university is not to be caught either by a list of its buildings or even – in a straightforward way – a list of its activities. A university is not even to be caught by a more discursive treatment, even by allusion to ideas, sentiments and hopes. It is not that these ideas, sentiments and hopes will clash – which they will – and that no agreed description of the university can be given. (Is the university an engine to help drive the economy forward or is it a major institution to promote enlightenment?) The fact that no consensus can be reached as to the purposes of the university is not the point here. Ultimately, a university is not the kind of entity that can be cashed out fully and adequately in language; it transcends language. It has an ineffable quality about it.

How is this? It is that a university has *being*. A university has its possibilities; *and* they are infinite. It has multiple options. Each university could be other than it is. But yet there are boundaries to what a university might be. Those boundaries have widened and are widening; and are becoming more open to negotiation. But still there are limits. Or, at least, the term 'university' has its place amid a horizon of ideas of university being. These ideas would include knowledge, truth, discussion, inquiry, authenticity, care, understanding, veracity, application, persons, critique, development and action. Strata of being overlay strata. Newer understandings of the university are caught by new clusters of sentiments, as to money, wealth, society, growth, control, problem nets, property, and power. Yet other understandings have formed of late around a sense of rules, regulations, audit, risk, procedures, systems and processes. And yet other understandings can be seen emerging, variously implied by life chances, the digital revolution, public engagement and citizenship.

There are layers attaching to the university's being, therefore. And these layers have time horizons associated with them. The title of Heidegger's ([1927] 1998) magnum opus, *Being and Time*, applies directly to the university. The university's being is in time, backwards and forwards; the past, the present and the future.

There is mystery here. Our words, however poetic, cannot be adequate to this complexity of being. The university eludes us. Descriptions of what it has been and what it is are difficult enough. But the university has its possibilities ahead of it. *Being possible* (Heidegger, 1998: 183). But what is its *being possible*? How is it to go forward? How might it go forward and still do some justice to the very idea of the university?

There is a double mystery here. There is mystery in the colloquial sense. 'It's a mystery' can mean simply that the matter at hand is too complex for our cognitive powers to comprehend it. That has to be the case here. But there is a deeper mystery.

The mystery of the university is that the sentiments, ideals and even practices with which it engages are in themselves mysterious. How is it that new ideas are formed? How is genuine teaching possible, so that students become themselves in new ways? How is it that students by and large maintain their will to go on learning? How is it that academics in different disciplines on occasions detect some rare thread that connects them to colleagues working in other fields such that universities are more than a collection of isolated departments? For all the understanding that we have of these matters, ultimately there is mystery here. In each case – and the cases could be multiplied – we are drawing in fundamental matters of human being, of life, of value.[4] These are not matters that are ever going to be completely susceptible to the empirical study of higher education.

The mystery of the university is ubiquitous, therefore. Wherever we can honestly call an institution 'a university', we are in the presence of mystery. Those fortunate enough to work or to have worked in universities surely know this. The university doubtless falls short of realising its possibilities in every moment but yet they can be glimpsed daily. The university conjures both limits and limitlessness all at once. New ideas appear; students become themselves in new ways and know that that is the case; worthwhile acts are undertaken and played out, without sense of any monetary return. Hovering in the background is a value framework of truth, discovery, service, becoming, friendship, hospitality, care and solicitude, a value background that is seldom articulated or put to the test. And so universities have their being, move from one day to another, on the basis of trust, trust not only between individuals but also as a form of institutional trust that there is substance to this value background. There is mystery in all of these dimensions of the life of universities.

Ending the mystery

Why this reflection on mystery in a chapter on 'the metaphysical university'? The connection is straightforward. In the metaphysical university, it was understood that its being was mysterious; that aspects of its being were beyond formal description and certainly beyond measurement. It was understood that the constitution of the university was layered. Yes, it had a physical presence, with its buildings; and yes, there were persons, masters and scholars, visibly present. But it was also understood that there were non-material presences associated with the university. It is unlikely that the popes and the kings who gave backing to the early universities in the West could have given an articulated account as to their understanding of 'university'.[5] It is true that that the individual colleges of the ancient universities were founded for specific purposes, but they were but a part of the larger university. And there, connotations of God, of service, of new understandings, and of contractual relationships with the wider realm had their presence.

The metaphysical university, therefore, almost by definition, was ultimately mysterious. It was seen as valuable, was granted value, even though full descriptions of it were out of range. They were out of range, admittedly, because in a semi-literate society, few possessed the cognitive and conceptual wherewithal even to essay a description. But anything approaching an articulate description of the metaphysical university was out of range, too. Its accompanying sentiments and insistent murmurings were too large and fuzzy to permit a clear description – a hinterland of God, Spirit, culture, being and the State forbade precision. And these presences worked their wonders to behold. How God, culture, being and the State came into play was never clear. But they were powerful presences none the less; presences that gave not just an extra-mural but an extra-worldly legitimacy to the university. All of that is lost; or almost so.

This is an age of explicitness. Matters have to be susceptible of measurement, of precise descriptions, and of rules, performance against which can be ascertained with objectivity. The assumption at work is that the world is completely available to man's purview: 'transparency' becomes a watchword of this order.[6] It is assumed that, given enough time – though time is seldom on one's side – a full inventory of the world could be made. No entities should or need be left unattended. All can come into our descriptions and measurements. The whole world, the whole universe indeed, can be accounted for.

This is both a modern (that is, post-seventeenth-century) way of understanding the world and man's relationship to it, and it is a particularly Western mode of thinking. On both counts, it is also associated with a scientific outlook and the rise of secularism. In all of this, there is a certain arrogance, with its sense that man can be the measure of all things; that nothing can or should escape his gaze. There need not be nor should there be any mystery left in the universe.

If this holds for the natural world, then it assuredly holds for man's invented social institutions such as universities. The very idea of mystery is repudiated.[7] It has been expunged from our formal language. Universities are now matter-of-fact places. Missions have explicitly to be set out; learning outcomes have to be stated; assessment rules have to be made fully transparent; likely employment routes have to be specified; the impact of research has to be spelt out even in advance of conducting the research; accounts have to rendered and risk has to be computed. Universities are no longer permitted to be places of mystery, of uncertainty, of the unknown. The mystery of universities has ended.

The loss of mystery

This passing of mystery is a double loss. Anyone seeking to suggest that the university is connected with ideas and sentiments that are beyond our descriptions is in for a hard time of it. They will be made to feel uncomfortable as their language discomforts the centres of power. Even talk of 'values' discomforts these days. There is a linguistic power structure at work that rules out a language that is not fully cashable in overt performance and measurement. The 'performative university' rules and with it comes a closing of the categories through which we might comprehend the university.

But this loss of metaphysics and mystery has a further aspect. In this closing of the language through which we can speak of the university, the university is itself diminished. Its possibilities are diminished. In turn, its very being is diminished. How it is, what it is, how it understands itself and its responsibilities in the world: all are diminished. In turn, what it might be, what it might become: these are diminished too.

We perhaps do not readily realise how limiting is this linguistic impoverishment. For in not being able to connect the university with sentiments of being, of spirit, of wonder or even of emancipation, the university shrinks. This is a pragmatic world, of living in this world. Imaginative possibilities for the university close off. Government policy statements on higher education and the future of universities are narrow, with anything in the way of a vision for the possibilities in front of universities being drawn in narrow terms.[8] University mission statements are, hardly surprising in such a context, often bland and relatively uniform.[9] But this failure of imagination, of imagining what a university might become is explicable. The categories with which the drafters of such statements work are themselves limited. The vocabulary is limited. The horizons are limited. The timeframes are limited. The drafting of any policy statement or university-wide strategy, accordingly, is hampered before it even starts. It never *could be* a daring, imaginative, creative document.

There is a particular and nice irony here. As implied, the university once stood for universal themes. While the connection between 'university' and 'universal' may not have been direct in the medieval origins of the European university, still universities were immediately associated with universal themes. It was understood that the understandings into which they enquired were of universal significance; indeed, of Godly significance. The truths with which they were associated had universal import.[10] The universities were an institutional means of gaining transcendence from this world.[11] Now, in contrast, universities fall back to categories that are very much of this world – of money, position, and competitiveness. Even their internationalism has a pragmatic edge: it is a matter of the universities surviving and being effective in this immediate world.

These are, of course, all signs of 'a loss of grand narratives' (Lyotard, [1979] 1987). Vast stories of man and his relationship to the world are no longer permissible; or certainly not encouraged. The world, it is presumed, is too complex, too fuzzy, to allow resort to be had to large ideas. To engage in talk of the university in categories of spirit, being, culture, emancipation and becoming is now outré; and, of course, here, God is dead. No such talk – with its metaphysical categories – can be tolerated any longer.

Yet, it is too easy to portray an unduly pessimistic picture of this linguistic and conceptual situation. The very complexity of the situation in which universities now find themselves brings up sharply the matter of responsibility. Now, perhaps for the first time, universities have to decide how they are to be in the world. This is an existential moment for universities. And in deciding that, they have to have recourse to a language about themselves. In this situation, either they can content themselves with simply describing and accounting for their being in the immediately given world, including the ideologies – of competition, efficiency, income generation and even 'wider participation' – that come to them *or* they can search for a different order of language through which they may hope to furnish some authenticity for themselves.

A new authenticity

So far, we have identified a number of themes: the being of a university and its challenges, the loss of a metaphysical background in which the idea of the university could be understood, the retreat of a sense of mystery attaching to the activities of universities, and the connection between the ideas of 'university' and 'universality'. In this opening chapter, I can only hope to expose these major issues confronting universities: we cannot do justice to these issues straightaway but shall have to go more deeply into these concerns in the chapters to come. Here, however, I want to open up the matter of authenticity.

Can we speak of *the authentic university*? This is perhaps the key challenge that universities face today: can they be authentic? After all, they are beset with large forces and ideologies. All across the world, universities are being enjoined to play their part in neo-liberal policies, they find themselves caught up in globalisation,[12] and they are bound to be players in the digital revolution, in which perhaps billions of messages circulate the world in an instant. Universities, so it may seem, have little space in which to be authentic. They simply play out roles that are given to them and they fragment into many different parts at once; or so it may appear.

There are two inter-linked stories here: the loss of the metaphysical university and the heavily circumscribed positions in which universities find themselves. We have also observed that, in the shrinking of the language and the concepts through which universities understand themselves, the ineffable character of a university's activities has been extinguished; or, at least, lost sight of. This loss of mystery provides a link between the two key features so far identified: (1) the loss of the metaphysical university; and (2) the apparently circumscribed positions in which universities find themselves. Universities play out their existence in circumscribed ways partly because of a lack of imagination – and courage – within themselves. Universities limit themselves largely to the here-and-now, shackling themselves, because they have abandoned any sense of a meta-reality in which they have their being.[13]

The 'metaphysical university' has therefore become 'the pragmatic university'. Once upon a time, the university recognised that it was not only linked to God, the universe and human being in fundamental senses but that it had responsibilities towards them. Why was it that the illuminated manuscripts of the medieval age were so lovingly cared for, and so carefully preserved if ever they were transported, and locked and chained in secure libraries? Why was so much time, effort and sheer resources spent on them (with pigments for the dyes being sourced across the world)? It was because such texts represented encounters with a meta-reality that provided a special order of meaning to such work. Such a sense of other-worldliness has dissipated. Universities have abandoned their metaphysical background – that background now being seen as pure baggage – as universities have embraced a pragmatic disposition.

As we observed, one justification for this narrowing of the university narrative lies in the way in which universities have come to be embedded in huge global and world-wide movements (of capital and knowledge generation): 'the learning economy' and 'global economy' are tide-like. They cannot be held back and nor is there any sign of their receding. Universities are caught in global networks: the world rankings portray a spurious sense of independence. In fact, only just beneath the veneer of those rankings, with universities carefully identified and separated, universities are interlinked at different levels: in parallel with the formal memoranda of understanding between universities across the globe, academics work with each other in international invisible colleges. And universities, in playing their part in the developing knowledge economy, work with industry and the private sector.

So the universities interpenetrate and are interpenetrated by the wider world. Universities are caught up in this world. They have their being in this overt world. For all their internationalism and globality, universities have become rather parochial. Their horizons have contracted. It is success – or at least survival – in this world as it presents in the public stories of the day that matters.

In this milieu, the idea of 'authenticity' has a hard time of it. Authenticity implies being unencumbered; or even attaining an unencumbered situation in which one can be truly oneself. How could such an idea gain purchase today in relation to the university? 'The pragmatic university'; 'the performative university'; 'the networked university': these, in contrast, as we have noted, seem to be the kinds of shorthand descriptions that do justice to the university today. Far from being unencumbered, this is a university that even seems to enjoy its interconnectedness. It proudly proclaims its embeddedness in society, whether at regional or national levels; or even across the world.

There are, though, two senses of being unencumbered that we should distinguish. First, there is the university that keeps itself-to-itself. This is the ivory-tower syndrome, into which universities slid for a comparatively brief period when they were characterised by 'donnish dominion' (Halsey, 1992). This is a university *in-itself*, with its being simply centred on the projects that it has chosen independently of a sense of the wider world. There is, however, a separate sense of being unencumbered. This is the university that actually lives in the world, but does so not through its simply living out others' expectations but through fashioning its projects (which are in the world) through its own values. This is a *university-for-the-Other* that frames itself and its possibilities in terms of the call of the wider society.

Here, we can perhaps just glimpse the possibilities of a new authenticity – and with it even a new kind of metaphysical university.

Regaining the metaphysical

In the light of these opening skirmishes, the key issue is this: can the idea of the metaphysical university hold any weight for universities in the twenty-first century? Or is it simply conceptual baggage that we should happily ditch, without any pangs of conscience?

We can, on the basis of these early reflections, distinguish two senses of 'the metaphysical university', one of which can still work for us. On the one hand, there is a sense of metaphysics as transcendence, that entry into a world of ideas, and that efforts to reach the truth, carry individuals into a world entirely separate from the here-and-now of this world. Whether it is an immediate encounter with Platonic forms, or whether it is God's revelation, or the participation in and fulfilment of Spirit, there is here the promise of an entry into a totally different world, separate from the physical reality of this world. This is not just a metaphysical world; it is a meta-physical world, a world in which the meta is separate from the physical. A hyphen has appeared, denoting the separateness of the meta-reality with which this university is connected.

This is a sense of the metaphysical university that we can abandon. It does not do any work for us today.

In contrast, we can point to a somewhat less intense sense of 'the metaphysical university'. *This* metaphysical university senses a world other than the present world and strives to bring that world into existence. This is a utopian university; its 'mission statement' harbours longings of a different world order, of a world in which groups live together with their differences and of a planet without serious injury to itself as a result of man's activities. This is a metaphysical university in a post-metaphysical age (Habermas, 1995),[14] which distances itself from the world, at least in its value structure, in order that it can act purposefully and in beneficence upon the world. It understands that the world could be more than that represented by its dominant ideologies, even if it contends with and in the world as it is. Even if it cannot give articulate expression to them, still large ideas such as fairness, freedom, care, solicitude and respectfulness inform its being in the world.

And what of mystery? Is there any mystery here? Does this metaphysical university possess any quality of mystery? *This* metaphysical university understands that it can never give a complete representation even of itself. Living in a counter-factual world, and wanting to play its part in ushering in a new world order, this university lives with a double mystery. On the one hand, it understands that the values and ideas that characterise it are inexhaustible: layers of contending meanings within itself are such that its own conceptual constitution must retain a core of mystery. On the other hand, it also understands that there can be no management formula by which an institution becomes this kind of institution: *this* university. There must remain an operational gap between the ideas that this university has of itself and its realisation of them. The assistant registrar's action plan and the risk audit can never capture all the elements of realising this kind of university. This is a university that is gossamer thin. Attempts to catch it will reveal its flimsiness. The mystery will have vanished; and with it, *this* university.

Conclusion

The metaphysical university has gone. The earliest form of the university (albeit one that lasted for some seven hundred years, from the twelfth to the nineteenth centuries), promised to give – through diligent inquiry and learning – access to God, to an immediate encounter with extra-worldly forms of understanding or to active participation in the unfolding of a universal Spirit. Now, in its place, we have the practical university, the performative university and the pragmatic university. However, we should not assume that this has to be our understanding of the university, that we understand the university only in terms of the here-and-now. This is a profane university, having a disregard for the non-worldly. The sacred university or the mystical university may yet be beyond us, beyond our modernity, but still we should not abandon the possibility that the categories of the mysterious or even the metaphysical can do real work for us.

At one level, this is hardly a controversial suggestion. After all, if it is the case that we now live in 'liquid modernity' (Bauman, 2000) or in 'virtual society' (Woolgar,

2002) or amid 'global complexity' (Urry, 2003), then perhaps any category that catches our imagination can be brought into play. But, in these opening reflections, a somewhat braver thought has opened. It is that, if an institution is to be worthy of the name of 'university', it has to be a metaphysical university – at least, of a kind. This is the kind of metaphysical university that lives beyond itself. It lives in hope of a better world, and understands that it has responsibilities towards that world. This is a metaphysical university in that it lives counterfactually in a world not of its own but of its yet-to-be-possibilities for humanity at large. This is a world of ideas, of possibilities, and of imagination. And these ideas are connected with large themes of truth, honesty, fairness and respect for the Other. It understands itself to be a steward of worthwhile inquiry put into the service of humanity. This university is itself a global citizen. It is a universal university.

The metaphysical university is yet, therefore, an idea that warrants our attention; not our amnesia. At least, in thinking that idea through, we will raise up the matter as to what it is to be a university today. Simply to give serious attention to the matter is implicitly to suggest that the forms of the university that have emerged over recent years do not need to exhaust the possibilities for the being of the university.

2 The scientific university

Introduction

Perhaps the first form of university to emerge after the dissolution of the metaphysical university was the *scientific* university.[1] As an appellation, 'the scientific university' is admittedly somewhat tendentious since the normal term of art here is 'the research university' (cf. Cole *et al.*, 1994) This form of university is roughly a hundred years old, and saw its origins in Germany and the USA in the nineteenth century. Over recent decades, however, and especially in the wake of the Second World War, it has become a defining form of university such that universities worldwide, in developed or developing countries, aspire towards it.

Why though use the term 'the scientific university' to stand in the place of the term 'the research university'? The matter is simple: science – that is to say, the physical sciences –overwhelmingly form the knowledge core of the research university. So much so that every decade or so a book appears with the title of 'the crisis in the humanities' (or something rather similar). In other words, in this respect, the term 'the research university' is disingenuous. For it masks the dominant position played by the hard sciences. The softer sciences and areas of study are obliged to find their place in the academic firmament in the shadow of the physical sciences.

Some will observe, too, that in the continental European university tradition, 'science' – 'Wissenschaft'[2] – was undivided in that the term stood for all systematic knowledge. It included much if not all of the social sciences and even the humanities. But that is not the point being made here. For, here, the term is used in its Anglo-Saxon sense, of referring to the natural sciences and those fields of study – such as engineering and medicine – that are built primarily on the natural sciences.

The natural sciences and their derivatives deserve special attention for five reasons. First, they have an underlying interest structure of their own – a 'knowledge constitutive interest', as Habermas put it ([1968] 1978) – namely in that of control.[3] In contrast, the knowledge constitutive interest of the humanities lies in mutual understanding. Second, the knowledge society is primarily interested in the knowledge produced within the natural sciences. The knowledge society is actually a skewed society, in its epistemological bearings. In the knowledge society, it is science that attracts high marks.[4] Third, university science has become deeply interconnected with both the state (including the military) and industry (especially in the technological oriented

as to form what has been termed a 'triple helix', exerting con-
on science policy (Etzkowitz and Leydesdorff, 2000).[5] Fourth,
teaching in the natural sciences account for a significant proportion
ersity's budget. Science is expensive. Fifth, and linked to this point about
nse, the perceived link between natural science, its technological applications and
economic growth are giving rise to a widening knowledge divide across countries.[6]

Against this background, it is hardly surprising that the modern research university
has come to be a largely 'scientific university'. It is a mode of university being into
which the university has slipped and commands attention world-wide.

Science and knowledge: problematic links

In contemporary society, 'science' has become almost synonymous with knowledge. This is explicable: after all, the idea of 'knowledge society' is felt to stand for a
society in which science is accorded a significant place; and arguably a hegemonic
place (Stehr, 1994).[7] In this society, science becomes the connection between reason
and culture: it is through science that society understands itself to be both a rational
society, its primary culture being that of scientific rationality (Gellner, 1992). So
the link between knowledge and science is understandable, as a form of social con-
ceptualisation.

In turn, two issues arise: is science entirely a form of knowledge? First, the nature of
science as such: is even science '*science*'? Does it live up to its own billing as supremely
rational? Does its place in modern society rather not owe something to faith, to faith
in science, namely 'our faith in the very extensive and important practical application of science' (ibid.: 109)? Even if science was once largely disinterested, perhaps
its direction of travel and orientation has given it a new orientation and shape?[8] Or
perhaps it has become shapeless – 'liquid science', as we might term it (after Bauman).
And second, what 'knowledge' stands outside science? Or, now, what knowledge*s*
stand outside science? To put the question another way, what is the shape and
configuration of the *epistemological space* of society?

Do these issues matter so far as the modern university is concerned? Why
not let the academics just pursue knowledge wherever it will take them? It matters
profoundly.

First, the wider society – through state agencies, professional bodies and public
opinion – is influencing, if not actually directing, the knowledge fields where resources
are to be placed. The academic field is shaped by the policy field. Second, through the
privileging of science,[9] the epistemological space of society becomes distorted. This is
not to say that other forms of knowledge are excluded but they come to be judged as if
they are putative sciences; and downvalued for not conducting themselves according
to the norms of science, when that may never have been part of their constitution or
teleology.[10] Science has become an ideology (Feyerabend, 1978: 106),[11] exerting huge
power in the knowledge society and skewing the epistemological territory (Rouse,
[1987] 1994).[12] It is like a football match played on a sloping pitch: the teams are there
playing their hearts out; but the situation favours one side and that side just assumes
that it is its right to play down the slope. Everything works in its favour.

These two phenomena have become part of the situation of universities and so universities are willy-nilly influenced by them. More humanistic and socially-oriented forms of research take their bearings from science. Quantitative studies, preferably conducted with large 'data-sets' and examined by teams of researchers, are encouraged while more reflective and interpretive enquiries are subtly (or not so subtly) marginalised. Research evaluations are skewed in the interests of science: particular attention is paid to criteria (such as project funding) and 'performance indicators' that are meaningful to the empirical sciences, so downvaluing research activities in the humanities. In turn, the term 'scholarly research' falls out of the academic lexicon. The term 'scholar' is now hardly to be seen and heard even less.

The key problem goes even deeper. The epistemological space in which universities have their being not just gives more space to science but shrinks at the same time. Non-science is given short shrift such that the discursive space in which universities understand their knowledge possibilities shrinks. Again, this is not to say that the non-sciences are neglected outright. At a casual glance, they may seem to be flourishing (and some of the non-sciences in particular). The point is about the context in which those other studies are understood and evaluated. But the situation is graver still. For the vocabulary within which our understanding of the world is developed dwindles. No longer – as we noted in the last chapter – is it easily possible to speak of 'wisdom', or 'wonder', or 'mystery' or to have a sense of an intertwined being with the natural world (Midgley, 1989; Cooper, 2002). A liquid world of knowledge it may be, but it is a liquidity that runs in some directions and away from others.

It may be said that this account exaggerates the situation. It is true, as I have just admitted, that not only have old non-sciences survived – still, philosophy and theology may be found in universities, even if in just an ever-small minority of universities.[13] It is true, too, as I have also just acknowledged, that new non-sciences and even quasi-sciences (in therapy, for example) are increasingly to be found on campus. The matter here is about the discursive context in which the university understands its knowledge possibilities. Actually, the signs are that that context is opening, that science is being asked to justify its hegemonic position and that space is widening now for other entrants.[14] But still, science will not surrender its hegemonic position lightly. On the contrary, as noted, its spokespeople – such as, in the UK, Richard Dawkins – exert their claims for science ever louder.

My concern here is less with science *per se* and more with the wider context in which science is understood *and* in which science understands itself. That science requires faith in order for it to proceed – faith in the intelligibility of the universe; faith in the universality of its phenomena; faith in the discreteness of its phenomena; faith in its being the arbiter of rationality; faith in its significance for practical life – is seldom acknowledged. On the contrary, the category of 'faith' is more or less banned in the wider academic life. Indeed, 'faith' is now coming in for an even harder time of it. Now, it invites suspicions of a harbouring of dogmatism, closure and even terror.

What is it to know something? Knowing itself has become tightly drawn. Originally, perhaps for good reason; to exclude dogma and irrationality. Science became thought to be the embodiment of right reason.[15] In the process, however, especially as science has taken hold and become more systematised but also as the whole edifice of academic knowing has grown, so it just may be that the rules of good and right know-ing have become unduly constraining. Those rules, for instance, may embed a sense of mankind separate from the world, as a spectator gazing on nature. Nature is out there and, by implication, available for man's activities. It then becomes but a short leap to technologising the world and to environmental pollution and decay (and man-induced climate change).[16] The sense, readily apparent in traditional societies, that mankind is in the world, is part of the world, has largely been lost; and with it has been lost a sense that mankind's fate is bound up with the fate of the world.[17]

Disenchantment with enchantment

I am suggesting, then, that the formation of the scientific university – and its accom-panying formalisation of knowledge – reflect and help to make firmer subtle assump-tions about the relationship of mankind to the world. If terms such as faith, mystery, wonder, wisdom and sensuousness and even imagination, illumination and insight have largely fallen out of the lexicon through which the academy understands what it is to know the world, that phenomenon is explicable, no less, as a process of disen-chantment with *enchantment*.

In these subtle movements, which have taken place over at least two hundred years, other shifts have occurred. For example, 'objectivity' has become an ideology. In the effort over time to secure valid forms of knowing, research methods have been systematically bound in by rules and procedures. A process of decontamination has taken place and continues apace (cf. Bulmer and Ocloo, 2009). But, in the process, possibilities are diminished for experiencing wonder, mystery and awe, and for seeing strange connections across forms of knowledge and for unbridled leaps of the imagi-nation. Now, rules have to be followed so that language and insight are vaporised; and cleansed of any possible contagion. All is safe; all is risk averse.[18]

Where is there space now for 'the scientist as rebel' (Dyson, 2006)? Where is there room for anarchic frames of thinking, of the kind espoused by Paul Feyerabend? The thought police have done their work. Even some of the humanities ape the sciences, with dissertations that have to have 'literature reviews', a 'presentation of findings', 'discussion' sections and neat 'conclusions'. These are not just matters concerning what it is to know in academic life. In a way, if the academics wish to censure their own thought and thinking styles, that might be felt to be simply the worse for them. But it matters to us all.

In his autobiography, Feyerabend observes: 'The world, including the world of sci-ence, is a complex and scattered entity that cannot be captured by theories and simple rules' (1995: 172). If this is right, this fact has profound consequences for our efforts to understand the world and our relationships to it and to each other. In turn, this fact carries large implications for what it is to be a university. If universities are seriously to be institutions that help us to understand the world, then they need to be such as to encourage daring, iconoclasm and strangeness. They seem, on the contrary, to be ever more rule-bound even as 'knowledge' enterprises. As organisations, they largely seem to assume that forms of knowing have come to exhibit stable patterns and systems.

Universities close off cognitive options. For example, 'multimodality' (Kress and Leuven, 2001) may be an interesting idea for school education but it has yet to penetrate the thinking of universities as organisations. The idea that universities might be institutions that sponsored multimodality has yet to take off. The possibility that research and teaching in universities might even be inspired by the concept of multimodality is barely on the horizon. The iconoclasm and rule-lessness that the idea of multimodality represents are neither entertained nor entertainable, it seems.

There are two linked phenomena at work here. On the one hand, science has an internal blankness about itself. It lacks a self-understanding and in turn develops a tightening of its own rules and procedures for knowing the world. On the other hand, science exerts its hegemony as the supreme form of knowing, so limiting the possibilities for new forms of knowing to emerge precisely at a time when more fluidity in knowledge forms is required. Those new forms of knowing might be interdisciplinary or even multimodal. The point is less about their form than about their emotional environment. It is now an epistemological regime characterised by fear. The courage to be totally 'off-the-wall' has been vanquished. The 'conquest of abundance' (Feyerabend, 1999) has been achieved.

Knowledge policies?

'Knowledge' is a badge of honour. Its use is characteristically a mark that implies one has arrived at, or is sure as to what constitutes, a valid relationship to the world. The idea of knowledge, accordingly, is not value-neutral.[19] It claims the high ground. By implication, any position not based on Knowledge is ephemeral, flimsy, non-rational and even dogmatic. To believe that one's position is based on Knowledge is tantamount to excluding other positions that do not match the knowledge criteria to which one is aligned. If not actually totalitarian, still the adherence to 'Knowledge' repudiates other positions.

Neither is this a point about relativism, nor is it to say that anything goes. It is rather that the belief that one has knowledge tends one towards an excluding position. To put the point another way, the assumption that one knows in general terms what is to count as knowledge reduces the range of cognitive options. The very idea of knowledge limits one. It puts one into a position where certain positions, certain perspectives, and certain holds on life and the world cannot be entertained. Here, there is solace for the faint-hearted. This is a comfortable position to be in; and doubly so. The limiting of one's cognitive options makes for an easy life. One does not have to be troubled by perspectives that appear to be at odds with one's own. There is both cognitive and emotional comfort here. But knowing what counts as knowledge enables one to assume the moral high ground. Here opens the way for the scientist as modern-day priest. The scientists rail against the priests when, all the time, they have become like priests themselves, espousing Truth. They make their pronouncements assuredly. Scientists have become the new priestly caste.

If this is not a point about relativism, neither is it a point critical of science *per se*. It is rather a point about the place of science in society. The knowledge society is largely the scientific society. In such a society, science can become sure of itself; sure of its right to hold sway in any claims to knowledge. Non-science can be relegated as non-knowledge.

The scientific university – that is, any contemporary multifaculty research-intensive university – is dominated by science (and science-based fields, so giving rise in the UK to the acronym STEM – that is, science, technology, engineering and mathematics). Universities' knowledge policies are, in effect, their research policies; and their research policies are substantially their policies in relation to the STEM disciplines.[20]

The research university, we may accordingly judge, is an institution for closing thought and understanding rather than opening thought. The proposition will seem heretical to many. But, to repeat, we only have to notice that many categories relating to thought and understanding are now – except in fringe activities – outlawed on campus: the sacred, the sublime, wonder, mystery, awe, wisdom, oneness and spirit. Categories such as these are largely repudiated. Their presence in papers submitted to journals would often cause a certain *frisson*. These are awkward, if not downright dangerous, categories.

What, then, would it entail for a university to develop a knowledge policy (Bergendahl, 1984) against this background? A knowledge policy for a research university that was seriously interested in knowledge would look to a widening of categories in which knowledge was framed, and not to a narrowing of the categories. That much is clear; but we can and should go further.

A university that is seriously interested in knowledge would be for *not*-knowledge. It would contend against what was taken for knowledge. It would seek to challenge, rebut and overturn knowledge. For the critique of knowledge can only yield fresh knowledge; the endorsement of knowledge, in contrast, leaves us where we are.

Again, heresy is voiced. A university is an institution for *not-knowledge*. A university is for the undoing of knowledge, but in order that knowledge can be rebuilt afresh, if only then to critique *that* knowledge. And so on and so on. This is not heretical. This is the way in which knowledge moves. Always rebuttal, critique and counter-argument; and the generation of new insights (and possibly revolutionary insights). The university in which such critical dialogue was not present would be no university. The heretical position – that the university is for not-knowledge – is, in fact, the orthodox position. The knowledge university welcomes epistemological mayhem.

How can this be? That the heretical position is the true position? This is because the university has to be for not-knowledge in order to be for knowledge. The university gains its knowledge spurs by being utterly focused on knowledge as such. Knowledge is knowledge after the critical dialogue; it is post-knowledge. The university – the research university at least – pursues knowledge by critiquing knowledge. It is incessantly pursuing its quarry, namely knowledge. It is restless in pursuit of knowledge; which is to say that it is never content with its knowledge positions. Such restlessness, such dissatisfaction with contemporary knowledge positions, reflects – in this university's best moments – the generous admission of strange forms of would-be knowing as bona fide knowledge. And so we arrive at the paradoxical but sure position: the knowledge university demonstrates its concern for knowledge by being for not-knowledge.

Any knowledge policy of the research university, therefore, has to be oriented towards opening processes of critical dialogue such that the knowledge structures in which it is engaged can come under the severest assaults. Disciplines would have to open themselves to each other; no discipline – or set of disciplines – could be accorded primary (and unassailable) status.[21] Vice-chancellors and rectors would have to become epistemologically sophisticated, sufficient to be able to form academic structures in which disciplines were liable fruitfully and imaginatively to collide with each other. Academic restructurings would be undertaken primarily with such epistemological imaginings in mind rather than through any administrative or economic optimisation or estates management.

A knowledge policy necessarily harbours both knowledge interests and knowledge responsibilities. However, these two terms – knowledge interests and knowledge responsibilities – have different logics. Whether it realises it or not, a research university stands for certain interests. Through its epistemological activities, it sustains and furthers certain knowledge *interests* – whether of understanding, of control of the environment, of ultimate economic value or of social utility. On the other hand, a research university does not have knowledge *responsibilities* in the same way. To say a research university, in its knowledge activities, has responsibilities is not to say that it is fulfilling those responsibilities or even that it is *trying* to fulfil those responsibilities. Interests are always present in action; responsibilities may not be present in action at all.

It follows that we can ask the question: what responsibilities might a research university seek to fulfil? What responsibilities should it recognise? However, danger lurks in answering the question. For, to answer the question in a substantive way, to identify responsibility x or y, would be to box the university in; to limit it epistemologically. It would be tantamount to the university declaring certain kinds of knowing or avenue of inquiry out of bounds. Such a university would not be a university for it would have abandoned the openness to universal knowledge that is – at least in its self-understanding – a necessary condition of the university being a 'university'. So the question: 'What responsibilities might be enjoined by the university?' has to be asked; but it is answered only at some peril. Knowledge responsibilities are always problematic.

Epistemological mayhem

There are two narratives running here: epistemological mayhem *and* responsibility. Can they be reconciled? On the one hand, there is the idea that serious knowledge and understanding can know no boundaries; that no *a priori* prohibitions should be present (and that no categories for understanding should be ruled out in advance); that all comers should have their say; that conditions of 'knowledge production' should be such as to encourage daring and imagination; that the very criteria as to what is to count *as* knowledge should always be open to critical appraisal; and that new perspectives should be permitted even if (or especially if) they frighten the old guard. On the other hand, there is the idea that knowledge activities should be pursued with some sense of responsibility. But how might the idea of responsibility gain a secure position in the company of epistemological mayhem?

We should distinguish between *substantive* epistemological mayhem and *procedural* epistemological mayhem. So far as *substantive* epistemological mayhem is concerned – the very ideas, perspectives and theories that might come into play – any attempt to delimit the range of offerings is in principle to be outlawed. Any attempt to curtail what might be proffered is anathema in a free society (cf. Feyerabend, [1978] 1982). And attempts of this kind are increasing within universities: limits to what can be said and how it can be said are being imposed, even if subtly. Academic claims and positions might embarrass the corporate university (see Chapter 4) or run counter to the position of strong academic factions or disturb the research funders (especially the government and its agencies and the large corporations). Academics come to guard their backs and censure their own utterances and, in the process, academic discourse shrinks. Such limitations are, in the long run, corrupting the academy.

On the other hand, so far as *procedural* epistemological mayhem is concerned – the processes in which knowledge offerings are put forward – some limits have to be entertained. It is a necessary condition of a collective freedom of expression that that freedom is lived out in a way that does not unduly curtail the freedom of individuals to utter. This reflection leads us towards Jürgen Habermas' (1989) 'validity claims', concerning truthfulness (participants are seriously striving for understanding), sincerity (participants mean what they say and are not trying to hoodwink others by inappropriate methods) and appropriateness (offerings are sensitive to context). These, we may note, are not really validity claims but conditions of and principles for rational debate.

This distinction between substantive epistemological mayhem (what can be said) and procedural epistemological mayhem (how matters can be expressed) is, of course, overly neat. In practical domains, in professional fields (such as surgery and engineering) and the performing arts, 'truths' are expressed *in situ*. In such areas of work, what is said and what is done are bound up together. What is said is partly and even more or less entirely performative. So the distinction between what is said and how it is said will not hold straightforwardly in all situations. Still, it has its usefulness as a heuristic device.

The general principle is this: we can be and should be generous and flexible in regard to *what people may wish to say*, but restrained in regard to *how people say what they want to say*. This distinction both allows anarchy and provides restraint. In regard to what people wish to say, we can encourage the most extreme innovation. Even to say that anything goes is too mild. For to say that 'anything goes' implies that we know in advance what 'goes', what is acceptable, what the rules of acceptability are. The phrase implies that we have a rough sense at least as to the kind of profferings that might come forward. But in a liquid age, knowledge itself is liquid, with new kinds of computer-based, iconic, performative, interpretive, creative, collective and interactive ways of understanding the world tumbling over each other.

In this age, we cannot lay down in advance what is to count as a valid knowledge offering. On the contrary, we need to open ourselves completely, to entirely new forms of knowledge and new ways of relating to the world and to other people. On the other hand, this apparent anarchy has to be restrained in the manner of its expression. The anarchists have to curb their anarchy, at least in the ways in which they present their wares. The anarchists have to be conventional, albeit in their mode of engaging with the world. Admittedly, new media – especially but not only the internet – are making possible new ways of reaching the different publics of the academy but still, the conditions of rational debate apply. Imaginative and daring in what it has to say; careful and sensitive to the norms of rational debate in the way in which it communicates its offerings: these surely have to be the epistemological norms of the academy.

Prospects for re-enchantment

Let us take stock. The knowledge university has dogmatised knowledge: knowledge has become a dogma (Nisbet, 1971). More knowledge and more knowledge still: this has become the mantra of the knowledge university. The knowledge university has, accordingly, become *the research university*; and by research is characteristically meant science; and big science at that. Paradoxically, we may note, the resources required for investigating the smallest structures are often enormous (witness, for example, the equipment and physical space needed for nanotechnology and the particle accelerators needed for atomic research).

These developments have had severe repercussions. This form of university being has fallen away from its self-rhetoric. The idea of the *university* is linked to *universal* knowledge but the knowledge forms associated with the research university are unduly limited. In its pursuit of scientific knowledge, categories of understanding – such as wisdom, awe, poetry and mystery – are diminished, if not downright repudiated. The humanities and related forms of knowledge and understanding struggle to gain a hearing. In fields linked to the caring professions – such as nursing – knowledge activities are corralled into a science-like form. At the same time, through the assumptions embedded in modern science, the world is seen as separate from man, available for his inspection and ultimately for his use. Enchantment has been taken out of this world. And it is but a short step to unstoppable climate change and also to a world in which people become objects and so liable to perpetual surveillance.

The knowledge university comes then to embed a certain kind of epistemology. Certainly, we have seen signs of new epistemologies finding a foothold. The 'Mode 2' thesis of Michael Gibbons and his associates (Gibbons *et al.*, 1994; Nowotny *et al.*, 2001) has been one attempt to press the idea that the dominant epistemology is already faced with a rival. Against formal propositional knowledge residing in academic journals attempting to describe the world (Mode 1) can be seen a mode of knowledge that springs from actions in the world: this Mode 2 knowledge is *in situ* and is intent on changing the world. What is odd about the interest shown in the Mode 2 thesis is not that it is particularly radical – as some believe – but that it is unduly conservative.

Why should it be thought that just two modes of knowledge offer a complete understanding of the world? In a globalised world, in a world in which cultures and traditions are colliding with each other, any number of knowledges will arise. The question is: what is to be the stance of the knowledge university towards multiple knowledges, especially given that one form of knowledge – scientific knowledge – has an especially dominant position? Can the knowledge university become epistemologically generous, such that no mode of knowledge is especially favoured?

There are two other ways of expressing this challenge, and they are linked. The first is to ask: what are the prospects for re-enchantment for the university, for its epistemologies to be connected with the world and with improving wellbeing in the world? The second is to ask: which are the networks with which the academy will connect in its knowing endeavours? After all, those networks are growing rapidly to include state agencies, industry, business and commerce, the professions, policy circles and political domains. So the academy is already widening its own networks.

Should there be any boundaries to the university's networks? Ecological and community groups, charities, third sector organisations and other groups that are concerned to improve the lot of individuals, communities and the physical world itself are already part of the university's networking – and their influence could grow. In this way, too, the university's epistemologies would be likely to widen. The world would no longer be seen as alien, in a way; to be described, analysed, and understood as if it was separate from mankind but mankind would resume its position – held in traditional societies – of being epistemologically in-the-world. In the process, too, in this journey back to enchantment, the university would come to understand itself as being-in-the-world.

Over the last century, the big epistemological question has come to be: to what extent do propositions correspond to the world? The correspondence theory of truth embeds the sense of a world separate from human beings (cf. Rorty, 1980; Austin, 1994). Traditional societies, in contrast, had – and have – much more of a sense of man-in-the-world. For such societies, their truths of the world said much about mankind; and it was understood that man was implicated in technologies arising from knowledge. In turn, with the rise of the scientific university, the academy has come tacitly to reflect in its knowledge policies a sense of knowledge separate from mankind. However, recent years have seen shifts in the epistemological positioning of universities.

As universities have come much more into society, so their epistemologies have become more practical, processual and performative in character (Eraut, 1994). It has come to be understood that professional knowledge, for example, relies as much on communicative understanding, on tacit knowledge and a knowledge-in-action that goes beyond the merely competent (Schön, 1983). The professions allied to medicine, the creative arts, the leisure and tourism industries, and the business and management fields are evident in these movements. It is also being recognised that long-standing professional fields – medicine, engineering and law – draw on forms of understanding that are not exhausted by propositional knowledge. It is not merely that there is a widening to encompass the performative aspects; the formal knowledges themselves expand and become blurred. 'Medicine and the humanities' emerges as a single field of interest. Science still remains the dominant field but that others are finding a place in the university demonstrates that the epistemological space of the academy has a certain permeability.

Knowledge and the world

This chapter has constituted an exploration of the epistemological positioning of the research university. We have noted a number of different epistemological positions, with perhaps the most significant being identified by the following two axes:

1   *Knowledge-for-itself/Knowledge-for-the-world*: This axis turns on considerations as to the *interest structure* at work: To what extent is it assumed that knowledge is valuable in itself? To what extent is it assumed that knowledge is valuable insofar as it has a utility in society?
2   *Knowledge-in-itself/Knowledge-in-the-world*: This axis turns on considerations as to the *location* of knowledge production: To what extent is it felt that knowledge is valuable insofar as it is generated in the academy? To what extent is it considered that it is knowledge that is generated in the 'real world' that counts?

We can put these two axes against each other, in the form of a grid (Figure 2.1).

1   *Quadrant (a): Knowledge-for-itself/Knowledge-in-itself*: This university is the 'ivory tower' university, intent on producing pure knowledge, irrespective of its utility in the world. The knowledge is produced apart from the world and is held apart from the world.
2   *Quadrant (b): Knowledge-for-itself/Knowledge-in-the-world*: We might call this university the 'professionalised university'. This is a university that is located in the world to a large extent – with the professions – but which conducts those knowledge activities so as to advance the university's own interests.
3   *Quadrant (c): Knowledge-in-itself/Knowledge-for-the-world*: Here is the 'entrepreneurial university' in its starkest form. This is a university characterised by a form of

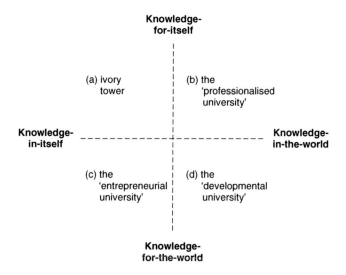

Figure 2.1 The university and its possible knowledge orientations

knowledge production held largely apart from the world but where the knowledge products are applied to – or sold to – the world so as to yield, characteristically, the highest economic return.

4   *Quadrant(d): Knowledge-in-the-world/Knowledge-for-the-world*: This university is both active in the world and is generating knowledge through those activities in the world. It is intent on helping to improve the world – its knowledges are put to work for-the-world. To pick up a phrase originally coined by James Coleman (1986), we can term this the 'developmental university'.

The dotted lines of the matrix are crucial for its divisions are porous *and* there is movement across them. The research university has been largely located in quadrant (a) (*Knowledge-for-itself* and *Knowledge-in-itself*), but it is moving in the directions both of quadrant (b) (*Knowledge-for-itself* and *Knowledge-in-the-world*) and quadrant (c) (*Knowledge-in-itself* and *Knowledge-for-the-world*). We might understand the distinction between quadrants (b) and (c) as a distinction between hard and soft forms of entrepreneurialism (a matter I explore in the next chapter). Quadrant (d) (*Knowledge-in-the-world* and *Knowledge-for-the-world*) lies rather empty but there are definite signs of universities moving in that direction, in which they are not just active in the world and are generating knowledge thereby but in which they are intent on putting those knowledge efforts in helping to improve the world.[22]

Conclusion

In a world of liquid knowledge, where knowledge has become knowledges jostling and even competing with each other, there are knowledge spaces: universities can approach knowledge – and are doing so – in radically different ways. Science still dominates the epistemological landscape but other forms of understanding are emerging, even as others have a hard time of it. Consequently, the range of interests fuelling the academy's knowledge enquiries is severely distorted.

In this situation, the university can no longer avoid its epistemological responsibilities. Universities have to be charged with developing knowledge policies for themselves. But what considerations might come into play in shaping those knowledge policies? For now, we can answer that question with a series of further questions: To what ends, if any, are the university's knowledge activities to be oriented? With which knowledge networks and communities is it to engage? Could it develop knowledge policies not just for itself but which might be deliberately aimed at helping to improve the wider world? We shall pursue these questions in the chapters to come, and we start by examining the idea of the entrepreneurial university.

3 The entrepreneurial university

Introduction

The idea of 'the entrepreneurial university' has taken off in recent years. Made substantial in the work of Burton Clark (1998; 2004), the term has been so extensively picked up that it has become part of the contemporary language of higher education (Shattock, 2009). Many believe that universities in general are set on the path to entrepreneurialism: far from being idiosyncratic, the 'entrepreneurial university' is becoming and *should* become ubiquitous. The idea transcends countries: across the world, it seems to offer a way of capturing common features of university development. It may be that, in many systems of higher education, the 'entrepreneurial university' is not much in evidence but the presumption is doubly that such universities are on the path to entrepreneurialism even if they are some way back *and* that this is the right path for them to take. In the idea of 'the entrepreneurial university', it can be said that universities – and university systems – are converging. All paths of university change lead to entrepreneurialism, it seems.

However, the concept of 'the entrepreneurial university' is far from clear. A wide range of activities and orientations might be brought within the ambit of the term; *or* a quite narrow set of activities. Despite or because of its fuzziness, the term gives rise to polarised views: some see in it the making of the university in the twenty-first century; others see it as heralding practices and conceptions that are anathema to anything that could be said to be constitutive of a university.

In this chapter, I want to tease out some modes of entrepreneurialism and I shall use, as a device, the idea of 'knowledge travel'. We cannot hope, through this latter idea, to exhaust the senses of 'the entrepreneurial university' but we may glimpse through it some provocative suggestions. It may be that, far from 'the entrepreneurial university' being a cameo of convergence across the globe, the idea of entrepreneurialism points towards increasing diversity among and optional choice for universities. In the idea of the entrepreneurial university are windows that open glimpses of quite different *possible* directions of travel. *Both* the optimists and the pessimists may be right: entrepreneurialism presents value choices that lead to contrasting ethical stances for the university.

Entrepreneurialism and risk

The entrepreneur is a go-between. He attempts to move or even take an entity X from point A to point B within a situation of some risk. He is willing to stake himself, his reputation and his capital in the venture in order to gain some profit; and he may be able to persuade a third party also to risk their capital and their reputation.

Capital, as Bourdieu (2000) reminded us, does not have to be financial. In the case of the university, it might be its cultural, intellectual or social capital that could be at stake and that is being put at risk. It might be its reputation that is risk; and since a university's reputation can itself act as a lever to garner resources, we can speak of its reputational capital being at risk. 'The entrepreneurial university' comes straightaway, therefore, to be a very large term indeed. For the entrepreneurial university could be engaged in risking any of these forms of capital; or some combination of them; or even all of them. The entrepreneurial university might be putting rather a lot at stake. The forms of capital that it can risk are many and complex.

However (and in keeping with entrepreneurs in general), the entrepreneurial university is concerned not so much to place its capital at stake as to generate some kind of return on its efforts. Characteristically, it wants its capital to grow. It may want its intellectual capital to expand (and to see the numbers of prize-winners among its staff rise); it may want to see its endowments increase and so improve its working financial capital; it may want to see an upward movement in its reputation (judged perhaps by an enlargement in the numbers of applications per student place at its disposal); or it may want to improve its social capital (and will count itself as having achieved this when it is accepted into the membership of a group of prestigious universities that it has its eye on, either within its own country or internationally).

Recently, the financial risk that the entrepreneurial university might run has attracted attention (and not only within the Rector's senior management team), but it is surely clear that other forms of risk may come into play. The university has many forms of capital at its disposal and all can attract risk. Ultimately, what is at stake is, as we may term it, 'mission risk', in which the university lays on the line its image, reputation, and positioning. 'Laying on the line' is an apt phrasing here, for it connotes both the paying of money and the taking of risk: the one act has both properties. There is a paying out, an expenditure of resources or effort of some kind and there is risk; and this – for the entrepreneurial university – may happen on a global scale. It may have a global reputation but that reputation may be at risk through *other* forms of its capital being put at risk.

The forms of capital of the entrepreneurial university and its forms of risk are, therefore, inter-connected; and multiple forms of capital and risk may be simultaneously evident. If its professoriate is unhappy with certain aspects of the university's new entrepreneurialism – for example, being asked to be themselves marketeers and to attract 'customers' for courses or even to design new market-sensitive courses – the global academic labour market lies waiting to capture the university's dissidents. At the same time, this university's intellectual capital *and* its reputational capital may be at risk. (Admittedly, risk can be overhyped. Since university entrepreneurialism is a global phenomenon, the dissidents who threaten to depart with much of the university's reputational and intellectual capital may find that the academic grass is not that much greener elsewhere and may surprisingly quickly become returning dissidents.)

There are, then, many different kinds of capital on which the university can potentially draw – even if the securing of credit may not be easy. In what follows in this chapter, I shall focus on entrepreneurship as it is exhibited through the accumulation of financial and intellectual capital; and I shall examine their interaction.

Change and risk

As implied, to say of a university that it is entrepreneurial is to invoke sentiments of undertaking, venture, risk and 'enterprise' (Marginson and Considine, 2000). In entrepreneurialism, there is a definite undertaking (by the entrepreneur), there is movement and change, the movement and change are imbued with some uncertainty, and (so) there is risk. The entrepreneurial university is prepared, indeed, is willing to become other than it is, and this at both surface and deep levels. At a surface level, its new ventures may take it into uncharted paths. It is 'enterprising'. Almost by definition, the venture in question has not been attempted before, certainly by this institution and possibly not by any other institution.

A university may decide, for example, to establish computer-based variants of all of its programmes of study, or even determine substantially to switch its 'portfolio' of courses in that direction. This will incur high up-front costs, not least in the training and development of its faculty, quite apart from the installation of the more physical infrastructure. The venture, undertaken seriously, has profound implications for the university: its pedagogies change, its educational relationships with its students change, the relationships that the students have with each other change (the students may become more interactive among themselves) and the pedagogical identity of the 'tutors' change (less a visible authority, aided by an immediate physical presence, and more an enabler of learning tasks and opportunities).

It follows that, in addition to the surface changes that entrepreneurialism heralds, changes also occur at a deep level. Indeed, in our present example, the university changes as such. It is not merely that the students are less visible on campus; now, this university is marked by new kinds of identity (of both students and tutors), relationships and communicative structures.[1]

Through entrepreneurialism, therefore, universities add to their repertoire of undertakings and undergo fairly visible *performative* change but, in the process, they may undergo *constitutive* change. Such constitutive change is not captured by talk of mission change. On the cards is the prospect that the university becomes a different *kind* of university. This reflection raises the question: under conditions of entrepreneurialism, are there any limits to the changes that might be wrought upon the university, even as it continues to claim the title of 'university'? After all, the entrepreneur, we may take it, will not be spending much time reminding himself of the 'idea of the university' as it has developed over the centuries, far less monitoring his entrepreneurial activities against that narrative. Instead, this entrepreneur will be keen to usher in change: his time horizons are largely in the future rather than the past. For now, it may be that 'anything goes' in this entrepreneurial dispensation.

It emerges, then, that the entrepreneurial university not merely exposes itself to risk but to *multilevelled* risk. At the surface or performative level, the risk may not pay off: the new students may not appear for those computer-based programmes. Human and physical resources are at risk here (as we have seen) but there may be opportunity costs as well. The capital – intellectual and financial – may be at risk: the university may run into financial deficit: staff may leave as they are called upon to take on their new pedagogical identities (and undergo 'training' in the process). But there is risk, as we noted, embedded at deeper levels. In the changing of its pedagogies, its academic and student identities, and its educational relationships, unpredictable changes are let loose. (Again, this unpredictability is a logical feature of 'risk'.) And, having been given momentum, such changes may be irreversible. Yes, the university may decide to return to conventional curricula and reassert itself as a conventional university, but human identities and institutional positioning, and their associated perceptions, values and orientations – both internal and external – once dislodged will not easily be morphed back to earlier configurations.

The entrepreneurial university may be risking more than it understands, for it may be risking itself. In coming to be a different kind of institution, it risks coming to live by new sets of institutional values. The risk may still be felt to be worthwhile, however, although that consideration implies that the risk to the university's value structure has actually been identified and assessed (and such an ethical audit is not something that is easily accomplished in the 'risk analysis' now being taken on by universities). Both an ethics of risk and a politics of risk attach to the entrepreneurial university (cf. Beck, [1987] 1992; Franklin, 1998).

The entrepreneurial university is between states of being, but no new stable state of being is available. A particular form of performative change may be identified as a goal and it may even be reached (the new campus is opened, perhaps even in another country) but the entrepreneurial university is never at rest. This is its characteristic mode of being, a restless mode of being; and this is part of its self-understanding. The entrepreneurial university delights in risk, but does it comprehend the risks that it is taking?

Forms of entrepreneurialism

Entrepreneurialism in universities comes in many shapes and sizes. The colloquialisms are justified here: entrepreneurialism takes on both shape and size on campus and beyond it. It may be present only to a marginal extent – in some departments, say, or as rhetoric emerging from the Senior Management Team – or it may have come to characterise an institution to a significant extent. So shape and size may be helpful metaphors here. We can envisage the university as a set of spaces and consider the penetration into the spaces of the entrepreneurial ethos and its practical manifestations.

How might those spaces be taken up by entrepreneurialism? I want to suggest *two sets of distinctions* that may help us understand the character of spaces that may exhibit an entrepreneurial presence, namely *hard* and *soft* entrepreneurialism; and entrepreneurialism under conditions of *strong state regulation*, on the one hand, and *strong markets*, on the other.

By 'hard' and 'soft' entrepreneurialism, I distinguish between those forms of entrepreneurialism where there is a definite intention to secure an economic return (preferably 'profit') as against those forms where the economic drive is much less evident or is absent altogether. After all, entrepreneurialism can be found in relation to different forms of academic capital (as we noted earlier); economic capital need not feature especially strongly. What is necessary, for entrepreneurialism to be present (so we also noted), is that there be some measure of risk involved. The university may risk its reputation, its intellectual capital, its position, its ethos, its educational character, its role as a cultural good, and so on.

Why, then, restrict the appellation 'hard entrepreneurialism' to the economic form? Because the economic form may not merely modify but even corrupt other forms: under market conditions, for example, the pedagogical relationship may be damaged by the undue presence of money: the transaction between teacher and taught may be irredeemably distorted, as the student becomes a customer seeking a return on her own financial investment and as staff sense more career advancement by pursuing avenues for research and consultancy that bear significant economic and status returns. In research, recognised methodologies may be short-circuited and 'outcomes' may be softened so as to satisfy private sector corporations funding the work in hand.[2]

We can offset this idea of soft-hard entrepreneurialism against a sense of the presence of markets. And here, we should distinguish between open markets and regulated markets; between situations where institutions offer the services they wish to offer at the maximum price that the market will bear among whatever customers can be found at those prices and situations where any of these three aspects of markets (services, prices and customers) are subject to some kind of regulation.[3] It is surely manifest both that open and regulated markets exist to a greater or lesser extent *and* that there is no sharp boundary between the two situations: open and regulated markets present us with a second axis, therefore.

In speaking of the presence of markets, clearly, too, the state looms into view. Open markets or regulated markets both arise characteristically as a result of state policies and actions in respect of higher education. (It is because the state in the United Kingdom, despite the ideological trappings of developing the market to higher education, remains a strong player in the evolution of higher education that, there, we should more properly talk of a 'quasi-market'.) In picking out the presence of markets to help our understanding of entrepreneurialism in higher education, the state, therefore, cannot be far from our analysis. In drawing out our two axes of entrepreneurialism, the state, accordingly, will form much of the canvas. If we place these two axes against each other, we open some of the spaces of entrepreneurialism (Figure 3.1).

In *Quadrant (a)*, a situation of soft entrepreneurialism in open markets, we have the case of an entrepreneurial university – or, say, an entrepreneurial department – that is keen to develop and promote itself in the public sphere. It is proactive and creative: its music department, say, is active in the multi-ethnic community (perhaps especially in cooperation with the local schools), exploring different music traditions as a way of developing multi-ethnic relationships in the community; its archaeology department is both widening intellectually to forge links with other departments (chemistry, biochemistry, computing, anthropology, statistics, anatomy and even theology) but

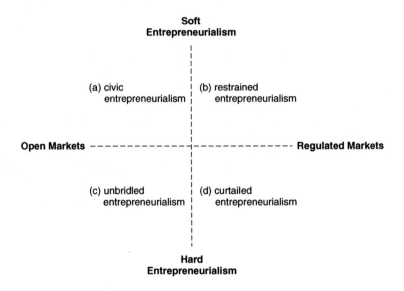

Figure 3.1 Forms of entrepreneurialism in higher education

is also engaged with projects in the wider society, perhaps on television, helping to broaden the interest in archaeology among the general public.

There may be income streams attaching to these activities – in fact, there will be – but that does not provide the major motivation or criterion of success. What counts here is the level of engagement with the social and public sphere. This institution wants really to be entrepreneurial but casts its entrepreneurialism widely so that it is unlimited in its entrepreneurial endeavours.

The level of risk here is significant but what risk there is, is not just economic in nature. The risk attaches to reputation (in seeming to 'sell out' to less academic opportunities and in working with the wider public), to opportunity costs in pursuing ventures that end in blind alleys, and also in running against the mainstream so that traditional academic outputs (in the form of papers in learned journals) might not be so readily achieved and, thereby, diminish a department's standing in national evaluations, especially but not only in research. Let us term this form of entrepreneurialism 'civic entrepreneurialism'. In this quadrant, therefore, lies a version of – as we may term it – 'the service university'.

In *Quadrant (b)*, soft entrepreneurialism but now operating in regulated markets, we have the case – at least in principle – of a university that is willing to essay forth (as in Quadrant (a)) but where it is severely regulated in its creative potential. It may be that institutions are here encouraged to compete with each other but are also, at the same time, expected to demonstrate that they are each playing their parts in widening participation in higher education across the social classes. Or it may be that institutions are encouraged to engage in research – or even 'third stream' activities (beyond 'research' and 'teaching') – but that they are also required to demonstrate societal benefit accruing from such activities. Or it may be that the state's marketisation agenda has to take account of other state agendas such as 'quality' (where a state's quality regime plays its part alongside market opportunities) or 'selectivity' (where a wish to deploy the state's resources to maximum effect limits the extent to which institutions can be involved in the teaching of students in 'costly' subjects, the registering of research students and being involved in research itself, especially in science and technologically-based subjects). In all these ways, the market would be regulated by the state for reasons that were connected with relevant public goods. Public capital, in other words, may vie with economic capital.

Under such circumstances, the incentives for an institution actually to become engaged in entrepreneurial activities would be diminished. After all, the risks here could be significant and the potential gains would be limited. An institution might be interested, in principle, in being entrepreneurial but it would surely hesitate in going in such a direction. Accordingly, let us call this entrepreneurialism a *restrained entrepreneurialism*. (The term 'restrained' is nicely ambiguous as to whether it is the state that is doing the restraining or it is the institution that is unduly restraining itself, in the face of the state's regulatory regime.)

In *Quadrant (c)*, a hard form of entrepreneurialism amid open markets, money counts; and money generating a surplus for the institution. This is the main driver. For instance, the message might go out to all members of staff that they were required to generate, say, three times their salary, both to cover the institution's overheads and to secure a profit. Here, the institution would understand itself to be a major source of exploitable knowledge capital in the wider 'knowledge economy' and it would seek to deploy that capital effectively and so secure the maximum financial return. Such a university would have become a player amid 'knowledge capitalism' (Peters, 2003).[4] It might well set monetary targets for third-stream activities in its corporate plans and a culture would be developed, department by department, in which ventures were created and seen through (perhaps with 'spin-off' companies, links with industry and the technological applications of research patented) that were intended to generate income (and, indeed, profit).[5]

This university would not just be business-*like* but would have become a business. This would be 'academic capitalism' (Slaughter and Leslie, 1997) in its purest (some might say starkest) form. Here, knowledge production would not be viewed as a public good but as an economic resource and as an intellectual property to be privatised.[6] This university would have every incentive to act in this way because, in this setting, the state would fully have opened markets to the higher education sector.[7] Under these conditions, our institution could charge whatever it felt able to charge, taking its own view of the market and the market attractiveness of its products and services. Let us – quite naturally – call this an *unbridled entrepreneurialism*.

In *Quadrant (d)*, a hard form of entrepreneurialism but now within a regulated market, institutions play out their entrepreneurialism in an environment in which the state in particular regulates the market, so that the most glaring excesses of unbridled entrepreneurialism are curbed. Either the amount of profit *or* the range of goods and services over which institutions could extend their entrepreneurial inclinations would be limited. Institutions might have their missions limited – or any monies derived from third-stream activities as additional income might be discounted against other core funding from the state – or institutions might not be permitted to charge the market rate either for their teaching or for their research. Or it might be that the extent to which institutions could borrow money would be limited if not denied altogether. Without credit facilities, an institution would not necessarily be unable to be 'entrepreneurial' but its capacities to be so would be severely limited.

In circumstances such as these, the incentives to engage in entrepreneurial activities would be limited by the state regulating the market (as in Quadrant (b)), but unlike Quadrant (b), where public or social goods were coming into play in the steering of the market, here, the market would be curtailed through the acting out of the state's own economic and political interests. We may call this a *curtailed entrepreneurialism.*

From this analysis, we see that entrepreneurialism can appear in several different forms. Indeed, in practice, hardly any one institution or even one department is going to be situated in any one single quadrant: it will itself spread across the box spaces (and within a multi-faculty university, different departments will be located in different quadrants); but there may be a dominant point or fulcrum, even amid the fuzziness of the outline, around which such an entrepreneurial university will be positioned.

'There is no alternative'

We should note, in regard to Figure 3.1, that *little rests on the two axes as such.* Other axes could have been chosen. By way of example, here are two further axes:

1   *Extractive–Providing*: The ends of this axis indicate institutions that are using their entrepreneurial activities to extract capital or profit from their environment *as against* institutions that are seeing their entrepreneurialism as a means of gifting their (often considerable) resources to the wider society and so adding value (instead of extracting it) from the wider society. The distinction here, we may say, is between *exploitative* entrepreneurialism and *beneficent* entrepreneurialism.

2   *External mission–Internal mission*: The ends of this axis indicate where an institution is focused primarily on the external environment and is seeking to engage anew with and in the wider society *as against* an institution that is seeking to be entrepreneurial through extending its inner academic activities (where, for instance, academics would continue to give external talks but would seek a fee on each occasion or where academics might, again for a fee, give advice to governmental committees). Through such an axis, we distinguish in effect an *other-oriented* entrepreneurialism from an *inner-oriented* entrepreneurialism.

We do not need to follow these distinctions through for the point surely is made. Entrepreneurialism comes in different forms but those differing forms themselves result from different kinds of values and interests, and their interplay.[8] 'Entrepreneurialism' turns out to be an umbrella term for a plethora of phenomena that are the surface manifestations of deep structures, which are in contention with each other. There is an archaeology at work[9] – at once conceptual, institutional and ideological – within the 'entrepreneurial university'. Accordingly, to label activities of the university as 'entrepreneurial' is merely to hint at spaces and textures that are configured by underlying structures.

Two crucial and related points follow from this analysis. The first is that the move on the part of a university in the direction of entrepreneurialism is not the end but the start of a new complex journey of institutional reasoning. For now, the university has to determine what forms – plural – of entrepreneurialism that it wishes to adopt, and in what balance: in which quadrants, and to what extent, does this entrepreneurial university wish to have its new being? Here, too, will lie all manner of political and ethical judgements: even if it is permitted to do so, will such a university accept donations from tobacco companies or from individuals holding strong political views? To what extent and under what conditions will it work with pharmaceutical companies that would attempt to limit the academic freedom of its academics (to publish freely under their own names research arising from the testing and evaluations of its products)? And universities will come to different judgements on these matters.

It follows, therefore, that any view that in entrepreneurialism lies a uniform global movement among universities should be resisted. There may be more differences than similarities across so-called 'entrepreneurial universities'. No simple convergence thesis can hold here.

The second point is that this depiction of entrepreneurialism as to so many contending forms of entrepreneurialism begins to suggest that there remain modes of being a university that lie outside entrepreneurialism. If 'entrepreneurialism' comes in hard and soft forms, if it can embrace self-interest and service to the community, perhaps there are options available to the university that are not to be captured by *any* notion of entrepreneurialism. Beguiling as it may seem, 'academic capitalism' should not be assumed to be an enveloping mode of being that waits – or even threatens – to engulf all universities. There is legitimate academic life still to be had outside entrepreneurialism and even possibly *inside* entrepreneurialism.

On both points (that entrepreneurialism turns out to a family of contesting ideas; and that there is space that universities can inhabit in the presence of entrepreneurialism), entrepreneurialism is no academic tsunami. The idea that there is no alternative to unbridled entrepreneurialism should be scotched.

Knowledge travel

Whatever changes are befalling universities worldwide – and amid the neo-liberal revolution there are many – universities remain knowledge institutions. What counts as knowledge may be widening or even changing, but we cannot comprehend the university independently of the concept of knowledge. Accordingly, we may understand entrepreneurialism to amount to an entreaty to academics and the academic community to engage in forms of 'knowledge travel' (cf. Barnett and Phipps, 2005). What is entrepreneurialism if, at its core, it is none other than an enjoinder to academics to create knowledge in new contexts, to use their knowledge in new ways, to find new ways of producing knowledge,[10] and to help new kinds of students to an understanding of this knowledge and to establish new knowledge partners? Epistemologically speaking, this is to travel in a new way. This is knowledge travel.

It follows, too, that the different structuring principles that we have encountered will lend themselves characteristically to different forms of knowledge travel. Is one travelling with an eye to the main chance, focusing on the potential economic gain, or has one embarked on the journey because it may be intrinsically interesting? Is one engaged on the journey because, through it, one may get to know others and speak their (academic) languages better, or is one on the journey simply as a form of personal aggrandisement?

Knowledge travel on a path to entrepreneurialism may be accomplished in different modes. Mode (a) is a particularly *academic* form of knowledge travel, and takes two sub-forms: either the crossing of existing knowledge fields through multidisciplinary and interdisciplinary ventures *or* through the development of new knowledge fields (Strathern, 2004). Both these forms of knowledge travel take place *within* the academy. Here, we may envisage – as academic and ethical virtues – both require epistemological courage, as our knowledge travellers venture into what are (for them, at least) new knowledge lands and, particularly in multidisciplinary inquiry, academic hospitality[11] or quizzical-ness or even some hostility, as they are received by academics in different tribes.

In Mode (b) knowledge travel, the traveller crosses into the *practical* domain. This form of knowledge travel is prompted where academic entrepreneurialism is addressed to the solving of practical problems. This knowledge traveller is active in the world and will take on a hybrid academic identity that consists of different relationships with the world being held together: the contemplative and the practical; understanding and action-in-the-world.

In Mode (c) knowledge travel, connections are made with the *public* realm (as in Quadrant (a), in Figure 3.1): this will call for communicative dexterity, spoken, visual or written. Interactions with groups in the local community, professional groups, the media and consumer groups: civic entrepreneurialism will call for productive engagement with all such manner of interest groups, each with their communicative challenges. Judgements will have to be made as to how to 'pitch things' for an audience: the style required for a television documentary may be quite different from that needed for a local community project.

In practice, many – or, indeed, all – of these forms of knowledge travel may be run together. A group drawn from a university department of engineers offering specialist advice in the construction of a huge project in another country may well find itself involved in interdisciplinary, practical and intercultural forms of knowledge travel. In turn, our engineering entrepreneurs may find themselves having to attend to their mode of self-presentation, their gestures, their dress sense and their communicative tone.

Ultimately, entrepreneurialism calls for complex academic identities.[12] What starts as a purely epistemological matter turns out to an ontological matter: what counts for effective entrepreneurialism is the mode of being that academic entrepreneurs are willing to embrace. If academics show a reluctance to take on an entrepreneurial spirit, it may reflect a disinclination to depart from or even to widen their own state of academic being. Resistant academics may be exhibiting not just an epistemological conservatism but also an ontological self-limitation; and the latter stance may just have some right on its side. The idea of 'academic integrity' may loom into view here.

But for those who are willing to become academic entrepreneurs, to venture into new epistemological and ontological lands, academic identities may be lost but they may also be reshaped into a richer, more complex form.[13] The logic here, of course, is that these epistemological entrepreneurs live happily with fluidity, a state of perpetual ontological voyaging. One just never knows which group or community one will be engaging with, from one day to another; one never knows the adjustment and nego-tiations one will have to make, in order to effect some kind of rapprochement. Our knowledge entrepreneurs have to think, and translate, and represent themselves in new and subtle ways 'on their feet'; and very often, literally so.

Academic entrepreneurs have to be able to empathise with new audiences. They are perpetual translators, effecting translations of their ideas, in new modes, for oth-ers to take them on board in settings that are new for all concerned; and they effect translations of others' work and language in assimilating them into their own language and frameworks. This is ontologically taxing: knowledge entrepreneurs must always be willing to go on remaking themselves in a continuing process of accommodation and assimilation. In turn, the individual changes.

But is it mere change or does the individual grow? Is the academic entrepreneur 'authentic' or 'inauthentic'? And is the academic entrepreneur a carrier of system-wide change that enhances society or diminishes it? Given our analysis, no general answer can safely be provided to such questions.

Here, however, we may conclude with the more prosaic observation that knowledge travel is endemic to academic entrepreneurialism but that it can move in profoundly different directions. Time and space are but intersecting dimensions revealing of these differences (cf. Robbins, 2008). The forms of knowledge travel and inter-communi-cation in which the engineers engage with their eye on definite time schedules and a precise design problem are a long way from anthropologists engaging in a long-term project with Amazonian Indians, which again is a long distance from archaeologists engaging with local councillors and planners on the occasion of a major 'find' in a city centre industrial site and turning the find into the foundation of a new museum of national importance.

Conclusion

The idea of 'the entrepreneurial university' may seem to point to a single form of university being, which is both unitary and inescapable. Both depictions are wrong. Under the banner of the entrepreneurial university sit many university forms, and many ways of being a university in the twenty-first century. Even so, despite its many and varied forms, entrepreneurialism is not all-encompassing. It cannot be a sin-gle movement threatening to capture all universities in its wake. Its boundaries are so fuzzy that there is space beyond which universities may also inhabit. Indeed, in some of its softer, more civic and public forms, and in its interdisciplinary shapings, entrepreneurialism offers generous spaces for new creative forms of academic life.

Folded within 'entrepreneurialism' stands, therefore, all manner of academic identity, of academic movement, of interplays between knowledge fields, of political and
social values, and ultimately of academic being itself. A decision to become an entrepreneurial university cannot be a way of ending or even limiting institutional judgement. On the contrary, such a decision is the harbinger of waves of issues that will
pose difficult if not intractable ethical issues. The work of the entrepreneurial university may never be complete; but nor are its value judgements. The entrepreneurial
university is constantly faced with choices. Being an entrepreneurial university opens
new possibilities but it also opens new dilemmas that – except at the price of institutional authenticity – cannot be avoided.

4   The bureaucratic university

Introduction

That the contemporary university has become bureaucratic is surely self-evident. Certainly, that is a widespread view among academics over the world who complain about the administrative burden to which they are subject. The surveys of university staff across countries testify to the point. The bureaucratic university is now with us. And yet this phenomenon is barely examined in the research literature. It is the elephant in the room situation. It is there but few in polite company dare mention it. It is business with a straight face. That signs of the university's increasing bureaucracy are ubiquitous are for the most part ignored in the overt interplay of academic life. And yet being a university cannot now be understood adequately without some consideration being given to this phenomenon of the insistent presence of bureaucracy in academic life.

There is another phenomenon that warrants attention in this chapter. This is the phenomenon of the emergence of what may be termed 'the corporate university'. The bureaucratic university and the corporate university are distinct but related phenomena. They have both affinities and tensions. Identifying those affinities and tensions may be instructive not only in understanding the contemporary university but also in opening imaginary possibilities for the future.

The rule of the proforma

It seems as if, for any activity in the university today, there are several proformas relating to the activity. Characteristically, the proformas are in electronic form: they have to be completed and submitted on-line. Sometimes, the computer programmes do not even permit or do not easily permit (where a table of columns runs across several screens) the proforma to be run off in paper copy. The person completing the form, who is very often an academic, becomes an extension of the computer, simply inputting data.

Just some of the features of academic life that are subject to bureaucratic procedures are student admissions, the appointment of staff, the balance of academic activities, examinations, research applications, curricula structures, recording of one's activities (especially research activities and research publications), teaching hours, meetings with research students, statements of immediate plans, research student *vivas*, internal quality audits, statements of expenditure and weekly diaries. This list is not static but grows in two senses: the list of procedures expands *and* each set of procedures becomes more complicated. The forms become more intricate and the entries become more numerous. Appointing a junior member of administrative staff (in support of an academic activity) may involve several rounds of completion of forms, and the entering of a judgemental score on each of a long series of criteria for each candidate even prior to an interview and both for 'shortlisting' purposes and then for the candidates actually called for interview.

There are two features of this enlargement of these bureaucratic processes that are immediately notable. First, increasingly, academic activities are being regulated. Of the extension of bureaucratic procedures, there shall – it seems – be no end. Second, and by extension, those who conduct those activities – the academics – are being regulated. By and large, it is not the administrative staff or the managers who are subject to the proformas. It is largely – although not entirely – a matter of bureaucratic procedures being designed by non-academic staff and completed by academic staff. In the UK, too, we may note, non-academic staff now outnumber academic staff.[1]

We are entitled to say that the bureaucratic university is also *the surveillance university*. Through its bureaucratic procedures, academic life is subject to increasing watchfulness. And this surveillance bears in on past activities (the recording of teaching and research and other activities already accomplished), present activities, immediately forthcoming activities (the completion of the proforma is necessary for the activity to happen) and probable future events (where one records the envisaged activities, either for the next week or even for the next year). This is a university life lived out by the proforma; it is the rule of the proforma.

All this has happened in a comparatively brief span, perhaps over the past forty years. It is evident in the considerable increase in non-academic staff, especially in personnel (now renamed 'human resources') departments, in finance, in quality audit and in marketing as well as in other functions. Financial data reveal this trend: the proportions of a university's expenditures now devoted to non-academic staff and their activities have grown quite disproportionately, compared to academic staff.[2] How can we account for this remarkable and significant change in the character of academic life?

The immediate answer – if this question were to be posed to a senior manager – might be that the data gathering exercises are required or are a necessary consequence of government-imposed systems. There is substance in this response. The arrival of the mass higher education system and a concern on the part of the state about state expenditures have brought about a determination to ensure 'value for money' and 'accountability'. In turn, the state places universities in a new regime of audit. (In the UK, university vice-chancellors are now the 'chief accounting officers' for their universities.) We see the arrival of the 'evaluative state', as Neave (1988) put it. Accordingly, it may be said, in installing bureaucratic procedures in-house, universities are simply responding rationally and prudently to the environment of accountability in which they find themselves.

As a complete answer, however, this rejoinder has to be found wanting. In looking in turn at each bureaucratic procedure and examining its presence as a response to the demands of the state, the link will be clear on occasions (for example, as in university procedures for national teaching or research evaluations) but on many other occasions, the link will surely be tenuous. So the alleged tight connection between particular internal procedures and the wider interests and accountability exercises on the part of the state will often be difficult, if not impossible, to sustain.

Here, a second justification for the panoply of bureaucratic procedures could be adduced, namely that the university has an interest in the efficient and effective management of its own resources. Universities have considerable resources, the most expensive of which are, for the most part, its academic staff. Accordingly, universities have an interest – and even a duty – in ensuring that those resources are yielding their maximum output. This response has some merit but it is also somewhat disingenuous. For – in the UK at least – it is evident, from many national audits and other such exercises, that, in international terms, the higher education system is working well in relation to both teaching and research. The evaluations of the national Quality Assurance Agency have found the higher education system – even at subject level – to be operating at high levels of quality (whatever might here be meant by 'quality') and the scores in the national student satisfaction survey show that students are largely happy with their student experience. Further, the arrival of the mass higher education system has been accomplished at the cost of a significantly lower level of the unit of resource. In research, it is evident too – in the UK – that its universities are highly productive and well regarded internationally.[3]

In short, it is known from the readily available data that – in the UK, at least – the higher education system is operating both efficiently and effectively. So a defence of the increased bureaucratic procedures in terms of a concern with the efficiency and effectiveness of the higher education system is disingenuous.

A yet third reason to justify a university's array of bureaucratic procedures takes note of the uncertain environment in which universities find themselves. Given the turbulence in the world, it might be said, the more information that the senior managers have to hand, the more adept the university can be in responding to unforeseen difficulties. Bureaucracy, so the argument runs, is a natural response to risk. A particular example of this phenomenon lies, it might be suggested, in the litigious environment playing upon universities. Not just students but many others – staff, suppliers of services and organisations who feel that their interests are prejudiced by the university – are prepared to seek legal remedies. The 'paper trail' provided by bureaucratic arrangements can help to offset any such risk, since the university will be thereby better able to defend itself. Again, the university has right on its side: risk and litigation are real factors in a marketised age. But the suspicion at least must be that these considerations are not those that – by and large – motivate the onward march of the bureaucratic university for the extent of the routines and procedures are surely disproportionate to the alleged risks.

Rather than looking for a *post hoc* reason or justification for the emergence of the bureaucratic university, then, it would be better to look for an explanation.

What rationality?

I have suggested that the bureaucratic university is also, in some of its contemporary manifestations, the surveillance university. Admittedly, the term 'surveillance' carries baggage.[4] A number of different senses can be attributed to surveillance as it is instantiated in the bureaucratic university.

Bureaucracies have – as Weber pointed out – virtue on their side. Through bureaucracy, like situations are treated in like ways. This is bureaucratic reason and it is *thoroughly* reasonable. Such reason brings efficiency. One no longer has to think when presented with situations. So long as the situation can be classified – a certain box ticked – it can be comprehended and the 'right' action taken. One does not have to waste time, as it might seem, weighing up a situation in and for itself. Its categorisation as being an X or a Y places boundaries around the scope of its management. Now seen as an X rather than a Y, it can be treated according to the set criteria for Xs. It is this kind of course rather than that kind of course; it is a piece of 'research' as distinct from a piece of 'consultancy'; it is supervising a research student rather than teaching on a Master's course. Seen in this way, the emergence of the bureaucratic university is entirely understandable: it is a supremely rational device with which to cope with the extraordinary complexity that is the contemporary university. Systems allow academic life to move on in an orderly and an efficient fashion. Not least, they enable the development of management information systems for the systematic collection of data to inform managers' decision-making.

But this set of reflections brings in a second meaning of surveillance. This surveillance is a necessary part of the bureaucratic procedure; of systems thinking. Individuals – or their actions, at least – have to be subject to surveillance in order that they and their actions can be categorised and the necessary further action taken. There is then a bureaucratic movement in play:

Action (1) → categorisation by bureaucratic procedure (BP) → action (2)

Action (2) – say, the agreement that a research proposal can be submitted to a research council or a new course unit can be started or that an individual is to be classified or not as 'research active' – is dependent on a prior bureaucratic procedure (BP), which is in turn dependent on action (1), namely, the submitting of the research proposal or the course proposal or the listing of one's publications. The BP is necessary in order to release the subsequent action (action (2)). Similarly, the completion of the catering proforma enables the lunch to be ready, or even wheeled along the corridor to a particular room. There is, therefore, an element of power embedded in such bureaucratic procedures.

This bureaucratic procedure constitutes a *generalised* form of surveillance. It allows 'intelligence' to be gathered about certain kinds of activities. And so, in an electronic age, more and more of the procedures are completed 'on-line' for that makes more easily possible the subsequent gathering of the intelligence data.[5] The amount of money sought and secured in research proposals, the number of new course proposals from different departments and faculties, the proportion and numbers of staff who are 'research active' and even the extent to which in-house events are needing to cater for vegetarians: all such matters can be readily computed.

We see, then, a three-fold structure to *this* bureaucracy. First, it is a measure of control: it narrows the options available, since an action (or a need or a want) has to be classifiable: it has to fall into some class or other. Second, it is a form of surveillance at two levels. It contains at least a diffuse form of surveillance in that it is a system intended to supply management information. This is a kind of lower case 'surveillance'. But there is also, even if less evident, a more personal form of surveillance, when individuals are required to undergo procedures that are designed to reveal themselves – their research output, their teaching activities or their performance over the past year (as for annual 'staff appraisal' exercises). This is 'Surveillance' with a capital S. Third, bureaucracy is a mode of academic life in which individuals are reminded of the presence of the institution as such. The elements of power and control inherent in bureaucratic procedures, in which the bureaucratic procedure makes possible a further action, remind individuals that they are subject to the institution that employs them. In the process, it just may be that the exterior eye of management may be internalised so that individuals come internally to monitor their activities for themselves.

The matter, here, is a philosophical one. What rationality is represented by the new systems? Jürgen Habermas (1989: 354–355) has observed that, in modern society, instrumental reason is tending to colonise the 'lifeworld'; that getting things done to fulfil ends comes to be more important that arriving at a deep interpersonal understanding of matters. We cannot straightforwardly apply that judgement to the situation in front of us. For here, I have suggested, we are faced not with instrumental reason but bureaucratic reason. The two are importantly different. Whereas, as stated, instrumental reason is intended to get things done and to find the most powerful means of achieving that end, bureaucratic reason is notorious for holding things up.[6] The research proposal is ready to go off and the deadline is pressing but it needs to be sanctioned by and needs the signature of the Pro-Vice-Chancellor for Research, who is away on other university business. Bureaucratic reason, as we have seen, is motivated not by getting things done but by exercising control and surveillance (albeit for other ends of greater institutional efficiency and effectiveness).

So might we say, then, in the wake of Habermas, that, in the university, it is bureaucratic reason that colonises communicative reason? Bureaucracy, it could be said, generates such a momentum that it supplies contours in which the features of universities are comprehended. Students are classified as of this or that ethnic community; staff are classified as research active or not, or regularly gain research funding or do not, or as efficient or not. Communication on campus comes itself to be curtailed for bureaucratic reason does not allow for poetry, for nuance, for colour.

Behind Habermas' observation – that instrumental reason colonises the lifeworld – lay a powerful sense that there is a fundamental human drive *mutually* to comprehend matters and to attend to the particularities of a situation; and to proceed by the force of the better argument; but that all these features of the rational life are being occluded by the desire simply to get on with things. How things are comes to seem more important than why they are as they are. Is there not something in this story for our understanding of the contemporary university? After all, is the university not society's institution *par excellence* for engendering communicative reason? And could it also be the case that the communicative reason on campus is threatened by the inexorable march of the bureaucratic university?

This is a tempting argument to follow but I think we should resist it. Inexorable and pervasive as the burgeoning of bureaucracy in the modern university may be, its significance lies not in its reducing the space for academic interchange and academic argument but elsewhere.

The corporate university

I suggested earlier that, alongside the emergence of the bureaucratic university, we have also witnessed the emergence of the corporate university; but I also suggested that there are both affinities and tensions between these two states of being of the university.

It will be recalled that, in positing in this book the presence or emergence of different forms of the university, I am not suggesting that any one state of being entirely characterises any one university. Within a single university can be found the research university, the entrepreneurial university, the bureaucratic university and now the corporate university. Even traces of the metaphysical university have a presence. In identifying these forms of what it is to be a university, I am pointing to dominant strains in the way the modern university has become. That the modern university is an amalgam in differing degrees of these states of being constitutes part of the argument of this book.

So, here, the bureaucratic university and the corporate university are to be found alongside each other. They are not coterminous but they have a close relationship. In the first place, the bureaucratic university is *necessary* for the emergence of the corporate university. By 'necessary', I am here pointing to the empirical conditions of our age. The bureaucratic university is the necessary means for the formation of the corporate university. In the bureaucratic university, as we have seen, individuals are subject to common procedures and their working lives are thereby rendered transparent.

Both of these aspects, the commonality and the transparency, are among the features of the corporate university. The corporate university is that form of the university that claims allegiance from its members. Its members – especially its academic members – are required to understand that the university is an entity in itself and that at least part of their identity is that of a member of a particular institution. After all, each university now has its own mission and has made that mission public. It may even have worked out a new 'corporate strategy' and made that public too. Copies have been despatched to its 'stakeholders' and it has been put onto the university's web pages on the internet.

So the university has its own being, independently of its members. It is *not* that 'the university is its members and its members are the university'. To the contrary, the corporate university is fashioned as an entity distinct from its members. That is its point. The old-style research university was 'loosely coupled' (Clark, 1983: 17): its members saw little in common among themselves and their relationship with their university was semi-detached. Their loyalty lay towards their discipline (Becher, 1989). The typical academic might know better and feel more connection with other researchers in his or her discipline on the other side of the world than with an academic in another discipline in the same university, even in the same building. So the corporate university is a vehicle through which to develop collective ties. Now, in the corporate university, every member of staff can – or should – feel themselves to be a part of the same enterprise.

With the arrival of the corporate university, therefore, has come the establishment of marketing departments. Each university seeks to forge a distinct identity – or 'brand – for itself. It adopts a new logo and ensures that all of its stationery and web pages bear the same imprint. Its academics will be encouraged or expected to use the same template for their PowerPoint presentations, especially in other places; a template that again carries the university's new logo and opening slides. 'Business cards' will be printed only providing that they conform to the new house style. There may well be university gifts for senior visiting academics and dignitaries and these, too, will often bear the logo as well as having been chosen to project the new corporate image.

Why is all this necessary? After all, wasn't the idea of 'academic community' precisely that individuals felt some identity with each other, even across disciplines? Weren't academics happy to feel that they were members of the University of X; and even proud to say so? Two quick points may be made. First, as Gandhi reputedly said of Western civilisation, academic community would be a good thing. In other words, academic community has been seen more in the breach than in its presence. The novels on academic life often displaying hostile in-fighting may be a more accurate picture of academic life than the academics' own rhetoric as to their collective spirit. Second, and as noted, academic community has been undermined by the burgeoning of academic disciplines and sub-disciplines, each claiming allegiance over its adherents.[7]

These are, though, rather minor points; and they could serve as legitimisations for the defenders of – or apologists for – the corporate university. For a fuller explanation of the sudden emergence of this new form of the university, we must surely turn elsewhere.

In the corporate university, it may be noticed that Professor X (head of a department) and Professor Y (head of an important research unit) refer to the university in which his department and her research unit are based precisely as 'the university'. Not to 'this university' or to 'our university'; but to '*the* university'. Their university is seen precisely as an entity separate from and standing over their activities. From the perspective of the senior staff, this is indicative of a semi-detached stance of Professor X and Professor Y. Accordingly, the web pages and the leaflets describing the activities of the department and the unit of these professors are scrutinised for any departures from the house style (the size, shape, font and relationships of the character of the university's logo all having been carefully chosen and now *de rigueur* for the whole institution).

The corporate university, then, is an entity that exerts claims upon the staff and their activities. Indeed, to some extent, the staff are required to subjugate their academic personae within the corporate persona (as with the business cards and the PowerPoint presentations). The corporate university can tolerate only so much idiosyncrasy.

Still, the question remains: why should such a form of the university arise? It would be tempting, again, to fall back on the idea of control: the corporate university is but a device to exert control over academics. The corporate university is an answer to the challenge of managing academics which, it is often said, is like herding cats. There is something in this idea but it is not the full answer; in itself, this suggestion is to mistake symptom for cause. Control of the academics is the outcome of a deeper presence.

The corporate university has arisen in a context that includes the emergence of globalisation, the world-wide knowledge economy, and the neo-liberal movements. Universities have been caught up in these dramatic shifts. Whether a university has a largely local, national or global reach, it is now part of a world-wide web of universities that compete with each other both for prestige and for income. The appearance of global rankings of universities is but an indication of these phenomena.

Universities are here caught in a pincer movement. On the one hand, amid 'knowledge capitalism' (Murphy, 2009), they are encouraged to identify and sell their knowledge products. New customers have to be formed for these knowledge products. Here arises the entrepreneurial university (see Chapter 3). But, also, on the other hand, within the knowledge economy, in which knowledge as such – especially in the so-called STEM subjects (Chapter 2) – plays such a pivotal role, universities are pitched up against each other. They compete on a global stage, the global rankings depending largely on their research reputations and achievements.

So the corporate university is inevitable. For the corporate university seeks to maximise its efforts, to pool its resources, to advance itself in the world, to enhance its reputation as a university. It is called into being by the currents that envelope it. It has little choice but to form itself as a corporate entity. The corporate university is entirely explicable.

And what of authenticity?

I have argued that 'the bureaucratic university' and 'the corporate university' are separable states of university being but are intimately associated with each other. In particular, 'the bureaucratic university' provides, in large measure, the foundations of 'the corporate university'. The bureaucratic university is a necessary formation for the corporate university to come into being. Through systematic bureaucratic procedures, the otherwise maverick academic personae are folded into a set of boundaries so that at least the fiction of a single corporate identity can appear.

This chapter could have been entitled, therefore, 'the corporate university'. But the bureaucratic university is not to be understood purely as a means of achieving the corporate university. It has a life of its own. The offices, the procedures, and the managers put in place to advance the corporate university will often come to enhance themselves. They will grow with their own dynamic. Here is a paradox. The very systems that were put in place to advance the university as a corporate entity take on a life of their own and become separate from the university. The purposes of many of the procedures become unclear, there seems to be no convincing rationale for the systems and the managers become caught up in their own roles, identities and purposes, independently of the university as a whole.[8] The bureaucratic university is a necessary means of achieving the corporate university; but all too easily, the bureaucratic university can be a means of the undoing of the corporate university.

Why the undoing? In bureaucracy taking on a life of its own, bureaucracy causes the splintering of the modern university. It is not at all clear how one set of procedures relate to another set. The procedures simply proliferate, uncoordinated. Their lack of coordination is not happenstance but is the very essence of bureaucratic systems coming to have a life of their own, independent of persons. That is precisely their nature.

But, what – so the above sub-heading asks – of authenticity? It is in the nature, too, of bureaucratic procedures that they usher in the inauthentic. In submitting myself to a procedure, I submit myself to a procedure that stands outside of myself. But, surely, so it may be objected, academics all the time submit themselves to procedures that stand outside of themselves. In research and scholarship, academics submit themselves to procedures and methods characteristic of a field. In teaching, academics submit themselves to ways of going on – of teaching, of curriculum 'design' – that have emerged in a community over time. So what is the point here about bureaucratic procedures?

The bureaucratic procedure not merely stands over academic life; it limits academic life; it even dictates to academic life. In research or teaching, in contrast, the procedure opens up possibilities. A university, after all, is nothing unless it is in part a space for structured inquiry. It has ways of going on. But these ways of going on are procedures that open a set of infinite spaces in which individuals – whether alone or in groups – can be creative.[9] A bureaucratic procedure, on the other hand, is in-itself; it is its-own-end. It is a closed system; there is nothing outside of it; no opportunity for spontaneity, for creativity, for nuance, or for personal inflection.

The bureaucratic procedure, accordingly, denies the possibility of authenticity. In the bureaucratic procedure, the self is subjugated to the procedure. In genuine research and teaching – research and teaching that have not become collection of routines – the academic is *opened* by the procedure.

We may note that Paul Feyerabend's (1978) book, *Against Method* (perhaps his most influential book), amounted to a passionate critique of the way in which method can work to reduce the space for originality and daring. How does Feyerabend's thesis play here? It surely plays nicely. For Feyerabend wanted even science to realise that it strapped itself in by its perspectives and procedures. And so he inveighed against Kuhn's (1970) account of science proceeding by a series of interspersed paradigms and revolutions. For Feyerabend, paradigms amounted to 'consolations for the specialist' ([1970] 1977): they were safety measures, which kept thought and experimentation cognitively safe. Authenticity – admittedly not a term that Feyerabend much used – would signal a freedom from procedure; and it would be exhibited in iconoclastic ideas, images and metaphors.

There are two views, then, of the university as an institution characterised by authentic inquiry. The first view is that procedures are an essential part of the university; they are indicative of the university at work. But for the procedures to be fitting, they have to be open-ended. They amount to a set of if–then principles. If one is intending to conduct physics or anthropology or philosophy, then the work in question should conform to certain principles. These principles are procedural and not substantive; they do not govern what one does but the manner of its doing. Disciplinary principles *enable* the activity to take place. In contrast, the university's bureaucratic procedures precisely spell out what is to be done and so limit what is to be done.[10]

The second view of *the authentic university* – as we may term it – is that of a space that encourages iconoclasm. The potentially suffocating or unduly binding character of procedures is understood and maverick thought and methods are welcomed.

These two views of authenticity in academic life differ in the significance that they attach to rules but *both* observe rules. In the first view, rules are to be followed. It is they that provide identity and security and justify claims to the rational life. In the second view, iconoclasm relies on rules, if only to break them. The contrast between academic life and bureaucracy, therefore, is not be found in the presence of rules.

To draw on a distinction made by Hannah Arendt (1958), bureaucracy calls for *labour* whereas the authentic work characteristic of academic life is *work*. It is not, as we have seen, that bureaucracy is characterised by procedures or routines. Authentic academic work has *its* procedures and its routines. The point is that the activity in bureaucracy stands outside of oneself. In subjecting oneself to a bureaucratic procedure, the academic is separated from that work. The fingers may be moving on the keyboard, and the proforma may be completed by the individual; but the bureaucratic activity does not come from within. It is not an intended act on the part of the academic. It is prescribed, required and regulated by the university. The academic is not the author of the activity. The academic cannot invest herself in the procedures and cannot find spaces for her own creativity. The compliance with the bureaucratic procedure is mere labour and not work. In the Marxist meaning of the term, the academic is *alienated* from the activity.

Leading to managerial possibilities

Although the managerial function has been present in this discussion, it has largely been implicit. Why might this be? There is much angst in the academic community, after all, over the emergence of management as a key feature of the modern university, the term 'managerialism' often being conjured as a term of opprobrium. In *this* exploration, alongside the bureaucratic university and the corporate university, '*the managed university*', however, has been perhaps strangely absent.

The absence of the idea of the managed university in this inquiry is explicable. Despite the febrile atmosphere that the juxtaposition of 'management' and 'university' may produce, the managerial presence is but a surface feature of both the bureaucratic university and the corporate university. Each of those latter two forms of the university require strong management. The establishment and the maintenance and refinement of bureaucratic procedures across a university require strong management; and so does the development of a vivid and unified corporate identity. For either the bureaucratic university or the corporate university, we may read the managed university. But, in either case, a strong management presence is not the main act;

it is merely a necessary condition of the *possibility* of the bureaucratic or the corporate university.

If 'management' has only been sighted in the shadows of this discussion, invisible has been the idea of 'leadership'. This, too, is explicable. The bureaucratic university requires no 'leadership': it (just) requires strong management in evolving and instituting robust procedures. The corporate university requires strong management too, in developing a strong institutional identity and in ensuring that the university remains solvent but merely a thin kind of leadership, and *sotto voce* at that. The academics need to be reminded of their allegiance to their university (that pays their salaries) and this widening of their 'academic identity' calls for academic leadership; but this academic leadership had better go about its task without calling attention to itself for it will only undermine its own efforts if its endeavours and purposes become overt. Accordingly, the recent transformations of the university have required strong management but, given the kinds of transformations in question here, the place and role of 'leadership' are debatable.

Both the ideas of management and of leadership are in some difficulty, therefore. On the one hand, management comes to be identified with a closing off of spaces, in its strong association with both the bureaucratic university and the corporate university. On the other hand, leadership comes to be but a thin concept, hardly able to gain much of a purchase. But both concepts – management and leadership – are crucial to any fulfilment of the idea of the university; to any advance toward what I have termed feasible utopias of the university. Universities are extraordinary *and* complex institutions, increasingly seeking funds from multiple sources and having their being in uncertain environments. They need and deserve exemplary management. *If feasible utopias are to be realised,* systems need to be developed and managed efficiently and new sources of income identified. The utopian university needs to be managed. But two riders are necessary.

First, the managed university can be legitimised only to the extent that its sources of funding and systems are managed against the horizon of the largest ideas as to the purposes of a university. It is here that the concept of leadership gains purchase, in identifying possibilities for a university and securing endorsement in taking the identified possibilities forward as collective endeavours.[11] 'Management' and 'leadership' therefore are entirely different concepts. 'Management' can only secure assent for its activities if it is framed *within* a concept of leadership, itself couched within an ambitious but realistic sense of a university's possibilities.

Second, the concepts of bureaucracy, corporatism, management and even leadership can never exhaust the challenges of helping to take an institution forward. The corporate university has to have time for individuals; bureaucratic and instrumental reason cannot be allowed to stand for the life of the university, still less to triumph over the life of the university. There remain spaces in the corporate university for individuals to be recognised as individual persons. The interpretive life, the felt life, remains as an integral part of the university not only on account of the care for all persons within the idea of the university but also on account of the fulfilment of any authentic idea of the university. In the end, individuals matter.[12]

Conclusion

The bureaucratic university and the corporate university are among the latest forms of the university to emerge. They are related but they are not the same. The bureaucratic university *supports* the corporate university: its systematic procedures enhance the university as a single entity that the corporate university yearns to be. Bureaucracy, however, has a tendency to become itself, to further its own ends. At least the corporate university can claim that it is acting both to further the interests of the university and to play up its part in society; the corporate university aids the entrepreneurial university (Chapter 3) and even the research university (Chapter 4). But the bureaucratic university has few such redeeming features. It tends to suffocate creativity and spontaneity; it limits academic identity; it corrals academic life into an undue uniformity; it allows no escape. And it reduces institutional energies instead of enlarging them.

However, the bureaucratic university is not without point and even virtue. The uniformity that is symptomatic of the bureaucratic university rules out undue departures from acceptable practices. The procedures, being universal, ensure that matters do not fall through the net. Universities, after all, are collectives. Their academics depend on each other. The procedures ensure that tasks are accomplished, and on time, and to an acceptable standard. Through bureaucratic procedures, academics are called to account.

So bureaucracy has its place in the modern university. But – as Winston Churchill reputedly said of the scientists – it can only be efficacious if it is on tap and not on top. It has its place; which is to say, it should be kept in its place. The corporate university arises on the foundations of the bureaucratic university and it emerges in both suffocating and empowering versions. The corporate university can opt to stifle dissent, strangeness, and quirkiness. Mavericks may not be tolerated (being not part of the corporate mission). But the corporate university may still harbour spaces for the recognition and affirmation of individuals. It can be the means by which academic identities can flourish and through which feasible utopias may just be brought off. As ever, in our inquiries, the university turns out to have options before it.

Part II

Contending concepts

5 Being and becoming

Being has not been given its due.

(Sartre, *Being and Nothingness*, [1943] 2003: 16)

Becoming is a verb with a consistency all its own . . . It is . . . a creative line of escape that says nothing other than what it is.

(Deleuze and Guattari, *Kafka: Towards a Minor Literature*, quoted in Guattari, 2005: 75)

Introduction

In Part I of this book, we saw that universities have had and continue to have different forms of being. Many of these forms will be found in a single university *at the same time*. Still, over time, *alternative* dominant forms of the university can be discerned. What it is to be a university in the twenty-first century is not what it was in the nineteenth century, and still less what it was, say, in medieval times.

But the matter as to what is it to be a university is not only a matter of historical and sociological interest. In part, too, it is a conceptual or even a philosophical issue; it raises the matter as to what the idea of university *could* mean. Here lies the purpose of Part II of this book, to inquire into concepts and ideas that might inform the development of the idea, or ideas, of the university. The strategy adopted is that of exploring sets of twin *contending* concepts. They are contending concepts in that, to some extent, the two concepts in each pair contend with each other; there are tensions between them. But they also, in their intimations, contend for possible new ideas of the university. Their conjunction may just help us to glimpse virtuous possibilities for the university.

In this, the first of these explorations, we begin with the fundamental question: just what is it to *be* a university? How might we understand the 'being' of a university? To pose such questions may seem strange. Are not universities already 'universities'? However, institutions may take the name of 'university' but may fall short of what it might mean to be a university. And so the question – what is it to be a university? – presses itself. But, then, further issues arise. If universities characteristically fall short of the fullest realisation of the possibilities inherent in the idea of 'university', then universities surely need to *become* fully 'universities'. But what, then, is this process of 'becoming'? 'Being' and 'becoming', therefore, are the contending concepts immediately before us.

Being possible

For Heidegger, as we noted at the outset, being is 'being-possible'. Being is only being insofar as it has possibilities in front of it:

> *Being-towards-possibilities* . . . is itself a potentiality-for-Being. [It] has its own possibility – that of developing itself.
>
> (Heidegger, [1927] 1998: 188)

Being, then, is a philosophical idea. It is open-ended. It has options in it and, then, responsibilities. Being weighs heavily on being, we may say.

In their being, in being 'universities', universities are full of possibilities. A university may not be able simply to ensure that it will appear in, say, the top hundred universities in the world-wide league tables. It may not be able to ensure that one of its academics will win a Nobel Prize. It may not be able to bring about the highest level of satisfaction among its students. But still its possibilities are infinite; that some possibilities are unattainable in no way dents the point that it has infinite possibilities. To what extent might it invest in information technology and to what end? How much relative effort does it wish to devote to research *and* to teaching? To what degree does a university see itself as serving society and being active in the community? How, if at all, will it reach out to potential students from non-traditional backgrounds? What is its formal structure to be and what groupings of departments might it have? Might its academic departments be encouraged to collaborate (and even witness a level of cross-subsidy among them) instead of competing against each other? The university has choices to make in all these and many other respects. And the options that can be taken up are of an infinite variety.

These opening reflections point to a subterranean set of dimensions that affects the way that the university is in the world. First, there are the *empirical conditions* of a university's being. What is the extent of its funding? To what degree can it raise additional income? How is it perceived in the world – or even by its own students and its own staff? There are limits to its possibilities; its being is constrained.

Second, there are the *ideological conditions* of its being. What is the dominant sense of a university in this society? To what degree is it expected to be entrepreneurial? To what degree is it expected to 'serve' society? These ideological conditions help to frame a landscape of possibilities.

Third, there are the *imaginative conditions* of its being: what are the visions that the university entertains for itself? What are the possibilities that it imagines for itself; (to use a term from Charles Taylor (2004)) its own 'imaginaries'?[1] Are those imaginative possibilities merely an extension of what it has been and is now; or is a quite different future envisaged for it?

Lastly, there is the *value background* (Taylor, 1969) against which each university has its being. Is a university mainly concerned to live within itself, a university *in-itself* (the research university); or to profit from the world – a university *for-itself* (the entrepreneurial university); or to attend to the wider society – a university *for-the-Other*? Does it believe that inquiry as such is valuable, is its 'own end' (as Newman (1976) put it) or does it believe that inquiry is only valuable insofar as it is demonstrably put to use in the world,[2] or can it identify a new relationship for itself with the world?

These four sets of conditions – empirical, ideological, imaginative and value conditions – form the structure of a university's being. They set limits and they supply promptings. They are in themselves a mix of the actual and the possible. In these conditions are real constraints; but in them, too, are possibilities, yearnings and strivings into the future. A university sensitive to its possibilities in these terms not merely thinks itself into the future but looks to advance the future. It may see the future largely in terms of its own fortune but it may also see the future much more in terms of the fortunes of the wider world, puzzling how – given its resources – it may help to improve that wider world.

These four sets of conditions are also increasingly more open to possibilities. The *empirical* conditions are largely given, though not entirely so. A university can reach out into the community to work with local schools and colleges to identify pupils who would benefit from a university education but who might not otherwise reach the normal entry requirements. It could choose to set up a modest fund to encourage its staff and students to be active in the local community, even though it does not receive state funding for such an activity. It may be a research-intensive university but find that it is rather lowly placed in a national survey of the 'student experience' and choose thereupon to offer a route to the title of 'professor' in which one's teaching profile could play a significant part. 'Empirical', therefore, need not mean wholly given. Universities often have latitude to alter to some degree the empirical conditions of their being.

Successively through the ideological, imaginative and value conditions of their being, this latitude expands. In the *ideological domain*, a university is confronted with collective interests of a higher education system, but it is not impotent. It can work to change the dominant ideas that spring from those interests: for example, it might work with its Students Union to address any emerging sense of students as 'consumers'. Despite such a conception – of students as consumers – being bound up with the incorporation of the university sector into the 'learning economy', the ideology is not totally binding. The university always has some room for manoeuvre.

In the *imaginative* domain, a university could set up fora for its staff, in which both its academic and all its support staff could come together to create new ideas for the university's development. In other words, it could seek to maximise the *imaginative capacities* available to it, as it identifies its future possibilities. And in the *value domain*, a university could reach out to others to glean external perceptions of its values, so as to leap out of itself in a reframing of its own value position. Its own values may be kept perpetually under critical self-review.

The university's being is always 'being possible', therefore. Its being lies behind it, within it and before it.

Becoming a university

What is the difference between the *being* of a university and its *becoming*? Is its becoming a university separate from being a university, or is *being* a university to be understood as a process of perpetually *becoming* a university? Being a university is always a matter of becoming a university. To put it cryptically, being a university is *always* unfinished business.

Being is always active. Being a university, therefore, is not a passive existence. In being a university, a university is not simply in the world. It is *active* in the world, and that includes being active *with* its own self. In being a university, the university has a concern for itself in the world. It reflects on itself as it acts in the world. Being a university is a matter of being engaged with the university's being.[3]

It follows that, in becoming a university, a university is seeking to become itself. In becoming itself, a university is always striving to take itself forward, attempting with all its energies to go in some self-determined direction, even against the swirling waters that would deflect it off its path. It is like the competitive canoeist, struggling to pass between the markers without touching them, all the while buffeted by the turbulent currents that seem to snatch it away from and keep its goal just out of reach.

A university can only fully become itself through taking its own self-understanding forward. It will, therefore, conduct inquiries into itself. Such self-inquiry goes far beyond the collection of 'management information' (Chapter 4) to embrace the most subtle self-understandings. Even 'research', ordinarily understood, cannot do full justice to the demands of the situation. It is notable that the 'scholarship of teaching and learning' movement, now underway across the world, plays up 'scholarship' rather than 'research'. Its morale, its ethos and culture, its sense of itself in the world, the changing character of the 'academic identities' within it, students' sense of themselves and what it is to be a student, the possibilities for a university's research and scholarly endeavours: all these and many other matters would form part of the growth of this university's self-understandings. Unfortunately, universities' interests in studying the world seldom extend *in this manner* to trying to understand themselves. But self-understanding is crucial for any university to edge seriously towards its full possibilities; to become itself.[4] Through such self-understanding, its possibilities are better disclosed to it.[5]

So being a university is becoming a university. In a way, there is no more to be said. In being a university of the kind I am arguing for, a university is always in play, in self-consciously forging its own becoming. There is no break between being a university and becoming a university.[6]

But it is worth dwelling on the idea of becoming. For becoming has its own possibilities and its own conditions. Perhaps the greatest modern account of becoming is that of Deleuze and Guattari in their (2004) book *A Thousand Plateaus*. For them, 'becoming is never imitating' (ibid.: 336). Neither is it 'to progress or regress along a series' (ibid.: 262). 'Becoming produces nothing other than itself' (ibid.: 262). But what is it to produce itself? What would that mean in relation to a university? Is there a self to be produced? 'Becoming is involutionary' (ibid.: 263). 'Involution' is contrasted with 'evolution': whereas evolution is to lead out from where a species is, 'involution is creative'. It is – we may say – both a going into itself and is creative all at once.[7]

A key idea in *A Thousand Plateaus* is that of 'rhizome'. 'There are no points or positions in a rhizome, such as found in a structure, tree or root' (ibid.: 9). As such, 'Any point of a rhizome can be connected to anything other.' We may still want to talk of structure in connection with universities – both within individual universities and across a higher education system – but the idea of a rhizome with its inter-connectivity is surely suggestive. Every part of a university – its languages, its genres, its practices – is connected both internally and externally with the world, even if many of those connections are to be described as tensions, antagonisms and ruptures. This *interconnectedness* of the university-as-rhizome within itself and with the wider world perhaps accounts for its longevity.

But, for our purposes, another – albeit connected – idea in *A Thousand Plateaus* is even more significant. It is that of *multiplicities*. For Deleuze and Guattari, multiplicities are definitely plural. There are forms of multiplicity. And we may observe that a university is a multiplicity in itself *and* that universities exhibit forms of multiplicity. 'Multiplicities are rhizomatic . . . There is no unity to serve as a pivot in the object' (ibid.: 8):

> A multiplicity is defined not by its elements, nor by a center of unification or comprehension. It is defined by the number of dimensions it has.
>
> (ibid.: 275)

And, we may observe, universities are multiplicities in themselves,[8] and have a myriad, really an infinite number of dimensions – including their relationships with the state, forms of knowledge, modes of learning, purposes of inquiry, and their orientation to public engagement. And universities work with each other and against each other: 'Thus packs, or multiplicities, continually transform themselves into each other, cross over into each other' (ibid.: 274).

Is this not a neat description of a university, its multiplicities 'cross(ing) over into each other' and 'continually transforming themselves'? The concepts held by its groups and its members – both its academics and its managers and other staff – and its activities continue to extend its shape on a daily basis. It moves this way and that across societal surfaces, always restless. Its 'thresholds' orient it in some directions, denying some potential movements and permitting others. Its doors may be opened, if individuals and groups possess the necessary keys.

But what of becoming? '[B]ecoming and multiplicity are the same thing' (ibid.: 275). So more becoming is more multiplicity: the university becomes itself by becoming even more of a multiplicity. But it isn't a multiplicity in itself. For what is involved, to draw finally on and to adapt another of the constructions of Deleuze and Guattari, is that of 'becoming-university'. 'Even blacks, as the Black Panthers said, must become-black' (ibid.: 321). Here, this blackness 'rises up' (ibid.: 321). In other words, we may say, a university becomes a university when it shares in a collective sense of 'university' that has been forged among universities. However, an individual university must come into this self-understanding in its own way. After all, 'becoming is never imitating.'

For the university, the challenges of its becoming, then, are turning out to be considerable. We have identified three challenges. First, a university has to become itself. This is, in the first place, not to say that a university has to have a simple conception of itself but that rather it does have to have some sense of itself and its possibilities. Second, a university becomes a university in virtue of coming into association with other institutions that share in a collective sense of the idea of 'university'.[9] Third, this becoming has to be achieved while the university is a multiplicity, weaving in and out of other multiplicities. Each of these three challenges is problematic; and their joint realisation is more problematic still.

Becoming itself

If in its being and becoming, a university has to become itself as a university, what could that mean? After all, the university is saturated with ideologies, imposed structures and narrow interests and is a set of complexes. Is there a self – that is the university – that can be recovered or uncovered? Or do we just allow the multiplicities – the powers, the flows of money, the languages, the activities – that constitute a university simply to collide with other interacting multiplicities? In these circumstances, can there be *any* idea through which universities might become themselves as universities?

I want to examine the possibility that the idea of *understanding* can begin to furnish such a normative function for the university. 'Understanding' works on a number of levels.

We can ask of an individual: 'and what is his understanding?' But we can also ask the question of a group or even a society: 'and what is *its* understanding?' In positing 'understanding' of a group or society, we are not implying unanimity. Provided that there is some degree of reciprocity among its members, we may still speak of a group's – or a society's – understanding of a matter even though there be disparate beliefs evident within it. Indeed, that there can be such disparate beliefs may be an indication that the level of understanding has some depth to it.

We are, though, only entitled to talk of a deep level of understanding when we are also able to assign a truth value to that understanding. 'Understanding' is an indication that the matters that are understood are in some way true. In an 'understanding', some kind of valid insight into the world has been formed.

Understandings do not just form in themselves for 'understanding' is a quality of *beliefs*. Beliefs may be held with greater or lesser understanding and with greater or lesser profundity (Elliott, 1975). Such beliefs, held with understanding, form via knowledge. The term 'via' is important, for knowledge offers a pathway to understandings. Characteristically, knowledge is an interlinked set of ideas, concepts and practices with some tradition behind them. These form 'disciplines' or fields of professional practice, and understandings form within such disciplines and fields.

The term 'understanding', then, points to a set of relationships between believers, understandings, beliefs, knowledge, truth and the world. Understanding links believers to the world, via knowledge.

We should note that, having brought into view the ideas of truth, knowledge and world, we do not have to take a stand on what is to count as truth, knowledge or the world. Indeed, it is important that we do not take a stand on those matters for debate on those matters has to be permanently on the table, so to speak, within 'the university'.

Where has this excursion into the nature of understanding taken us? If we now suggest that the idea of understanding furnishes a unifying idea for the becoming of the university, we are saying very much. For it now becomes the task of universities to help advance understanding *as far as practicable*. That is to say, it is the task of universities to help bring potential believers into valid knowing relationships with the world, *wherever those potential believers may be in the world*. We have noted that understanding can be shallow and it can be profound. Accordingly, to speak of understanding in this way is to point to the task of universities in advancing public understanding in the world. There is no limit to the deepening or growth of understanding in the world, or as to whom might form well-founded beliefs and to whom the university might seek to reach out; so there is no limit to the work of universities.

We noted earlier that understanding can be an attribute of individuals, groups or society itself. It follows that to make a strong connection between 'university' and 'understanding' opens a path into the ways in which universities might help to develop society's understanding of matters; indeed, the world's understandings of matters. The world *is* its oyster.

It will be noticed that, in making these remarks about 'understanding', we have mentioned neither research nor teaching. We have not needed to do so. For 'understanding' applies both to research and teaching. 'Understanding' is, therefore, a much larger concept than either research or teaching.

To suggest that a university is *sui generis* connected with the growth of understanding is to say, implicitly, that it has to do all in its capacity to help understanding to grow. That is to say, the university will be active to this end in all of its possible connections to the world. A university will not arbitrarily limit – or accept arbitrary limits being placed upon – its endeavours to help the growth of understanding. Those endeavours may be direct efforts, in helping individuals or groups to advance their understandings; or they may be indirect efforts, putting ideas and knowledge into the public domain across the world to help in widening the conceptual resources and primary knowledge that might in turn further those individuals' and groups' understandings.

The idea of understanding, then, is a potent idea in trying to discern a unifying idea for the university and an idea that furnishes a special role for the university. A multiplicity the university may be; and intersecting in uncertain ways with other multiplicities. Still, there remains the possibility that some unifying idea may be gleaned. 'Understanding', seen as understanding in and across the world, may be one such idea.

Other contenders

A number of other suggestions have been made recently as to what it might be to be a university. Those ideas include 'wisdom', 'inquiry', 'virtue' and 'dissensus'. A brief comment on each one may help to bring out further the particular characteristics of 'understanding'.

Surely the most significant contemporary advocate of the idea of wisdom is that of Nicholas Maxwell. For over thirty years, Maxwell has argued that the turn to knowledge in the Enlightenment has proved to be a costly mistake. Instead, a move towards wisdom should have been made,

> [W]isdom being understood to be the capacity to realize what is of value in life for oneself and others (and thus including knowledge, know-how and understanding).
>
> (2008: 2)

Accordingly, educational institutions, including and perhaps especially universities, should be oriented not towards 'knowledge-inquiry' but towards 'wisdom-inquiry'. This would 'articulate our problems of living (personal, social and global) and propose and critically assess possible solutions, possible actions' (ibid.: 16–17).

This is an argument powerfully worked out by Maxwell. There are, perhaps, two inter-related difficulties that it prompts. First, it is not at all clear that 'what is of value in life' will command any consensus. There will be never-ending dispute on the matter. Second, it is part of the nature of the university that it sustains argument. Without argument, we are not in the presence of a university but of a totalitarian state. What is to count as wise thought and wise action, therefore, are precisely matters over which it is part of the university to sustain a critical debate. On both points, it is unclear as to how wisdom-inquiry as such could ever get going, given that the university is an institution characterised by never-ending critical debate. All this is tantamount to saying that it is part of the purposes of the university to provide a space in which the search for ever more refined *understandings* can be continued and it is a well-populated space.

This possibility of never-ending critical debate takes us to Readings' (1996) idea of dissensus. Readings sees the idea of the post-historical university as lying not in communication as such but in a 'community of dissensus':

> Such a community . . . that presupposes nothing in common, would not be dedicated either to the project of a full self-understanding (autonomy) or to a communicational consensus as to the nature of its unity. Rather, it would seek to make its heteronomy, its differences, more complex.
>
> (ibid.: 190)

The university will sustain such a dissensus through its possessing 'a shifting disciplinary structure that holds open the question of whether and how thoughts fit together' (ibid.: 191).

That the university holds within itself differences we have already noted in this inquiry. It is a set of multiplicities, of unkempt borders, of disruptions and antagonisms. But this reflection seems to constitute no good reason, as Readings implies, to repudiate consensus. For the kind of dissensus that Readings points to *relies on* a consensual set of understandings, namely over the terms of the debate through which the parties will form their dissensus. Furthermore, it just may be that, on occasions at least, in striving for understanding, individuals and groups will come to agree. They may even come to see the world in entirely new ways and agree on a conceptually innovative perspective that still does justice to their earlier disparate understandings.

Understanding, therefore, remains a concept prior to either wisdom or dissensus. Let us at least try to reach an understanding, and let it be as true and as valid and as insightful and as nuanced as possible; and still allow for our different viewpoints. Let *this* understanding do new justice to the world, letting us see the world in new, worthwhile and innovative ways.

Is this not, though, the same as 'enquiry', a term developed in a series of books by Stephen Rowland? Understanding and enquiry *are* close and even overlapping concepts. For Rowland,

> [The] concept of enquiry . . . encompasses and extends beyond discovery. . . . Intellectual love is its key component and . . . it forms a basis for both teaching and research. Enquiry (quest for the truth from the Latin *quaere verum*) involves seeking. Pedagogically, perhaps the most important task of the teacher is to develop an atmosphere or an attitude in which students seek . . . Similarly, for the researcher, enquiry provides the ground for discovering new knowledge.
>
> (2006: 109)

Here, 'enquiry' is surely somewhat lacking in evaluative criteria. I can enquire into the state of play in a game of cricket; I can enquire into the reason as to why workmen are digging a hole in the road; and I can enquire into the likelihood of its raining later today. In all these cases, I may be satisfied at the first answer I receive or I may receive an answer that I find unsatisfactory. If I am satisfied, I may have no means of judging if I have been given a sound or true answer; if I am not satisfied, my understanding has not been taken forward. I may seek a further response but still I shall have no way of judging that response. In other words, enquiry may be lacking judgement. An enquirer is too easily satisfied.

The idea of understanding, in contrast, is multilayered. It incorporates a reference to the world and the relationships between the world and accounts of it. It posits relationships between those accounts and their veracity. In a university, my understandings have also not only to be assessable as true but they have to be *my* understandings. 'Understanding', therefore, is a much more demanding concept than 'enquiry'.

The virtuous university

Virtue has been examined in depth by Alisdair MacIntyre. MacIntyre's argument is complex and eludes any brief summary. Still, it is important that we acknowledge it, in however an incomplete form. Crudely, MacIntyre's argument turns on an interweaving of the ideas of virtue, practice, internal goods, tradition and institution:

> A virtue is an acquired human quality the possession and exercise of which tends to enable us to achieve those goods which are internal to practices and the lack of which effectively prevents us from achieving any such goods.
>
> (MacIntyre, 1985: 191)

Characteristic of the goods internal to practices is that 'their achievement is a good for the whole community' and characteristic of practices is that they involve 'standards of excellence and obedience to rules as well as the achievement of [internal] goods' (ibid.: 190). It follows that:

> Practices must not be confused with institutions. Chess, physics and medicine are practices; chess clubs, laboratories, universities and hospitals are institutions. Institutions are characteristically concerned with . . . external goods . . . acquiring money and other material goods [and] structured in terms of power and status.
>
> (ibid.: 194)

Lest it be thought that, here, MacIntyre has only a negative view of institutions, he is explicit that 'no practices can survive for any length of time unsustained by institutions' (ibid.: 194). But it is the case that institutions 'have corrupting power' (ibid.: 194). Accordingly, 'we [are] unable to write a true history of practices and institutions unless that history is also one of virtues and vices' (ibid.: 195).

What, then, for MacIntyre are the 'peculiar goods' that universities serve? Universities are 'places where conceptions of and standards of rational justification are elaborated, put to work in the detailed practices of enquiry, and themselves rationally evaluated ' (MacIntyre, 1990: 222). But that view can be plausibly advanced

> only when and insofar as the university is a place where rival and antagonistic views of rational justification . . . are afforded the opportunity to . . . develop their own enquiries . . . and to conduct their intellectual and moral warfare.
>
> (ibid.: 222)

MacIntyre immediately adds that:

> It is precisely because universities have not been such places . . . that the official responses of both the appointed leaders and the working members of university communities to their recent external critics have been so lamentable.
>
> (ibid.: 222)

More recent voices following in MacIntyre's (Aristotelian) footsteps are that of Bruce Macfarlane and Jon Nixon. Macfarlane has developed, in a series of books (2004; 2009), a conception of universities as built around sets of virtues in relation, separately, to teaching and to research,[10] while Nixon's (2008) book offers as the foundations of the virtuous university the virtues of truthfulness, respect, authenticity and magnanimity.

What might we make of this virtue-based approach to the idea of the university? It is surely a powerful idea and in the hands of Macfarlane and Nixon, the idea is worked out such that we see what it might mean in the day-to-day practices of institutions. There is, though, a problem that any virtue-based account of the university has to face and it is this: what is the status of the proposed 'virtues'? Are they held to be valuable in their own right and that, therefore, universities should do what they can to uphold them? In that case, what is special about universities? OR is it that the virtues are held to be inherent in the kinds of practices characteristic of universities? But since universities are complex institutions, why should it be felt that there would be collective assent to the alleged virtues being inherent in university practices?

Weak meta-strategies

MacIntyre worked through issues, I think, close to these and it was his sense that Western society has seen a dissolution of any consensus as to there being characteristic virtues that attach to roles. The title of his book, *After Virtue*, is testimony to the point: on what basis are virtues to be identified in an age that is 'after virtue'? And so, when he came to examine universities, it was part of the logic of MacIntyre's philosophy that all that could be offered for the university was a kind of meta-virtue: the university was – as we saw – to be a place 'where rival and antagonistic views of rational justification . . . are afforded the opportunity to . . . develop their own enquiries . . . and to conduct their intellectual and moral warfare'. This is a view that mirrors Bill Readings' idea of 'dissensus' and, while it is a helpful *aide-mémoire*, it is a rather thin idea of the university; and it is doubly thin.

On the one hand, the meta-idea of a university as a place of rational conflict is insufficiently sensitive to the challenges faced by universities in modern times, challenges at both national and global levels (of open interactive electronic media, globalisation, the knowledge economy, and so forth). The idea of the university as a place of rational conflict presumes that the university can seclude itself and establish intellectual borders between itself and the wider world so as to preserve its argumentative integrity. But that world has passed. Now, the world is in the university and the university is in the world. The university-as-debating-society separate from the world is now an inadequate idea of the university.

On the other hand, this debating society idea of the university is imaginatively weak. The challenges that the university faces are placing new stresses on the idea of the university. The contemporary university is fluid, interspersed in the currents of the age; it lacks definition and any kind of unity it seems.

It is surely through sensitivity to such matters that scholars such as MacIntyre, Readings and Derrida have resorted to a meta-strategy, that of trying to find a stratospheric description of the university – as a place of intellectual conflict, or dissensus, or as a place where questions can be asked as to what the responsibilities of the university might be. The difficulties of saying anything substantive about a university – as to what its virtues might be or its culture or its responsibilities might be – lead to the meta-strategy.

In each case, what is proposed is a description of the kinds of conversation characteristic of 'a university'. In turn, we lack any imaginative depiction, even at the level of general principles, as to the *being* of the university. However sympathetic, it is by no means clear that a vice-chancellor or rector, on reading any of the texts of these scholars, could have much in the way of promptings as to how to develop a university as 'a university'. What is to be done on the Monday would remain far from clear.

There is a programmatic and imaginative thinness that attaches to the concern with the character of the university's conversations.

Conclusion

A university is not entirely autonomous such that it can determine its being and its unfolding by itself or for itself. It is caught in its own empirical circumstances, at once local and global, and at once ethical, intellectual, financial and material. To a large extent, the university is in the world and of the world. There are pragmatic conditions of its being but there are also imaginative possibilities. All universities have some space in which to identify their feasible options. Characteristically, universities draw those options rather narrowly.

Admittedly, being imaginative about a university's future is no simple task. It calls for an interweaving of the singular and the collective and of the present and the past and the future. It calls for sensitivity to the intricate nature of a university, its own multiplicities interconnected via continuous data streams with other multiplicities across the nation and across the world. It calls for a sensitivity to the responsibilities that attach to being part of the collective community of universities. It calls for hopes and glimpses of a better world and of the university helping to bring about that vision. And it calls for courage to strike out for sets of values that contend with 'the self-images of the age'.[11]

Are there any lights by which to steer a university's becoming in an uncertain and fluid world? Two gambits are available in the literature. On the one hand, the virtue approach: a university can strive to be and become a university through upholding fundamental ethical virtues and concerns. A wide array of virtues has been proposed and each one has its own worth; its own virtue, indeed. But they pose difficulties. Once begun, it is not clear why there should be an end to the listing of virtues. In turn, it is clear neither that any virtue will attract a consensus nor as to its status as a uniquely defining characteristic of universities.

Faced with the difficulties of saying anything substantive as to what it is to be a university, modern philosophers have resorted on the other hand to an alternative gambit, falling back on a meta-strategy, on high-blown depictions of the communicative processes of 'the university'. In general, these processes should be such as to make possible rational discourse, systematic rational reflection, argumentative conflict, conversation and dissensus. The difficulty here is that these depictions exhibit a programmatic and imaginative thinness. They offer little help as to how to go on being and becoming a university, especially given the interconnections of the university with the world.

Is there an intermediate way through here (one hesitates to say 'a third way') that will avoid the dual difficulties of adding to a question-begging list of dispositions and virtues, on the one hand, and, on the other, of offering a stratospheric depiction of the university's conversational processes that do little to help in the development of a programme of action? I have suggested that the idea of 'understanding' may be helpful here. 'Understanding' is neither a virtue or disposition on the part of the university nor is it a depiction of its communicative processes as such. Rather, 'understanding' begins to indicate the *intentional space* of the university. The university has a fundamental interest in promoting understanding, *and* so understanding can begin to offer a way forward in a university's self-reflections.

A university that took hold of the concept of understanding – as part of its own sense of itself – would be faced with the challenges of determining the scope of its concern with understanding (how far is it going to reach out to publics nationally and globally in furthering their understanding?) and of the conditions on which it was going to make those forays (how far, for instance, would it wish to generate 'profits' from such activities?). The idea of understanding offers no simple solution to the problems of being a university, therefore. But yet, it just may be that the idea of 'understanding' can begin to help institutions have a clearer sense as to what it is to be and become a university.

6   Space and time

Introduction

Outside the university's library, dare an academic be seen reading an academic book on campus, even in the academic's 'own office'? The question is a nice cameo of the intermingling of time and space. For the reading of a book represents certain kinds of time *and* space. The activity calls for some duration of time and characteristically – as in the phrase 'reading a book' – a slow pace of time. The book's argument has to be comprehended, its nuances observed. But where is this activity to take place, if at all?

The library was a designated space for reading but, now, in some universities, libraries are noisy places, as groups of students gather around large tables jointly to pursue their undergraduate projects. But the academic cannot easily retreat to her room to read. Her room, after all, is not hers: if she is fortunate enough still to enjoy a room to herself, she may be aware that her room is a university space, and subject to the university's space usage calculations and the reading of books is not seen as a *bone fide* activity in such calculations. She may feel too the press of the university's developing ethos of busyness, of explicit actions, of setting goals and having timelines. In this milieu, the reading of a book is an expression of anarchy, running against the currents of the academic age. It is a private and interior activity, requiring its own space, and calling for a slow pacing. The apparently simple activity of reading a book either in an academic's room or in a public space – a single book, and not the quick assimilation of great quantities of books and papers for a 'literature review – is an anarchic act. It interposes private thinking and a personal duration and pacing of time into the organisational spaces and pacings of time of the university.

In the university of the twenty-first century, space and time are, therefore, intimately connected; inter-connected, indeed. It was also thus, of course, ever since the modern university's inception in the Middle Ages. Then, the scholars of Europe travelled across those countries and were conscious of the temporal conditions of their calling not least as they discovered the work of Aristotle and other Greeks. These scholars lived in time; they understood themselves against a horizon of time. But the university still lives in time, while also living in the space attaching to being a global institution. Perhaps the contemporary university has lost much of its memory, forgetting – and not being much interested in – its past. Now, it lives much more in the future, thinking about its forward journey. It is also aware of its geographical contexts, at once regional, national and world-wide. And these two dimensions – of space and time – intersect, and even contend with each other, so making even more intricate their effects on the university.

Despite these dimensions of the contemporary university having being ubiquitous, there has been rather little examination of them.[1] The university in space and time, therefore, is the matter before us in this chapter.

The narrative of simultaneity

> [T]ime becomes human time to the extent to which it is organized after the manner of a narrative; narrative, in turn, is meaningful to the extent that it portrays the features of temporal existence.
>
> (Paul Ricoeur, [1984] 1990: 3)

Does the university understand the ways in which it is held in time? Can it do so? The university can be understood as intermingling sets of narratives of itself that have been laid down over time. The strata that form the narratives are not neatly layered on each other: they are just like rock formations, the separate strata being visible but also running into each other, with old strata reaching up into the new. And so, suddenly, a scholar who has stumbled anew on a centuries-old manuscript of a composer or writer becomes headline news. The scholarly university of old breaks through the research and the entrepreneurial university of today.

But, today, the university lives in time and space in ways that may be beyond our comprehension. We can no longer content ourselves with getting out our old tools and equipment to peer into the interplay of the narrative strata.

Assume a multi-faculty university with some 20,000 souls in it who are part of the academic enterprise – students, academics, researchers and many others. Assume there is that same number of computers connected with the university (many of which will be portable computers and so will not necessarily be on campus). Assume that characteristically many if not most of those computers are, during the course of a single day, are connected to networks across the world. Those networks will typically be interactive and so, at any one moment, the university is caught in, engaged in, networks on a global scale. Here is 'chronoscopic time', as Robert Hassan has termed it (after Virilio):

> The meter of chronological clock time that has underscored our industrial, social and cultural institutions, and has been the temporality through which we have made sense of the world, is being supplanted by a digitally compressed temporality [that is, chronoscopic time] . . . Through the increasing density of data networks and human interconnectivity we are in the process of creating a whole new temporal ecology based on the constant now.
>
> (Hassan, 2003: 111)

This is time that shatters time. An incessant simultaneity of time. And from these reflections, Hassan develops an indictment of the effects of this supra-fast time on academic life and the student experience. In this speeded-up temporal milieu, as knowledge is reduced to mere data, space for contemplative thought and even reflexivity evaporates and deep learning – of the kind caught in the German concept of *Bildung* – is diminished (cf. Levy, 2007). Insofar as we may still speak of knowledge, it is now 'commodified',[2] where knowledge for understanding gives way to knowledge as a force for production.

There is much in this analysis. Universities are now nodes, concentrations of flows of information generation and processing. Their multiple information networks are active 24 hours a day. The academic life struggles to gain a purchase in such swift moving currents. Opportunities for slower, and genuine, communication shrink. As university buildings are refurbished, room is no longer possible for convivial meeting spaces. But the analysis can be overdrawn.

In her (1996) examination of *Time: The Modern and Postmodern Experience*, Helga Nowotny points to 'the illusion of simultaneity'. Even though it comes with its own credentials of critique, the narrative of simultaneity should not itself be accepted uncritically. By 'the illusion of time', Nowotny wants to draw attention to two phenomena. First, time has not been abolished. Time's arrow still runs; and in one direction, namely forward and 'it is now composed of many, recurring cycles' (ibid.: 54). Consequently, 'the plurality of times . . . also increases' (ibid.: 59). Second, the fast time in which many are immersed, especially in academic life, has an uneven spread. Not all are implicated in this instantaneity to the same extent.

Both of these caveats are crucial to an understanding of the contemporary university. It is *not* the case that slow time has been replaced by instantaneous time; time working by itself; time that continuously brings global spaces into the academic's work. Such 'chronoscopic time' is present but it is not the full temporal story. For today's university lives amid *multiple* time-spans, and time-speeds. If the contemporary university is to be understood as a layering of different forms of the university, then it is hardly surprising that it lives amid multiple timeframes. The scholar still lives on, with thought processes that resist quickening, even as his or her emails intone their arrival often expecting an early reply; the archaeologists and the historians have their being in the past; the large research teams are embarked on their research programmes lasting several years into the future; a seminar series is laid out for the coming year; and the university itself produces its various strategies that stretch over numbers of years and even decades. (One UK university has a 30-year estates strategy.) The university lives with all of these timeframes and rhythms contemporaneously; and many more besides. There is no one clock that the university follows.

Pace and time horizon *both* vary in the university. Activities have shorter or longer durations: hitting the 'delete' button can be done in a second; writing a book takes somewhat longer; and a major scientific study may last several years, even decades. But activities have characteristic rhythms too: fast time (there is only two weeks with which to put together a major and complex research bid, perhaps involving partners in other countries); and slow time (despite the publisher's deadline and the press of the research assessment exercise, the writing of that book resists quickening; thinking has it own pace). Academic life bears out Gaston Bachelard's (2000) dictum that 'the concept of rhythm is the fundamental concept of time'.

And there are yet other forms of time attesting to its rhythms and pacing: for instance, there is *measured* time or even *surveilled* time (the academics account for their time in the work 'transparency' exercises); and there is *intense* time (the consultancy project has attracted political interest and the public gaze turned upon it imparts an intensity to the way time is experienced). There is also – as depicted in the example at the beginning of this chapter – *private* and *public* time. As noted, reading is understood to be a personal activity to be undertaken in one's 'private' time, and in one's personal spaces, off-campus. On-campus, it presents a pollution of time. And so it is rendered invisible, and tacitly banished from the public space and time of the university precincts.

Academic time exerts its presence in another way. Time is a resource and also demands of academics that they become resources to other ends. Their time is, as just noted, measured. Academics become human resources, whose time is to be accounted. Is thinking time to be accounted? Is reading time to be accounted? The accountancy of academic life finds these activities difficult to categorise. There is an accounting of time; an accountancy of time. In *this* balance sheet of time, judgements are made: what is the cost of spending time on this or that activity? The academic lives by the clock.

As we have observed, there are multiple clocks running at once, with their rhythms and pace. And these rhythms intersect. Sometimes one cuts across another; characteristically, slow time gives way to fast time; and the long-term gives way to the short-term. But these patterns are far from uniform. Sometimes, too, a unit of resource – as we may term it – may be copied from one timeframe into another. The idea that occurred in a single teaching session is taken up in a research project and suddenly sustains a line of activity over weeks or even months.

There is, then, in academic time, a 'dialectic of duration', to use Gaston Bachelard's (2000) phrase. Time is interrupted, fragmented, running at differing paces. These are timeframes, tilting at different angles. The walk across the campus is interrupted by a chance meeting, and news is relayed of a seminar about to take place, or a 'have you heard about x's new finding in y university?' The browsing on the internet suddenly brings up a reference to a line of research in another country that impinges on the report, just being completed. Time has many arrows, flying in contrasting directions. 'Rhythms are overlaid and interdependent' (ibid.: 130).

We may judge, therefore, that the narrative of simultaneity is a temptation to which we should not fall prey. Academic time is *variegated*, marked by 'a plurality of durations' (ibid.: 47). To allow the narrative of simultaneity to form the temporal story of academic life will only serve to limit the temporal options available. That academic time is comprised of multiple timeframes may just, therefore, allow choice in the deployment of those timeframes.

Spaces of the university

Bachelard's text on 'the dialectic of duration' urges a sense of time as discontinuous but it also speaks of 'repose' and 'harmony': 'Without harmony, without a well-ordered dialectic, without rhythm, life and thought cannot be stable and secure:

repose is a happy vibration' (ibid.: 21). Is such 'repose' available in academic time? May 'a well-ordered dialectic' still be possible? Such 'harmony' is in doubt: 'There is, then, above lived time, thought time. This thought time is more aerial and free, more easily disrupted too' (ibid.: 37).

The phrasing 'aerial and free' is pertinent to our theme.[3] In it are metaphors of space. We can easily enough talk of spacious time. In academic life, spacious time is less and less in evidence: time is crowded, dense, thickly populated. Academics are bound to 'multi-task', and to find ways in which a single activity can work towards multiple ends. The space of academic time even expands; literally so, as academics work into the evenings and the weekends.[4] But, in this expansion of time, time itself becomes clogged. The demands of academic life – in teaching, marking, evaluating, reading, researching, writing, conducting fieldwork or experiments, fulfilling administrative requirements and income generation, not to mention seeing visitors, running open days, forging links with local schools, colleges, firms and organisations – reduce time's spaciousness.[5]

But yet, academic time can open spaces. A university may not have many agreements – 'memoranda of understanding' – with other universities around the world but its academics will still be engaged with others in distant lands. It was always thus but, now, with the internet, the world crowds onto the academic's desk – or wherever the laptop is currently placed.

These reflections as to the multiplicity of frames of academic time have parallels in academic *space*. In his (1991) magisterial opus on *The Production of Space*, Henri Lefebvre observes that, in the analysis of space, spaces have tended to multiply. So Lefebvre points to 'a geographical space, an ethnological space, a demographic space, a space peculiar to the information sciences, and so on ad infinitum. Elsewhere we hear of pictural, musical or plastic spaces' (ibid.: 91).

If we were to adopt this approach in identifying the spaces of the university, perhaps we might reasonably point to the following spaces as significant:

1   *Intellectual and discursive space*: This is space accorded to the academics to make a contribution to social discourse and the wider public sphere. Societies differ in the regard with which they hold the intellectual life to be valuable and this regard may change within a society. Here, we should note a distinction between opportunity and performance: it may be that the civil sphere would welcome a larger degree of participation by academics – in broadening the public understanding of issues – but that the scholars prefer to keep their own company. After all, one can never know how the interview with the reporter will appear in print; or so the rationalisation might run.

2   *Epistemological space*: By 'epistemological space', I refer to the space available to academics to pursue their own research interests. Such research endeavours may be influenced if not shaped by available income streams and external evaluation systems. *Both* private sector and state bodies may direct research in addressing particular problems and they may exert control over the publication of the output. As universities work in and for the knowledge economy (now widened to envelop public services), space for untrammelled research shrinks. Now knowl-

edge has to have impact and show some kind of return. So questions arise, or should do so, as to the extent to which such epistemological space is constrained – by partial interests, by financial return – even as the space also expands. Here, then, arises an issue as to the *shape* of the scholarly space available: is it oriented in a particular direction?

3   *Pedagogical and curricular space*: Pedagogical space and curricula space differ but they may legitimately be put together here. In *pedagogical* space, two issues are key: what space do tutors and course teams have to attempt new pedagogies, with alternative kinds of pedagogical relationships? And just what spaces are to be granted to students such that they may strive authentically to become their own persons? In *curricular* space, one matter dominates: what space do course teams have in which to initiate new kinds of course, free from ideological or discursive or even power-laden constraint (not dictated by frozen ideas of 'skills' or 'outcomes')? These two spaces are intertwined. In the end, adventurous curricula will be brought off through daring pedagogies and, in turn, imaginative pedagogies ultimately point to curricula transformation.[6]

4   *Ontological space*: By 'ontological space', I refer to the space in which academics have their being *as* academics. This is the space of *being* an academic.[7] As implied (see Chapter 3), this space is opening and becoming more fluid, as academics are invited, encouraged or even cajoled to take on wider identities.[8] Its boundaries with the wider world become more porous. The roles of academic as entrepreneur, manager, quality assessor, mentor, facilitator and curriculum designer (and others) stretch out the ontological space of academic being so much so that some who are on the full-time 'academic' payroll of universities are hesitant to see themselves as 'academics'. The very term 'academic' carries connotations of an overly limited and clerkly identity which they determinedly do not wish to inhabit. Does such a widening of the ontological space of academic life amount to a corruption of academic being or its liberation? Is its implied choice a widening or a diminution of the existential space for authentic life in universities? In this fluid ontological space, individuals may carry several academic identities but what might be the resultant psychological and institutional repercussions? The widening of universities' ontological space may bring both peril *and* liberation.

We have identified these four sets of spaces – intellectual and discursive; epistemological and scholarly; curricula and pedagogical; and ontological – having noted a string of spaces that Lefebvre had identified. But we should note that Lefebvre sees here merely 'partial representations . . . continually abandoning any global perspective, accepting fragmentation and so coming up with mere shards of knowledge'. He goes on to suggest that: 'What is . . . required here is . . . [a] knowledge of the production of space. Such a knowledge . . . may be expected to rediscover *time* . . . in and through space' (1991: 91). In short, we have little sense of the interplay of space and time in today's world. If this is so, then we have little sense of the interplay of space and time in today's university.

Academic poets

Universities bestride the world, living with their competing timeframes. The virtual university living in cyber-space lives globally; and it moves both in fast time and slower time. On a corridor, there may be a member of staff engaged with institutions – whether for research or for teaching purposes – in the immediate region. This academic will live in timeframes, plural, but timeframes of those local institutions. Strategies over the course of the year, projects for the next six months, and meetings on a fortnightly basis, interspersed with email correspondence may all be evident. But in the next room, there may be a colleague who has just returned from an overseas trip, to plan a joint research study with another university stretching over the next few years. And the research partners may also be communicating with other research teams around the world. And, one day, the two colleagues exchange pleasantries, only to realise that there is some hitherto unseen connection between their activities. Just a single concept may jump into the conversation and be felt to have some carry-over from one domain to another.

So both time zones and space zones intersect, at crazy and unforeseen angles. The university, accordingly, may be seen as a region precisely of intersecting time zones and space zones; and intersecting without a common pattern.

Admittedly, some of these time zones and space zones may be constrained and even policed. Entry into global space may be curtailed for those not at the cutting edge of research. Real space too is most definitely limited. Senior administrators periodically conduct their room usage surveys as they attempt to gain maximum 'occupancy' from the available physical space. In some parts of the university, academics may be asked to share rooms or even to 'hotdesk', while their personal libraries are vanquished. Entry into spacious time zones may be also limited. Departmental common rooms disappear as collective open time disappears.

Shifting patterns; awkward patterns; patterns laid upon patterns: these are the characteristics of academic time and space. Here lies congestion. Both space and time are limited. But yet space, and with it too, time, expand. Expansion and contraction; both movements are apparent.

We can now distinguish three kinds of time/space formations:

1   *Practical time/practical space*: This is the felt time and visible space, the time that forms the work diary (for individual academics and for universities) and the visible spaces in which the identified activities take place. Both time and space here are crowded. The days in individuals' diaries, now increasingly publicly available on the university's intranet, are full of activities; the university calendar is also overflowing with events. It is this time/space formation that has come to dominate collective understandings of time and space in modern universities.

2   *Virtual time/virtual space*: This is time and space in the margins, half-hidden or entirely hidden. It is liminal time and space. Included are the communications and the foraging on the internet, the papers and books written at home, and the reading accomplished on the train to work. This virtual time and space are, it seems, almost infinitely expandable. Their invisibility and their private character

render them unaccounted and so they attract little interest.[9] It is through the expansion of this time/space complex that concerns over the life/work balance arise for here professional time intrudes into both the time and spaces of the life-world.

3   *Imagined time/imagined space*: This is time and space conjured in the imagination. In this space, the mind leaps ahead of and out of itself. It conjures possibilities. In this time, the mind brings into itself new spaces and timeframes. Universities can do all of this. A 'corporate strategy', at its best, is just such a making vivid a set of imaginative possibilities, stretching over frames of time.

These three sets of space/time formations are *dynamically* inter-related. Form (1), real time and real space spill over into form (2), virtual time and virtual space. As a result, form (3), imagined time and imagined space, dwindles as the space and time for imagination is diminished.[10] This is an impoverishment of the university's time/space.

This time/space impoverishment is one feature of the contemporary nature of the university. It leads to a shrinking of the imagined possibilities for the university and so to a limitation of the university. As fast time and short-term time come to dominate the university, the university becomes a shadow of what it might be. And yet, while the *imagined possibilities* are diminished, perhaps the *possibilities for imagination* are expanded. The two ideas are significantly different.

In the university, time and space are not given, but are to a significant degree created and imagined. So there is a poetics of time and space:

> Til when the ties loosen,
> All but the ties eternal, time and space,
> Nor darkness, gravitation, sense, nor any bounds bounding us.
> Then we burst forth, we float,
> In time and space O soul, prepared for them,
> Equal, equipt at last, (O joy! O fruit of all!) them to fulfil O soul.
>
> (Walt Whitman, *Towards the Unknown Region*)

Time and space are, for the university, unknown regions. They are unknown sociologically, full of happenstance. But they are unknown philosophically. For, to a significant extent, space can be imagined anew; and with it, new time can be created.

The prison writings of intellectuals such as Bonhoeffer and Gramsci are further testimony to the matter: confined by their prison walls, they still managed to produce texts of profundity and hope. The human spirit need not succumb to tyranny: the most constrained time can still leave open the possibility of emancipated time and space.

The researcher thinking about tomorrow's experiment; the scholar planning a book; the course leader engaged in designing a course: these academics live in their own created zones of time and space. These academics are academic poets, imaginatively bringing into being new worlds. In a discussion as to 'Why Poets?', Heidegger suggests that:

the interior of unwonted consciousness remains the interior space in which everything, for us, is beyond the numbering . . . of calculation and, freed from these
barriers, can overflow into the unbarred entirety of the open. . . . The inwardli-
ness of world inner space unbars the open for us.

(Heidegger, 2002: 229, 231)

A challenge, therefore, to the contemporary university is that of inserting spaces for
openness, for dwelling and for imagination about the university itself. Here lies a role
for leadership rather than management (Chapter 4). Lunch-time fora, for example,
can be offered, in which all staff (not only 'academics') are invited to come together
to reflect on the university's future – perhaps in a reworking of its corporate strategy
– and individuals could be encouraged to develop their own ideas as to the university's
possibilities; and such cross-institutional debate could be set up on the institution's
intranet. In such dialogue, collective imagination would be stimulated. The imaginative
space/time of the university is not fixed: if it can be shrunk, it can also be expanded.

The courage of academic travel

Academics are travellers in time and space, limited in large part by their imaginations.
Of course, in a world beset with unequal power, time can impose itself on academic
being; we may even talk – as we noted earlier – of surveilled time. And academics can
be expected and even required to work in regions not of their own choosing (literally
so at times – the academic may be required to teach in or participate in a 'student fair'
in another country). But no matter how constrained both space and time are, academics still enjoy infinite spaces and thereby infinite time horizons.

Academic travel requires a willingness to live with uncertainty for, in academic travel,
academics put themselves forward into new spaces. Giving a talk in an international
conference in another country may carry its uncertainties of the local etiquette: perhaps
one is called upon to make an impromptu speech to thank one's hosts but the rules of
that speechmaking may be unclear. Having an idea for an innovative new programme
of study, perhaps with the students taking a large measure of responsibility for their
learning, or with the assessment regime hinged around practice-based assignments,
may also require fortitude, as continuing resistance is encountered. After all, the regulations do not allow for such curricula or assessment patterns; or so it will be alleged.

To academic travel, therefore, attaches both epistemological and ontological dimensions (cf. Barnett and Phipps, 2005). Knowledge ventures here into new
regions; individuals stretch their identities into unexplored fields. Again, space and
time intermingle.

A university is, then, an institutional space that makes possible spaces stretching across time horizons. The 'making-possible' has to be interpreted generously. It
may be helpful for academics to be reminded that their calling presupposes creative
endeavour, apparent at least in the criteria for promotion; and the criteria may distinguish the different arenas in which such journeying may be manifest (perhaps in
teaching, research, income generation, service to the university itself, and service to
the wider academic community and even to society itself). But the prompting will be

most effective in the culture of the institution; a culture in which creative endeavour is not just permitted but encouraged.

Accepting that challenge, travelling into 'unknown regions' (to call up Walt Whitman's words) – to reiterate – requires courage. Many will shrink from such a challenge. Such souls may benefit from some support to enthuse and stiffen the professional sinews. A university is a mansion with unlimited rooms, all of which have windows. Is the necessary courage present so as to pass through a window into the unknown?

The passing-through may be a collective endeavour. Dare a course team strike out for its own view of its new course? Can it transport itself into a future that it can barely glimpse? For it cannot be sure precisely which students might be attracted to the course and how the pedagogies and curricula will work in practice.

We may speak here of *institutional courage*. A corporate strategy is nothing other than an attempt on the part of a university to frame a set of futures for itself. To set out such a set of futures in a public document requires courage. For such a document constitutes a set of *hopeful fictions*. The university glimpses a new set of possibilities for itself. The possibilities set out in its strategy – if they are truly imaginative and significant and are doing full justice to the extraordinary potential that is a university – never could be completely realised. It is a document full of hope for and in the future.[11] But the stories that the university weaves for itself are, to some extent, bound to be fictitious. In an uncertain world, it cannot be sure of realising its ambitions. Living in space and time opens the way for daring, and imagination, but it is bound to bring uncertainty. The corporate strategy carries a necessary lack of assurance on the part of the university.

The will to live in creative spaces and their associated temporal rhythms require positive courage; the courage to live in the future and take on tasks that have to be uncertain as to their outcomes. But such a will requires a negative form of courage as well. Characteristically, it requires the courage to withdraw from or forgo certain options. The working mother decides to register for that PhD that she has long wanted to pursue; the research group determines a theme around which it constructs its intellectual project; the university sets itself off on a path of 'global citizenship' (which it interprets both in relation to its students and to the entire university). In the adoption of these choices, other possibilities are set aside. The mother is unable to spend much time at school events watching her children in their various evening activities; the research group foregoes the study of a theme that enthuses some of its members and which just might become the global theme of tomorrow; the university drops a strategic option that it had been contemplating.

Free spirits

Of space and time in the university, *space has emerged here as the dominant category*. This suggestion is a logical point, to do with the concept of the university. What is a university if not an entreaty, and a licence, to enter new spaces? Each space, however, has its characteristic time horizon. In entering a space, one enters a time horizon.

How is it that space is the dominant category? After all, have we not seen repeatedly here not only that time and space interweave but that time is a significant category in itself? Time can make possible ventures or it can close them off. And it can make possible authentic actions or demand inauthentic actions: 'Is Time not the name for the ontological opening?' (Žižek, 2003: 14). So why give the palm to space? It is because, as stated, that a university is the making possible of spaces. We might be tempted to suggest that it is the making possible of time-spaces; but that would make matters unduly complicated. A university is the making possible of, and the opening of, and the encouragement towards spaces: new spaces.

To have a thought is to enter a new space. Totalitarianism is the robbing of spaces and the university is a bulwark against totalitarianism. It is a space for free spirits. The idea of the university is that of an invitation to roam, to wander. After all, many – perhaps too many – journal abstracts contain the verb 'explore', as in 'This paper explores . . .'. In 're-search', one searches and searches again: it is, as Heidegger (2002: 65) noted, 'constant activity'.

Even though there be much activity – in a teaching situation, in research or in consultancy – for the creative act to occur, there has to be a moment of repose (to pick up Bachelard's word). The extent to which a considerable elapse of time-in-repose is necessary for creativity to occur is an empirical matter; but it may not be much. The comment that 'I am too busy to write that book (or even to write that paper)' may be borne out by the everyday busyness of the academic. But the academics' plea should not be accepted *tout court*; for the academics' plea is often a rationalisation to themselves. They are saved the authentic act; they hide behind the press of institutional life; behind the 'they' (to borrow a term from Heidegger). For, as remarked, the authentic act takes courage; requires a definite act of will; necessitates the individual to stake a claim for their own academic being. Being a free spirit is hard work.

The university is an institution that is significantly placed in bringing about 'the rational society', as Habermas put it (1972). But more even than that, it is an institution that has in its being the creative generation of spaces. That is to say, the university is an institution capable of societal creativity, of imagination, of new thinking. Such a source of iconoclasm in society might engender suspicion; or at least a nervousness. Dare society tolerate such encouragement to free spirits? Perhaps there is here a rationale for the ways in which so-called mass higher education systems are in practice characteristically differentiated, with some institutions permitted more space than others to be iconoclastic, not that any often live up to such a billing.

Conclusion

Our first conclusion is not that the university lives in multiple spaces and timeframes (although it does) but that it has its being amid multiple space and timeframe *options*. These options extend into the future; that much is clear. Which futures will the university entertain? But its time-space options extend also into its past. Which stories of its past does it play up? Which values, which positioning, in its history does it now encourage in its 'collective memory'? Our focus on this occasion, though, has been the university's *future* options. How might it go forward? Into which spaces are its academics encouraged to move? Into more intensive teaching? Into income-bearing research? Into profit-generating entrepreneurialism? Into creative ways of expanding society's self-understanding? Into helping to widen the public sphere?[12] More especially, to what degree are its academics – and its students – encouraged to open up spaces of their own? The university's spaces are not given but have, after all, to be constructed.

The university is not autonomous, however. And its academics do not enjoy untrammelled 'academic freedom'. Academic space, at the levels both of the university and of teams and individuals within it, is curtailed. And there is reason to believe that those constraints both from without and within the university are heightening. But there is no zero sum of space here. That spaces shrink, and that there is the associated press of deadlines, at the different levels of university life, do not mean that the category of the infinite has to be relinquished. Universities and their members have to hand unlimited space: an expanding universe of space. Their ideas, their perspectives, their theories and their ways of going on in their disciplines are all still open and are *opening further*, which is to say that universities and their members live in the realm of the infinite.

There lurks in the university, however, a fear of the infinite. Windows are to hand waiting only to be opened but it is safer to remain within the familiar walls; and it is more comfortable still, even if the room is crowded and the walls are drawing in. To open the windows, and to pass through, is to pass into the 'unknown region'. This fear of the infinite is two-fold. First, there is the fear of the infinite itself: the infinite is cold, lonely, and without a map. The path forward is unclear for there is no given way forward. Second, there is the fear of the authentic, which is associated with the infinite. For in moving into the infinite, one is obliged to strike out by oneself; to declare oneself, even in the face of hostility from one's epistemological community. In coming out with a new theory, or a new perspective, or a new way of teaching, or a new kind of university, resentment from the timid is likely to be a response. Being authentic in the spaces afforded by the university takes courage.

On this analysis, the phrase 'managing one's *time*' has to be seen as an injunction to determine the *spaces* that one is going to inhabit. One attends to the short-term tasks because in doing so one can avoid the anxiety that the spaces of the larger tasks open up. A problem of space is converted into a problem of time because therein lies a rationale for one's lack of courage. The busy mother who has always hankered to pursue that PhD has limited time, to be sure, but the fundamental issue is: does she possess the courage to embark on that journey? Her registration may indicate not so much that she has found the *time* but has rather found the courage to enter the learning *space*. Correspondingly, the university has pressing issues of the moment – in its finances, and student numbers – but the question in front of it as it turns to prepare its new 'corporate strategy' is: does it possess the courage to move into hugely challenging new spaces? So-called problems of academic time should be understood as problems of space, and the courage that moving into such spaces calls for.

We may conclude, finally that we are still entitled to draw on the category of the infinite in understanding the idea of academic space. The university still has infinite spaces as potentialities, even as its autonomies are in some doubt. Its members, too, still have infinite spaces as their potentialities, even as some of their spaces are shrinking. There is in fact good reason to suggest that this infinity of spaces is expanding, much like an expanding universe, even as space also shrinks.

7 Culture and anarchy

Introduction

Culture and Anarchy, by Matthew Arnold (published in 1869 and very influential in the middle of the twentieth century), has been described by Michael Tanner (2000: 23) as 'that shallow and influential pamphlet'. Perhaps that is not an unfair depiction of the book but, if only in its title, Arnold bequeathed a provocative juxtaposition of terms of value to us here. 'Culture' and 'anarchy': placed against each other, the two terms open a space for explorations helpful to our present inquiry.

In 'culture', Arnold saw a bulwark against anarchy. Culture offered 'as a defence against anarchy' that of 'right reason, ideas, light', culture understood as 'the single-minded love of perfection' (Arnold, 1969: 45, 60, 85). Culture is pitched against anarchy. Light and dark. Now, in the twenty-first century, 'culture' is understood in manifold ways. Yet, there remain surely two dominant interpretations. On the one hand, culture is understood as with a capital 'C' as it were. Culture is here a value-laden term, representing those ideas and forms of life held dominantly to be valuable in a society. On the other hand, culture is a much less sonorous term, a much lighter concept, referring to those valued ways of going on in any society or large group or organisation.

Arnold was working with and defending the first meaning of culture: he was not just wanting to identify it with 'perfection' but was sure that he knew the general form that that perfection took. Today, there is less sureness that any set of ideas or forms of life can be securely held to offer perfection and so the second, and more restrained, idea of culture has arisen. Now, it is felt that societies and large groupings – social classes, ethnic groups, and so on – have their own valued forms of life and there is a reluctance to legislate between them. Culture in the twenty-first century is divisible, consisting of many cultures: many if not all forms of life and meaning warrant recognition. It is against such cultural generosity that the idea of the 'multicultural' has its place. A complex society is a space for many groupings and networks: it is a home of many cultures.

Culture, then, implies some kind of unity, some kind of stability, some sense of the enduring. Even if culture is changing over time, still the process happens in a relatively measured way. Groups buy into the proceedings. In a situation of anarchy, in contrast, all bets are off. The rules – that enable forms of life to be recognised as culture – dissolve. Pitching 'culture' and 'anarchy' against each other – as did Arnold – not only implies that perfection (whatever that might mean) is impossible under conditions of anarchy but that darkness falls: the light of which Arnold spoke disappears from view.

What might the implications of this set of ideas be for our understanding of the university in the twenty-first century?

The call of anarchy

The first point to make is that Arnold drew the terms of this debate in an unnecessarily restricted way. Anarchy is often seen as a chaotic situation, a situation of mayhem and selfishness, as individuals play out their wants in a free-for-all. But both characterisations – of mayhem and of selfishness – are by no means necessary features of anarchy. For the self-declared anarchist, Errico Malatesta, anarchy is: 'the creation of a society of free and equal members based on a harmony of interests and the voluntary participation of everybody in carrying out social responsibilities' (Malatesta, [1891] 2001: 17). 'Harmony' *and* 'the voluntary participation of everybody in carrying out social responsibilities': we could hardly have a more explicit repudiation of anarchy as a situation of either mayhem or selfishness.

How did Malatesta envisage such a happy state of affairs coming about? By the 'abolition of the State' (ibid.: 17) or, as he preferred to term it, the abolition of government. We might just raise an eyebrow at the belief that the absence of government (or the state) would be likely to propel society or, indeed, the world, towards such a harmonious situation but Malatesta has a response to hand. For him: 'Human struggle . . . tends always to widen the association among men, their community of interests, and to develop the feeling of love of man for his fellows' (ibid.: 29).

Why should this be so? It is because mankind is fundamentally oriented towards 'solidarity': it is 'the goal towards which human evolution advances'. And by 'solidarity', Malatesta has in mind:

> the harmony of interests and feelings, the coming together of individuals for the wellbeing of all, and of all for the wellbeing of each . . . [this solidarity] is the only environment in which Man can express his personality and achieve his optimum development and enjoy the greatest wellbeing.
>
> (ibid.: 29)

We might be tempted to think that 'wellbeing' is a supremely modern and even postmodern term, characteristic of a century – the current century – in which individuals are shorn of large ideologies and have to fall back on their own resources; their own 'wellbeing' (cf. Vernon, 2008). But in Arnold, in the first half of the twentieth century, we see the term in full throttle.

Here, then, in this depiction of anarchy, is a particular cluster of ideas: solidarity, freedom, wellbeing, harmony, and social responsibility. This conception of anarchy is coupled with the belief that mankind has a natural tendency towards a state of social affairs characterised by this cluster of ideas. It is also coupled with the belief that the

state is a malign presence and all too often acts – even if through unintended consequences – to propel mankind in the opposite direction of individualism, competitiveness, and a gross falling short of what might be.

Culture or anarchy *OR* culture *and* anarchy?

For Arnold, it will be recalled, culture and anarchy were set off against each other.
Culture offered a defence against anarchy. But that reading only makes sense in the
company of unduly limited notions both of culture and of anarchy. On the one hand,
Arnold had in mind high culture, culture with a capital C, culture as being that of
'perfection' rather than the more relaxed sense of culture more prevalent today. On
the other hand, by anarchy, Arnold seemed to have in mind lawlessness and unbridled
individualism. Malatesta offers a quite different reading of anarchy: for him, anarchy
is that state of affairs in which mankind is liberated from the oppressive hand of the
state and finds its freedom. And in such a state, mankind is likely to evince solidarity
and social responsibility.

There are immediate implications here for any understanding of the contemporary
university. So far as 'culture' is concerned, by and large, there is a hesitancy to think of
the university as a site of culture.[1] In their different ways, both the conservatives (witness Allan Bloom (1987)) and the radicals (witness Bill Readings (1996)) lament the
absence of culture in the university. On the one hand, we receive a picture of cultural
degradation in the university in the wake of epistemological and cultural relativism
(associated in Bloom's (1987) picture of the impoverishment of student values and
student life). In modern society and reflected in the university, on this account, lies a
disinclination to believe that some aspects of human life – especially in its creative literary endeavours – are better than others and warrant value judgements. On the other
hand, we receive a picture (drawn by Readings (1996)) of the cultural dissolution of
the university, as a result of a hollowing-out of the cognitive role of the university
in modern society, a hollowing-out aided by the vapid character of state-run quality
methods with its empty adherence to the term 'excellence'.

Both of these laments, conservative and radical, share more in common than may
at first be evident. Both viewpoints begin from a sense that culture on campus is,
or should be, a kind of project. Culture is very much an upper case 'Culture' here,
in either camp. Bloom would uphold his idea of culture through a resurrection of a
great books 'canon'. Readings is less clear but, in looking back to nineteenth-century
Germany and the then articulation of the idea of *Bildung*, observed the university 'taking on [a] . . . cultural function for the state' (Readings, 1996: 68). In this situation:
'The state protects the action of the University; the University safeguards the thought
of the state. And each strives to realize the idea of national culture' (ibid.: 69).

It is, for Readings, the disappearance of the nation-state that makes problematic
any such conception of the university in relation to culture. And so – Readings suggests – in the current situation, where 'culture ceases to be the animating principle of
the University', we have witnessed the emergence of cultural studies in universities.
It is much to the point, too, that the kind of cultural studies that has emerged has no
'disciplinary specificity' in itself but has become merely a methodology that can be

turned on 'anything at all'. The problem is that cultural studies has come to take 'culture as the object of the University's desire for knowledge, rather than as the object that the University produces' (ibid.: 99).

For both Bloom and Readings, culture within the university is a project and a project to be *prized*. That many today shrink from seeing a link between culture and the university helps to explain the intensity of both of their accounts, different as they are. *Both* Bloom and Readings see themselves as inveighing against the loss of culture as a project for the contemporary university. In this sense, too, they keep company with Arnold, who saw the barbarians at the gate: for Bloom, the barbarians were those who declared against traditional standards of literary taste and judgement; for Readings, the barbarians were the state and its apparatuses in their hollowing out of the cultural space of the university.

It will be recalled that Arnold was counterposing culture and anarchy. Culture was a bulwark against anarchy. If either Bloom or Readings are right, the same juxtaposition presents itself today. If we are faced with a cultural void – as both Bloom and Readings would have us believe – are we then faced also with anarchy?

But here, we have to remember Malatesta's admonition. Anarchy does not have to be understood only as mayhem, as disorder, as rule-lessness. It can stand for a positive freedom, the kind of freedom and social responsibility that might emerge in the absence of the oppressive hand of the state.[2] Instead of culture being juxtaposed to anarchy, it might be that culture can actually thrive in a situation of anarchy. Not culture or anarchy but culture *and* anarchy.

The anarchic university?

The contemporary university is excessively a rule-governed institution. Every activity, as we observed in Chapter 4 ('the bureaucratic university'), is accompanied with not merely a rule but often many rules; a rule book, indeed. Terms of reference, codes of practice, regulations, frameworks: these are part of the language and the governance of higher education. The contemporary university is far from anarchic, at least in the anarchy-as-mayhem reading of the term. Rule keeping has become part of the symbolic structure of the contemporary university; part of its 'culture'.

But what then of anarchy as personal and social freedom in the absence of government? Here, the situation is more nuanced. Internally, as already implied, the university is heavily 'governed'. Rules, procedures, systems and frameworks are not merely produced continually but are maintained and revised and developed by the university's increasing number of professional managers. In the process, university 'governance' has become a major topic of policy and management interest. Externally, however, the state characteristically stands in an ambivalent relationship to its universities. In its encouraging of some kind of 'marketisation' of higher education (albeit a quasi-market), the state characteristically stands back from detailed control of its universities. Quality regimes move with a light touch; now the onus is more on students themselves – as informed 'customers' – to come to rational decisions as to the merits of particular courses and institutions in the light of the information available. 'Let the customer beware' seems to be the watchword in this dispensation. Institutions, too, are seldom asked for detailed 'corporate' plans, and if they are, such plans are not infrequently treated to a cursory treatment. In a market, after all, the onus falls on the providers to win the day for themselves against their competitors. It seems as if, if not quite yet an absence of government, still the state in the emerging 'neo-liberal' order wants to allow its universities room to prosper in their own ways.

But the situation is, as stated, ambiguous. For universities, and the higher education that they offer, are now crucial – or, at any rate, are thought to be crucial – to the place of a nation in the developing global economy.[3] And so matters cannot be left to the serendipity of the marketplace. Accordingly, the state continues with various monitoring and surveillance regimes, concerned with teaching, research, governance and financial audit. An unremarked aspect of this situation is that, like the large banks, it seems that universities cannot be permitted to fail. Unlike the banks, however, the universities are (still) subject to quite intense forms of scrutiny and accountability even if – as Readings observed – much, though by no means all, of that scrutiny has merely symbolic substance.[4] The idea of excellence, called up to act as a banner for such exercises, heralds little.

Our temporary conclusion, then, has to be the following: whether as (a) *anarchy-as-mayhem* or (b) *anarchy-as-collective-solidarity in the absence of the weight of government*, 'university' and 'anarchy' are concepts that sit in tension with each other. On either reading of 'anarchy', universities are far from anarchic. *The anarchic university is not with us* and nor is there any such prospect of this being so.

Culture in the university

What might be meant by 'culture in the university'? Might it point to lunch-time music recitals (perhaps by a resident quartet), to works of art in the open spaces and corridors (perhaps produced in part by the creative art students), to museums on campus (be they scientific, anthropological, or downright quirky)? Might it point to the 'culture' present in academic disciplines, with their own forms of life and value structures – as Tony Becher pointed to (Becher, 1989; cf. McCarthy, 1996)? Might it rather point to even more elusive aspects of academic life, dimly apparent in its social practices, its dominant discourses, its tacit assumptions and 'repertoires' and its implicit theories (of knowledge, truth, 'research' and 'teaching') (Trowler, 2008)? Might it point to culture-as-capital, to culture as power? Here, as advanced by Bourdieu (e.g. 1990b: 146), culture is a means by which groups of academics advance their separate interests from within their own socio-spatial positions or 'habitus'. Might culture refer to '*Bildung*', the acquisition on the part of the student of certain dispositions and qualities accompanying his or her epistemological journey?[5] Might 'culture' refer to the characteristic culinary, dress and even religious practices of different communities on campus? Might culture in the university be a self-avowed project of maintaining the university as 'a centre of consciousness and human responsibility for a civilized world; . . . a creative centre of civilization' (Leavis, 1969)?

That one can readily go on in this way and still not begin to exhaust the possible sightings of culture on campus is testimony to the essential *elusiveness* of culture. But perhaps it is testimony, too, to another feature of culture which we have been touching on in this chapter. There is a reluctance and even a kind of squeamishness to hold onto the very idea of culture. As an idea, it seems, perhaps, to be too messy, too nebulous, too inchoate to be able to do any serious work. But more than that, an unease over the very appearance of the term 'culture' comes about surely as a *Weltanschauung* of 'cultural pessimism' (Bennett, 2001). There is a sense that 'culture' stands all too often for Western culture at a very moment in which the West has become uncertain of its cultural position in a globalised age. It is not just that the G8 of Western countries has expanded into the G20; much more tellingly here, the placing of the Olympics are now, it appears, alternating between western and non-western nations. The West, in short, is losing its cultural hegemony and, in turn, the very idea of culture becomes a problematic category. It presumes judgements, the bases of which are far from sure.

'Culture' is in difficulty, therefore. It is elusive *and* it seems to call for value-laden judgements that are suspect anyway and particularly so in a university setting. Affixing the term 'culture' to any activity or form of expression leads also to arbitrary and unnecessary divisions in academic life, divisions that should always – in a university – be subject to continuous review.

Dual cul-de-sacs or open doors?

We seem to have reached something of an impasse in relation both to 'anarchy' and 'culture'. *Both* terms seem to lead into cul-de-sacs in comprehending the contemporary university and its possibilities. On the one hand, far from being sites of anarchy, the contemporary university is becoming more and more organised and more and more governed. For every action, there shall be a system or framework or risk analysis in which it is situated. Instead of the anarchic university, we have the corporate university and even the governed university. In its developing relationship with the state, too, the university is embraced by ever more articulated framings of its mission by the state itself, even if those framings often encourage the university to become more entrepreneurial. The idea that the university could be free of government and for its freedom and those of its academics to flourish – and so exhibit anarchy in *that* sense – becomes a delusion.

On the other hand, so far as culture is concerned, the university is variously held to be devoid of culture, or awash with cultures (plural)[6] or existing in a kind of culture-free zone such that to put 'university' and 'culture' together in the same breath is to exhibit a category mistake. Like 'university' and 'God', 'university' and 'culture' sit uneasily together.

It is also apparent, too, that if there is such a problematic state of affairs in relation to 'anarchy' and 'culture' separately in their possible connections with the university, even more so is the case so far as their keeping company together is concerned. If our inquiries into 'anarchy' and 'culture' separately are running into the sands, putting the two concepts together – 'anarchy and culture' – can hardly take us any further forward.

Is that the end of the matter then: the sense both that 'culture' and 'anarchy' can do no useful work for us in understanding the university in the twenty-first century and that there is no relationship between the two terms that can help our inquiry?

Perhaps this inquiry is set up entirely awry. And perhaps it is all Arnold's fault. Suppose, instead of pitting culture against anarchy, we see them as working together. Such a turnaround might launch us in the direction of Readings' (1996) idea of 'dissensus' or, going back a little further, Gouldner's (1979) idea of a 'culture of critical discourse'. The university, on this view, is to be characterised precisely as a site of argument. The story, presumably, would run on to suggest, for example, that a 'dissensus' or a 'critical discourse' – if either idea is to have substance – would require certain conditions to be filled. High on such a list of such necessary conditions would be those of freedom and tolerance. The story would presumably run on still further to suggest that where such conditions were being fulfilled, so then would the university become a site of epistemological adventurism. The maxim would be, of course: 'let a thousand flowers bloom', and if there is a riot of colour and if the flowers are a pretty ill-fitting bunch, so much to the good.

Both culture and anarchy, it will be insisted, are present here. The culture lies in the anarchy: the anarchy *is* the culture. The profusion of ideas and frameworks generated here would be anarchic, and the anarchy would be part of the value structure of this kind of university; part of its culture. This university would work towards bringing disparate groups and disciplines together, even or especially where there were few if any overt connections and would encourage dispute, believing that something quite novel might emerge. Anarchy would be doubly present, both in the bizarre combination of perspectives thrown against each other *and* in the ensuing ideas that might result. Culture would be doubly present too. This university would define itself partly in virtue of its being a site of open argument. It lives to furnish not just views but competing views; it likes the sparks to fly. This is how it understands itself. But it also understands itself as holding out dissensus to the wider society as a valuable form of life more generally. It believes in the virtues of dissensus, or critical discourse, not merely as part of its own mission – with the accompanying page or so in the corporate handbook – but it believes in such dissensus or critical discourse *as such*. The university of dissensus sees itself as a model of the open society.

Such an anarchic university is the kind of university that Paul Feyerabend might have held out for. It would be a university that was both epistemologically iconoclastic and generous. It would do all it could not to be confined within cognitive boundaries and would aim towards that goal by exposing disciplines to each other. As Feyerabend remarked, 'contact changes the parties involved' (1999: 268). All his intellectual life, Feyerabend strove to show that (even) science had an unduly restricted view of itself, especially of its methods. Famously, Feyerabend was 'against method' (although he disputed he ever said as much in those terms). For him, science works through fecundity, through daring, through imagination, through playfulness. Any attempt to crystallise science as a strict rule-following set of procedures amounts to 'a conquest of abundance' and any attempt to claim a high status in society on the basis of such a limited notion amounted, for Feyerabend, to an ideology (1982).

So we see here, surely, the opening up of a sense of a culture that is anarchic. Culture not separated from anarchy; not counterposed to anarchy, but identified by anarchy. Culture and anarchy as one, together.

If the two ideas are understood in this way – as mutually supportive of each other – instead of closing doors, the relationship between 'culture' and 'anarchy' can be seen to open doors. Anarchy, as a concern for open dispute and an interest in fostering it, can be a university culture. Of course, there is nothing new here, for the medieval disputations were ritualised means of stimulating argument. Certainly, they were not free-for-alls. They were governed by rules of procedure. Restraint was built into the process. But they performed the function of engendering dispute, of bringing hetero-doxy – and even a little heresy – into a situation where conformity was the norm.[7]

Beyond culture

Culture tends to be inward-looking. It betokens a concern for socially meaningful values and activities within a group, organisation or society. It offers a non-violent means of securing order *internally*. The idea of the 'multicultural', seen in this way, is simply a recognition that, in a complex society, there are many and even compet-ing frames of social meaning. That has long been the case but a dominant culture overshadowed other cultures. Now, there is a sense that many if not all cultures, all forms of life and meaning, deserve recognition. Their internal ways of going on are all worthy of respect.

So much is, I think, standard stuff. But what is missing from this account is an *exterior* sense of culture. While it is oriented internally, offering some sense of stable meanings within a group or society, it gains its bearings through the *difference* that it sets up with other cultures. A culture is this culture and not that culture. So culture naturally tends towards rivalry and even conflict. Correspondingly, the contempo-rary urgings that human beings have to find ways of living with each other gain their weight from a sense of differences established partly by culture; by a recognition of cultures, plural, living in the same eco-space.

This point, it may be felt, is merely a repetition, albeit from a different angle, of the matter we raised earlier: do we understand the university through the idea of Culture or through the idea of cultures? The one or the many? Is there a dominant culture that should characterise the university or, to the contrary, is the university to be character-ised by its being a home to many cultures? The university as a single-minded institu-tion on the one hand and the university as epistemologically and socially generous on the other hand.[8]

There is a link here to that issue but the point emerging is slightly different. Culture gains its bearings from its relationship to the Other. Culture is Other-oriented. It asserts itself against other cultures. It places itself in the world and yet separate from the world. But, in the contemporary world, to speak of 'other cultures' is to be open to the infinite. Ultimately, the 'multicultural' knows no cultural boundaries. Here lies a particular anarchy: a rule without rulers but this time also without cultural anchors. For culture now opens itself to the winds of other possible cultures.

And so, the anarchic university now becomes a university that is culturally open, culturally fecund. Does it have no cultural anchor, not even, say, those of definite 'rational' procedures – perhaps of the kind suggested by Habermas in the 'validity claims' of his ideal speech situation? Here, anything goes, *provided* that it is proffered amid a discursive situation that conditions utterances and offerings to conform to quasi-ethical principles of truthfulness, sincerity and sensitivity to context. Or are even the rules of the academic game to be negotiable, pliable even?[9]

These matters may seem arcane but they are of profound importance in searching for, in reaching for, an idea of the university in the twenty-first century. How might we understand culture in the university in the global world of the twenty-first century? To speak of the global world of the twenty-first century plunges us into a context of turmoil, fast and turbulently flowing currents, a liquid age, indeed (Bauman, 2000). The stability that 'culture' offers can, at best, only have purchase at a meta-level of the university. No matter which activities in which 'the university' is engaged, still those activities should comply with certain standards not of right reason but of right reasoning. Substantively, this university is without government; no one form of knowing should be allowed to dominate. This is a university of epistemological abundance, always holding itself out to new cognitive and experiential possibilities. On the surface, this is an anarchic institution, awash with competing perspectives. At a deeper level, however, the university hangs onto its title of 'university' through its adherence to norms of social reasoning. The *anarchy* is to be found at one level, the surface level; the *culture* is to be found at a deeper level, at a foundational level. Culture and anarchy can coexist after all.

But this is overly neat. For it presumes the validity of the conditions of right reasoning when just they have to be on the table for scrutiny. It assumes 'rightness' before the tribunal has got underway. In the liquid age, all epistemological bets are off. What is to count as a valid way of even encountering the world has itself to be available for interrogation. The 'culture of critical discourse' is taking on the appearance of a mirage: as we approach its foundations, they appear to recede and be out of reach.

The contemporary world seems to be propelling forward the anarchic university, *and* it is a university beyond culture.[10] At least, it seems impossible to fill out substantively what 'culture' might mean here.[11] Even at the level of discursive procedures, short of a unsubstantiated philosophical sleight-of-hand, solid foundations for a university-of-culture seem no longer to be available. Anarchy yes, but culture no. That seems to be the position.

Where's the passion?

A further set of considerations here lies in Nietzsche. Nietzsche inveighed against both the culture of the wider (German) society and against that of universities. And these diatribes were linked:

> [W]hat appals me [is] how German seriousness, German profundity, German passion in spiritual things is more and more on the decline . . . I come into contact now and then with German universities: what an atmosphere prevails among its scholars, what a barren spirituality, grown how contented and luke-warm! . . . Our culture suffers from nothing more than it suffers from the super-abundance of presumptuous journeymen and fragments of humanity; our universities

are, against their will, the actual forcing-houses for this kind of spiritual instinct atrophy.

(Nietzsche, [1889] 2003: 73)

The cultures of both universities and the wider society suffer from 'a barren spirituality' and a lack of 'passion', and both are atrophying as a result. And the universities are especially to blame for this impoverished state of affairs.

If that was the case in Nietzsche's day, surely still more is it true today. The bureaucratic university (Chapter 4) – albeit unwittingly – limits creativity and curtails passion. Here, then, we can glimpse a possible unity between anarchy and culture. In a liquid world, culture is not to be found through rules, even the rules of 'critical discourse' or 'dissensus'. For such a path arbitrarily puts *a priori* boundaries around the epistemological fecundity to which the university has to be open. The university has to be epistemologically ungoverned and even ungovernable. It has to be anarchic.

In these circumstances, the only culture available to the university is a Nietzschean-type of passion: an indefatigable boldness and adventurousness. This fearsomeness is not to be caught in rules of a Habermasian or Rawlsian kind but is to be hinted at – at most – in the institutional dispositions and qualities that mark out this kind of university. The culture of this anarchic university is one of fearlessness, even a fierce fearlessness. Seen in this way, it may be just possible for the university of the future to be characterised by both culture and anarchy.

Conclusion

Arnold was not wholly wrong. 'Culture' and 'anarchy' do present problems when put together. Culture may seem effete or cuddly or safe; anarchy may seem violent, not for the faint-hearted, and full of the unexpected. To put them in the same phrase seems to present a 'category mistake'. Like oil and water, they simply do not mix.

Correspondingly, that their conjunction has anything to offer in understanding the idea of the university may seem hard to fathom. Both the idea of culture and the idea of anarchy are complex. They each give rise not just to multiple interpretations but to competing interpretations. And those separate interpretations would point to alternative paths for the university. Put together, and the problems so multiply that they may seem insuperable. Culture offers some stability; anarchy offers unpredictability. Culture points to judgement; anarchy shrinks from judgement. Culture reflects collective meanings; anarchy stands for a preparedness to break any such bounds of collectivism. Culture and anarchy seem to point the university in opposite directions. Their conjunction summons a picture of the university like one of those optical illusions where a figure can be seen in two unlike ways but not simultaneously.

And yet we surely have to find a way of holding them before us in the one viewing. We cannot do without either the concept of culture *or* the concept of anarchy in apprehending the future university. It has to be a place of collective meanings and valuations; in this sense, it has to be a place of culture. And, if it is to be worthy of the name of 'university', it has to be somewhat anarchic. It has to have some element that goes beyond rules and sure method: it must always be possible, within a university, to confront the given. Perhaps if we are to give an initial response to Derrida's question (Chapter 8) – as to the responsibility of the university – it is that the responsibility of the university lies in its preparedness always to confront the given, even its methods, and even its own culture. The university will not just tolerate the unexpected but will *engender* it.

Nietzsche may be our saviour here. The culture of the anarchic university is not to be found in rules or perspectives of 'right reasoning'. It is to be found, if at all, in the passion and the will and even generosity that drive such an institution forward, even against its own bureaucratic and dogmatic tendencies. Sustained by a will always to illuminate with new insights and new actions, culture and anarchy may just live together in the being of the university.

8   Authenticity and responsibility

Introduction

The two concepts of authenticity and responsibility each pose difficulties. Is 'authenticity' a helpful term in the contemporary world? In a liquid world, aren't we obliged to take on different personas such that there is no self to which to be true so as to be authentic? On the other hand, 'responsibility' implies an allegiance to some larger cause or calling beyond oneself, but what might this be in the modern world? Isn't the whole thrust of postmodernism and relativism precisely a set of claims to the effect that no one set of claims can snare us in this way? 'Responsibility' implies obligation, but there being any principle on which an obligation might be founded is in doubt. The foundations of 'responsibility' seem to be crumbling.

Turning to the university, we may at least be able with some assuredness to identify what it might be to be an *in*authentic university or an *ir*responsible university. The inauthentic university is one that loses sight of its calling as a university. It fails to uphold standards; it closes inquiry; it reduces opportunities for learning. It not merely shrinks the space that it inhabits but it corrupts those spaces. The irresponsible university acts purely to advance its balance sheet; it acts in its own interests; it puts the pursuit of money before the pursuit of truthfulness; it runs the risk of losing sight of the public sphere.

Yet if it is a relatively straightforward matter to identify inauthenticity and irresponsibility, saying anything substantive about authenticity and responsibility is much more challenging.[1] Partly, the reason for this double difficulty lies in the contemporary reluctance to press for substantive large ideas in general (the postmodern disinclination to declare allegiance to so-called 'grand narratives' just touched upon). But in part, too, and almost contradictorily, it betrays the way in which the contemporary university has become snared by large forces – of the state, and the corporate world – *and* the concurrent felt need for the university to be adept in the contemporary world. Talk of authenticity and responsibility simply do not play too well in the vice-chancellor's regular meetings of the senior management team.

The problems multiply in trying to conjoin authenticity and responsibility. Can the university really be both authentic and responsible at the same time? Much as with 'anarchy' and 'culture', so do 'authenticity' and 'responsibility' seem to contend with each other. 'Authenticity' seems to be inner-directed. The authentic person is one who is true to him or herself. 'Responsibility', on the other hand, seems to be other-directed. It looks out from self and it has a care or concern for a world beyond. So is it possible for the university to be both authentic and responsible at the same time? Answering this question is the main challenge before us in this chapter.

The authentic university

The authentic university is one that is true to itself. But what does this mean? Is there a true or real self to which the university might be true?

David Cooper (2002) has drawn attention to two ideas of authenticity. In one variant, I am free insofar as I am disencumbered from potential constraint, and so am free to be myself. In the other variant – the variant favoured by Cooper – I am free insofar as 'I lean on nothing' and I therefore rely only on myself. I am thereby – in the neologism invented by Cooper – 'disincumbenced' (ibid.: 153). It might be said that these are negative and positive versions of authenticity; and both speak to the position of universities. These days, universities are beset by all manner of pressures, expectations and requirements, from the state, their students, their various funding agencies, professional bodies and the world of work. They are, therefore, very much encumbered. But, in the process, with the emergence of stakeholders, universities find it hard, if not impossible, to reach a stance in which they lean on nothing. They have become severely *reliant*.

Seen against the background of either variant of authenticity, universities no longer enjoy, if indeed they ever did, an autonomy in which they can be fully themselves. Authenticity seems to be beyond them. It is a concept that can do no work for us here, it seems, except perhaps serving as a critical standard, against which the university's developing must appear to be a situation of severe shortcomings.

After all, what would it mean for a university either to be unencumbered *or* leaning on nothing? A university cannot have its being in a space purely of its own, disconnected with the world. Even a university devoted to inquiry and understanding would be linked to disciplines that bestride the world in 'invisible colleges'. The connection that used frequently to be made between the university and critique depends on a sense of a world beyond the university that it might critique. Such critique ties the university to society. And the university of the twenty-first century is *ipso facto* bound to be linked to discourses, institutions, work, knowledge production across society and different publics.

But perhaps this way of construing the university's authenticity, as a matter of its being unencumbered, is misguided. Suppose that a university's authenticity lies precisely through its recognising that it is encumbered, and that it is truly itself when it is beset by other presences. Its authenticity would then be a matter of the way in which it engaged with those other presences. Or, rather, to put it slightly differently, its authenticity would depend upon the conditions under which those other presences were permitted to play their part in the university's space.

To speak, though, of the university's own space (in which it can be authentic) begs the question: to what extent does the university have any space of its own? The purposes on which its income streams are to be spent are largely pre-determined for it is subject to the power structures of the wider society; the providers of its income present the university with their expectations if not their demands. But, for the most part around the world, no matter how severe the regulatory regimes in operation, academics are not told precisely what to teach, or when to teach, or how to teach; there is a significant level of openness to the pedagogical relationship. Neither are they are told on which topics to conduct their research or their scholarly inquiries (no matter too how constraining the disciplinary cultures or the society's dominant knowledge policies). And nor, where they conduct income-generating activities, are universities often directed as to how they should seek and interact with their clients or how to go about attaining the intended aim of the activity (for example, how a consultancy report might be written). So, admittedly to considerably varying degrees, universities have pools of autonomy still open to them.

Further still, though it may not seem to be the case, those pools of autonomy are widening, even if they are *also* narrowing. Multiple income streams offer universities room for manoeuvre as to how to deploy their monies; the emergence of self-regulation – frequently a concomitant of reducing state intervention – places a measure of responsibility on universities to determine the character of their educational activities for themselves (and any associated internal monitoring arrangements); the intimate link to research and scholarship (to be found even in teaching intensive universities) generates an ethos of individual and collective criticality; governance arrangements that ensure that there is a variety of centres of decision-making (even if rectors come to see themselves as 'chief executives'); and the coming of the digital age, in which academics are linked in real time across the world 24 hours of the day. In and through all of these dimensions, it can be plausibly said that the university space opens further.

This widening of the university space is not entirely happenstance for the state, in the fluid conditions of the twenty-first century, has an interest in its having a number of knowledge-oriented institutions ('universities') that are to a significant degree open institutions. That this openness is monitored and even curtailed by the state – it gives with one hand and takes away with the other – is very much the case. Even as the state wishes to ensure that some of its 'public' institutions have a high degree of freedom to become themselves in the global 'knowledge economy', still it becomes nervous at the prospect and spasmodically twitches. Research and scholarship are highly desirable and help with the global rankings, *provided* that they yield demonstrable 'impact'. But, notwithstanding the caveats – as to state interest, the influence of the market, the constraining character of the circulating discourses – it remains the case that universities enjoy considerable pools of autonomy. We can still speak of a university space; and so the matter of their authenticity remains on the table.

Both space *and* the presences of others (the state, the corporate world, students cast as 'customers' and all their often strident and conflicting discourses): this surely is the situation of most universities across the world. And this combination of circumstances is, we can observe, precisely the conditions in which it makes sense seriously to speak of 'authenticity'. For 'authenticity' would not amount to much if there was no devil tempting one away from the path of true authenticity. Authenticity gains its spurs when it is in the company of malign influences that would encourage one from one's true self. Authenticity is the courageous and resilient sticking fast to the true self when the surrounding circumstances are pointing in another direction. The authentic university is one that has not yet fully fallen prey to those malign influences and temptations.

The university being true to itself

So, perhaps somewhat surprisingly, the conditions are in place for the university to be authentic. But still we are in the dark as to what substantively the authentic university might look like. The picture has opened up of the university retaining and possibly widening and certainly deploying its autonomies. In a networked world (Castells, 1997), a university becomes a node in which it is not just receiving messages, but is itself a source of its own messages outwards into the world.[2] The concept of authenticity, therefore, could be worked out by means of such a systems approach. What kinds of messages? What would be their velocity, trajectories and target audiences? With which other nodes would the authentic university especially interact in order to secure its authenticity? These are not superficial questions but by themselves they would evade the main issue and that is whether or not we can begin to fill in the substance of a university's authenticity.

An easy and beguiling option here is to say that, in a complex world, in which universities are differentially positioned, each university has to work out its own authenticity. Or, more formally, each university has to work out the conditions of the realisation of its authenticity: what does it have to do if it is to be genuinely authentic? This gambit amounts to saying that there is little in general terms that can be said about authenticity.

But that is too easy an option and it would underplay the concept of authenticity. For 'authenticity' cannot be solely a matter of a singularity living out itself, its whims, its fancies. While authenticity springs from within, and is particular, still it has its place in a horizon of the ethical (Taylor, 1991). The idea of the authentic has its limits. However faintly, it contains within itself a trace of an appeal to a value system beyond the individual. There is a thread of the collective in the concept of authenticity, much as it plays up the aspect of individual realisation (Guignon, 2004). We are, therefore, *required* to pose the question: is there anything – any project, any value, any activity, any aspiration – that every 'university' needs to heed if it is to be authentic? Even given the particularity of the position of each university – presence of research, spread of disciplines, proportion of non-state income, socio-economic status of its students, and so on – it just might be the case that there is some value or purpose to which any authentic university has to give its allegiance. It may turn out not to be the case but at least the question should be posed.

Earlier, I suggested that a core idea for the university might lie in the idea of understanding. Suppose we try to take that suggestion further and see if, under the umbrella of 'understanding', there is a cluster – or 'constellation' – of ideas or concepts (cf. R. J. Bernstein, 1991) through which the university might establish its authenticity. Suppose we consider that no idea of authenticity can be worked out for the university without some reference to 'learning' and 'inquiry'. Perhaps other concepts might come into view, such as 'truth', 'scholarship', 'critical thought', 'standards (of judgement)' and even, say, 'society'; but all these carry more baggage than either 'learning' or 'inquiry'. In the spirit of Ockham's razor,[3] let us not therefore multiply entities unnecessarily, especially when there are snares clearly associated with those other terms.

And what of 'teaching' and 'research'?, or so it might be asked. We must put these terms to one side as simply being labels attaching to the institutional forms that 'learning' and 'inquiry' have come to take in universities. 'Teaching' and 'research' do no work for us beyond that of 'learning' and 'inquiry'. Rather, 'learning' and 'inquiry', being concepts that are operating at a wider level of generality, can do much more for us here.

Keeping then, to 'learning' and 'inquiry', the question becomes: under what conditions might 'learning' and 'inquiry' furnish the basis – if at all – for the authentic university? The idea of the university has connections with those of totality, infinity and the universal. The university understands that it is connected with a world of knowledge (even if it is a specialist university and digs in one corner of the epistemological universe). The kind of knowledge in which a university is interested has universal validity and value. These are connected but different ideas. The ideas promulgated in a university are testable publicly and come, ultimately, to reside in (public) publications. They are tested against criteria that supply a universal warrant. At least, that used to be the case.

To some degree, the university's universalism has been undermined in recent years as individual universities have become more entrepreneurial and more practical in their orientation. Consequently, the university has become somewhat parochial. Its knowledges are tending to be knowledges of this region, of this set of companies, of this particular sub-group within a profession, or of this range of activities. In this parochialism is to be found the emergence of the performative university. But, still, in its self-understanding, the university wants to believe that it is more than concerned than with the here-and-now. It is not merely a local college dealing with local matters and interests. It has presentiments of itself being connected with larger judgemental criteria which, if not timeless, have both an enduring and a global significance.

This sediment of universal validity that lies within the university has its counterpart in the sense of universal value that attaches to the university. Again, the university may have become or be on the way to becoming parochial in all the ways just identified, and yet others as well (in its staff and student recruitment patterns, for example). Indeed, a 'university' may project itself and position itself in large part in local or regional ways. Still, it is likely to harbour hopes and beliefs that its work has a wider value, connecting with at least large if not worldwide themes of emancipation, growth of understanding, and even societal transformation.

'Learning' and 'inquiry' have to be placed under the umbrella of the ideas of universal validity and universal value if any substantive idea of authenticity is to take shape. If we now place this penumbra of ideas into the context of the twenty-first century, with its interconnectedness and porosity, an idea can just be glimpsed of the university playing out its interests in inquiry and learning in a global context. The authentic university may be one that so seriously takes its concerns for inquiry and learning that it sees its activities as being played out on a global stage. Those activities may be mainly parochial in their immediate character but this kind of university recognises them and may nuance them from time to time so as to acknowledge the global context in which those activities are played out.

The authentic university is a university, therefore, that fulfils its interests in inquiry and learning by realising them in a global context (however local in their overt character they may be). An interest in radiography in a health region is seen in the context of radiography worldwide; an interest in teaching potential school teachers for local urban settings is worked out via a concern for urban education across the globe (and perhaps the class is put into contact with a corresponding class in a different country).

This is a strong set of claims – as to interconnections between authenticity, understanding, inquiry, learning, and universalism – and deserves our further attention.

The responsible university – according to Derrida

Seldom is the question raised: what is or might be the responsibility (or responsibilities) of the university? University corporate strategies and mission statements may identify their strategic priorities and even offer a set of institutional values but of the university's responsibilities – as it sees them – such texts are usually silent.

Jacques Derrida did confront the issue of the responsibility of the university. He himself said that he 'still believe[d] in the task of [a] discourse on university responsibility' (Derrida, 2004: 92). What might this look like, in the face of recent and contemporary 'upheavals' (ibid.: 91) attending the university? 'Is a new type of university responsibility possible?' (ibid.: 91). So the task of identifying the responsibility of the university lies before us; it is not to hand. But:

> It is not certain that the university itself, from within, from its idea, is equal to this task [of identifying and pursuing the responsibility of the university] . . . and this is the problem, that of the breach in the university's system, in the internal coherence of its concept. For there may be no inside possible for the internal coherence for its concept.
>
> (ibid.: 92)

Does Derrida offer us a substantive way out of the dilemma, the aporia, that he identifies? I cannot see that he does. He goes on to make the problem even more complex, in referring to the 'contradictions' (ibid.: 93) in the university, in the loss of boundaries between itself and the outside world, in the university 'no longer (remaining) at the center of knowledge', in the collapse of knowledge and power, of reason and performativity, and metaphysics and technical mastery. The internal coherence that might just have supplied an anchor and a source of the university's responsibility seems to have dissolved. Noting the way in which the university has allowed itself to be guided by a notion of 'performativity', Derrida admits that he does 'not know if there exists today a pure concept of *the* university responsibility' (ibid.: 101–102). If we are to find such a concept, it 'has to require a new questioning about responsibility, a questioning that no longer relies on codes inherited from politics or ethics' (ibid.: 102). How might we go about the task?

We live in a world where the foundation of a new law (droit) – in particular a new university law – is necessary. To call it necessary is to say in this case at one and the same time that one has to take responsibility for it, a new kind of responsibility, and that this foundation is already well on the way, and irresistibly so.

Derrida develops the point, suggesting that: 'the university will have to walk on two feet, left and right, each foot having to support the other as it rises and with each step makes the leap'. Do we not see, in these quotations, Derrida raising the profound matter of the responsibility of the university, seeing its difficulties, wanting to take matters forward (to realise a new type of university responsibility) but being able to do so only elliptically, through metaphor?[4] Is this not the predictable outcome of a philosophy of deconstruction, we might be tempted to ask? For deconstruction forbids grand gestures, denies the building up of substantive new concepts: all a philosopher can do, at best, is to speak through metaphors – or become a poet.[5] But Derrida notices and seeks to head off just this response:

> Though too political in the eyes of some, deconstruction can seem demobilizing in the eyes of those who recognize the political only with the help of pre-war road signs. Deconstruction is limited neither to a methodological reform that would reassure the given organization nor, inversely, to a parade of irresponsible or irresponsibilizing destruction, whose surest effect would be to leave everything as is, consolidating the most immobile forces of the university.
>
> (ibid.: 103)

So the metaphorical is, or may be, politically powerful. If we are alert to it, there may be much in what Derrida has said, even though it may seem at first to amount to rather little.

I draw two things from Derrida; they are, though, susceptible to an interweaving that makes them even stronger. First, the term 'responsibility' is deployed in more than one way. In particular, it refers to the responsibilities that the university might uphold, *and* it refers to taking responsibility within a university. So the responsibility of the university is upheld – at least in part – through the taking of responsibility itself! This is a crucial insight for our present inquiry. Second, the value of the metaphor of walking through the action of feet that in turn support each other is also potent. We advance through our own efforts. We bear our own weight. The university, we can say, takes on and fulfils its responsibility through it taking responsibility for itself; not on meeting the claims of others or on fulfilling a destiny that it feels is given to it or that lies outside of itself. The university gains strength and momentum in just this way, through its own efforts. Shades (again) of Nietzsche.

Still, is this not a thin outcome so far? The university is to be responsible to itself. It moves forward through its own momentum. Is this all the new law of the university's responsibility amounts to? But in which direction are the university's steps to be taken? If everything is not to be left as it is, how are matters to be changed; even transformed? With what sense of purpose is the 'leap' to be made? Derrida gives us, I think, no answers to these questions. Despite his acknowledgement that deconstruction can leave everything as it is, we are not being offered by Derrida anything substantive here as to the university's 'responsibility'. Here, surely, we see the limitations of deconstruction: it has no resources in itself to construct anything of substance. There is a responsibility to say here more about responsibility.

Authenticity and responsibility

'Authenticity' and 'responsibility' are both large concepts. And both are crucial for comprehending the university in the twenty-first century. They also pull the university in different directions. 'Authenticity' looks inwards, to the university's inner being, its inner calling. 'Responsibility' looks at least partly outwards; it harbours a sense that the university just may have responsibilities beyond itself.

Both terms, we have seen, present difficulties. So far as *authenticity* is concerned, we are faced as to whether or not we can speak of the university's inner being, its inner calling. Earlier, I was proposing that it may still make sense to construe the university in this way. The authentic university in the twenty-first century, I was suggesting, may be a university that fulfils its natural interests in furthering understanding through promoting inquiry and learning. It takes inquiry and learning seriously. It has a concern with standards, while all the time itself keeping those standards under critical scrutiny. As I write this, news breaks of an inquiry being mounted by a British university into the operation of its world-famous centre for monitoring climate change, there being allegations as to the probity of its knowledge management processes. In a university setting, inquiry and learning are intimately bound up with the maintenance and evolution of standards.

So far as *responsibility* is concerned, the matter is still largely before us. It is not at all clear as to the basis on which the 'new kind of responsibility' that Derrida (rightly) calls for is to be founded. The idea of 'responsibility' invites the question: responsive to what? If the concept is to do work, it must refer to something beyond itself. But what might that be? Let us say boldly that the university is responsible to nothing other than to the world (which includes the university itself). The university has a universalism written into it. It bestrides the world. Even if its academics are not bumping into each other in the airports of the world, still its academic offerings are published in media accessible across the globe (in print and digital form). For many universities, too, their student body is comprised of a significant proportion of international students. In its conversations, activities and academic identities, the university is in part a global institution. Whatever, therefore, its local and its national obligations may be, the university has responsibilities that are worldwide. They are worldwide in that its activities and conversations are worldwide. The academics' texts are available around the world; its students arrive from every corner of the globe.

But the university's responsibilities are also *worldly*. Even if a university is national or regional in its positioning, still its offerings are offerings that have a worldly dimension. The tests of truth of its utterances are worldwide and, in turn, its utterances have a worldly significance, however parochial they may seem on the surface. All universities are world institutions: ultimately, they connect with concerns of the world and they are institutions for the world.

The reminders to universities that they are world institutions represented by the international 'league tables' both affirms but also undermines the point being made here. The global league tables tacitly confirm that universities understand very well that they are institutions of the world and that they will be and are judged against standards that have meaning across the world. On the other hand, the global league tables exacerbate cross-national competitiveness between universities (and their host nations) and, in the process, reduce universities' sense of responsibility to their own global possibilities.

The league tables also reduce a sense of universities' responsibilities to each other. The desire on the part of institutions of higher education to be granted the title 'university' (whether in the so-called public or private sectors) is indicative of the public value of the title. It follows that universities bear a responsibility to each other across the world in upholding collective standards to which the title of 'university' testifies.[6] The term 'university' does not, therefore, denote simply a number of discrete institutions that are named as universities but also refers to a collective set of institutions that owe much to each other in each being a 'university'. This reflection still leaves open, however, the substance of the responsibilities that universities owe to each other.

If, separately, authenticity and responsibility pose difficulties, together their challenges multiply.[7] In effect, in our explorations here, a grid space has opened (Figure 8.1). *A priori*, it would be possible for the university to be (a) authentic but not responsible; (b) neither authentic nor responsible; (c) responsible but not authentic; or (d) both authentic and responsible. In being (a), *authentic but not responsible*, a university would attend to its interests in learning and inquiry and would uphold severe standards in the pursuit of those interests. It would not, however, care much for the problems of the world. This is the position for which Kenneth Minogue argued in his (1973) *The Concept of the University*. It is not, however, a position that is feasible in the contemporary world. Over the past fifty years or so, the university has been called into the world, whether it likes it or not. Position (a) can therefore be ruled out as a feasible position.

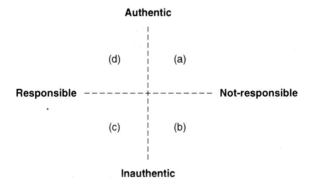

Figure 8.1 The university in the contexts of authenticity and responsibility

In being (b), *neither authentic nor responsible*, the university would be intent on its own interests. It might be highly entrepreneurial, with all of its faculty charged with the target of generating income two or three times that of their salaries (to allow for 'overheads'). It would not be overly concerned with maintaining collective standards and might even permit assessment practices to develop that helped to ensure that students were awarded their degrees.

In being (c), *responsible but not authentic*, the university would be highly responsive to the opportunities that presented themselves, perhaps for institutional advancement or for improving the balance sheet. It would not, however, be overly concerned with what it is or might be to be a university. Such niceties would not detain its management team.

Finally, in being (d), *both authentic and responsible*, the university would look both inwards and beyond itself. Here lies the dual challenge and the dual prize. This is not a comfortable position for it calls for judgement and carefulness, as the twin urgings of otherness and inwardness are heeded and reconciled.

Responsible authenticity

Can we see position (d), that of authenticity *and* responsibility, as a viable position for the university? Might a rapprochement between authenticity and responsibility be available? Authenticity seems to look inwards, here to a university's true calling. Responsibility looks outwards, to the obligations that a university has beyond itself, beyond its own immediate interests. Inner-directed and other-directed: authenticity and responsibility would seem to point the university in opposite directions.

However, if the university is placed in, and understands itself in, the global context, the two callings of authenticity and responsibility may just coincide. If the university's own inner self rests on a concern for learning and inquiry, and if the university understands that it has its being in the global context, then we can say that the university can be its authentic self in attending to its concerns for learning and inquiry by living out those concerns on the world stage. The university's authenticity may be safeguarded and its responsibility may be fulfilled at the same time and through the same set of acts. Authenticity and responsibility can be realised together.

A position for the university of *responsible authenticity* opens here. It fulfils its inner callings by playing them out on the world stage. In playing out its inner callings – of learning and inquiry – on the world stage, the university hears the voices of the world. This university is 'othered' – it is aware of the concerns of the world and brings its resources to meeting those concerns (even if a particular university plays out those responsibilities on a more local stage).

In this responsible authenticity, the university realises a space between the Scylla and Charybdis of internal and external ideologies. It is aware of both snares and acts to safeguard against them. In being authentic, it is alert to internal ideologies – of 'academic freedom' and 'academic community'. In being responsible, it is alert to external ideologies – of entrepreneurialism and the provision of 'transferable skills'. In being simultaneously responsible *and* authentic, the university attends to its interests in learning and inquiry by placing those interests in a global context. 'Learning' now becomes, for example, a matter of developing its students as 'global citizens'; inquiry now becomes a matter of developing global understandings of matters of significance.

This is a university that understands that its concerns, its activities and its resources are not merely 'private' but are public goods (cf. Chambers, 2005). My learning that x is such and such does not rob you of your possibilities and rights for *also* learning – in your own way – that x is such and such.[8] But the idea of the university as being the originator of public goods opens up much further both its responsibilities and its authenticity. This is a university that will be hesitant about becoming a player in markets, and will do what it can to mitigate the effects of the markets in which it does play, for it will be alert to the natural tendency of markets not merely to allocate goods according to preferences but to reflect and to enhance inequalities.

More positively though, this university, at once authentic and responsible, will seek – within the compass of its traditions, resources, epistemologies and positioning – to maximise the scope of its learning and inquiry. Potentially, the whole world becomes its stage. All of its activities are now interpreted and envisioned in this context. The idea of 'service' becomes a self-entreaty to serve the world (a small college might have just one project in the developing world); the idea of enhancing 'public understanding' becomes a project to advance the public sphere across the world (as much as possible of the university's output is placed on the internet and its academics in their own way develop their roles as public intellectuals[9]).

Conclusion

Both authenticity and responsibility are large concepts in understanding the university. Separately, they pose considerable difficulties. Can we any longer, given the university's complex position in the world, speak of 'authenticity'? Can we identify a 'responsibility' that the university should uphold in virtue of its being a university? If this is the case, that they pose difficulties separately, how much more so must it be the case that their conjunction poses difficulties. For authenticity demands of the university that it be true to itself; responsibility, in contrast, demands of the university that it have a sense of a world beyond itself, and of aspects of the world to which it should give its allegiance.

Paradoxically, putting the two concepts of authenticity and responsibility together, we may discern a way forward that allows the university to go some way to realising both callings simultaneously. Precisely by understanding that the contemporary university has its being through advancing learning and inquiry in and across the world, it may be possible to identify a space in which the university can be both authentic and responsible. In such a space, we may talk not so much of the student as a global citizen but rather of *the university as a global citizen*. The authentic university and the responsible university may happily co-exist in such an institution and at the same time.

Part III

Becoming possible

9   The liquid university

Introduction

The university has both substantive form and ideational form. It is both an institution in society and it reflects and embodies and, indeed, sometimes challenges ideas of the university. Ideas of the university do not exhaust our understanding of the university; far from it. But the university cannot be understood independently of the ideas it embodies.

Both form and ideas of the university have changed over time. We might wonder, as have philosophers from Aristotle onwards, as to whether an entity remains the same entity if every part of it changes over time. If the university as it is today bears no resemblance to that of its medieval predecessors, it is still the same institution? Does it have any *substance* of its own? That, though, is not the situation that faces us. The contemporary university never completely shrugs off its former stages. Within a single 'university', the research university is still present, even as the entrepreneurial university seeks to supplant it. But the metaphysical university can still be seen today, too, especially in the humanities. Not only are scholars still to be found, their books and materials crowding out their offices (much to the irritation of the estates managers), but these scholars will often want to see their endeavours in the horizon of large human ends. Enlightenment, culture, intelligence (a favourite term of Leavis[1]), humanity, and criticality: these are but some of the themes still to be heard in the corridors and the journals of scholars.

And so the university moves on, and often by adding layers of form and meaning to its existing forms and meanings. To look deeply into the contemporary university is to see a multi-layering of strata of self-images *of* the university, evident in the different practices and self-understandings of its incumbents. In earlier chapters (Part I), we identified some of the main ideas and forms through which this long history of successive layerings of the university might be understood, bringing the story to the present day (in noticing the entrepreneurial university and the bureaucratic and corporate university).

So the university has its being in time (Chapter 6): we cannot understand the university outside of the horizon of time. That reflection, though, prompts the further thought that we can try to discern the forms and associated ideas of the university *as it continues to unfold*, since locating the university in a horizon of time leads to a heightened sense that there are *possibilities* ahead of the university. We come back again to that phrase of Heidegger's: we can speak of the university's 'being-possible'. But then, in turn, the reflection arises that there is a *responsibility* to engage in this inquiry. There being options ahead of the university, we are ethically obliged to attempt not only to identify possibilities for the university but to attempt a kind of ethical audit of its possibilities.

In the remaining (four) chapters of this book, I shall identify in each one a keystone idea for the possibilities before the university (cf. Wyatt, 1990). Each idea offers a glimpse of the 'being possible' of the university. Each chapter, therefore, will form a case study of a feasible utopia, not only possible but adroit in its accommodations to the challenges of its age. Each one will be *prima facie* an attractive idea but we shall assess each one, to identify in each case its limits. Here – and taking our cue from the metaphor of the liquid articulated in a series of books by Zygmunt Bauman – we start with *the liquid university*.

The liquid university

The liquid university beckons. In fact, it is with us already to a large extent. And it comes full of promise. But it presents with its challenges.

The liquid university is amoeba-like. It is always on the move and interacting with its environment. It is not exactly shapeless; rather, it is a never-ending succession of shapes. The liquid university reaches out here, and then there. It touches, it feels its environment, and responds. It moves on, assuming a new shape, but only fleetingly. Reflective of Piaget's (1972) epistemology, it is an institutional example of a continuous process of *assimilation* and *accommodation*. The university encounters its environment. New income opportunities from a state agency, changes in a funding stream, a major departure in a discipline in which the university has a presence, incoming students presenting with unusual expectations: the university largely *assimilates* these happenings. It may grow or shrink a little but, even as it is interacting dynamically with its environment, it remains largely the same and in more or less the same place. The university is sufficiently complex and adaptable to move through such processes of assimilation effortlessly, for no significant changes are involved. And, in the process, those entities may themselves be subject to modification.

But some events and experiences place larger demands on the university. A funding stream may be shut or severely restricted; an external audit report is so critical that major changes have to be put in place before the agency returns; a cluster of transdisciplinary concerns bubble up in social policy such that a re-organisation of faculties and departments is called for if the university is to make the most of the opportunities that now present. In responding to such events and situations, the university undergoes change in itself. It *accommodates* to the changed environment in which it finds itself. It looks for new income-generating activities to meet the funding shortfall; it sets up an internal 'quality' office that seeks more data from its departments on a systematic basis; despite resistance from some of the departments concerned, it establishes a new faculty and it requires evidence that the departments involved are working on cross-disciplinary activities; and it may even close a department (or two) altogether. In accommodating to such changes in the university's environment, the university not merely moves on but takes on a new shape and forms new relationships with its environment.

Less obvious but even more significant are the changes that a university makes in accommodating to its environment *over time*. Successive efforts by the state to bring about 'efficiency gains' (say, an increase in the student:staff ratios, or a faster 'throughput' of students) are instrumental in changing the pedagogical relationship. Tutors become less accessible and students become subject to more monitoring of their progress. Efforts by the state to induce more of a student market encourage students to see their educational experience as presented, rather than as co-constructed. The pedagogical relationship takes on an instrumental tinge. The changes are not evident on a day-to-day basis or even across a year but work themselves out over perhaps two decades or more and, in these processes of accommodation, the university moves not merely into a different place but into a different configuration.

Time, therefore, is a crucial element in the making of the liquid university. As noted, this liquid university has its being in several timeframes all at once. Its corporate strategy peers five years ahead and it may have an estates strategy stretching thirty years into the distance. But a newspaper story of today requires a response today and the emails that fly into academics' in-boxes tacitly seek a response within hours. Other time horizons – of days, weeks and years – attach variously to different teaching, research and developmental activities. The university's temporal frames are, though, unequal in their press. Fast time tends to crowd out slow time; the short term tends to occlude the longer term. The liquid university is characterised by its ability to move quickly.

Rhizome or squid?

Here, we can return to Deleuze and Guattari who, in their philosophy of becoming, speak of being as a rhizome:

> A rhizome may be broken, shattered at a given spot, but it will start up again on one of its old lines, or on new lines . . . Every rhizome contains lines of segmentarity according to which it is stratified, territorialized, organized, signified, attributed, etc., as well as lines of deterritorialization down which it constantly flees.
>
> (Deleuze and Guattari, 2004: 10)

Is this not a nice description of the emerging university? The liquid university is faced suddenly with a crisis – an internationally famous research team is accused of overstretching its research claims, the state reduces its direct funding by 30 per cent overnight, an audit report speaks of 'limited confidence' in the institution, an overseas campus has been placed in a country suddenly experiencing a civil war – and the university appears temporarily at least to be 'broken, shattered' at that 'given spot'. But it is able to regroup through its existing 'lines of segmentarity'. It may even wish to 'deterritorialize' itself of certain elements: it disinvests itself of particular departments that are not performing adequately and of its off-shore campus. But it cannot so easily divest itself of its internationally-renowned research team. The matter has to be carefully investigated. Perhaps a working party will be established. Perhaps the research team can modify its practices in the future; perhaps it can be connected with another research team:

> The rhizome is altogether different, a map and not a tracing . . . it is entirely oriented toward an experimentation in contact with the real . . . it fosters connections between fields . . . The map is open and connectable in all of its dimensions: it is detachable, reversible, susceptible to constant modification. It can be torn, reversed, adapted to any kind of mounting.
>
> (ibid.: 13)

The liquid university moves in different directions all at once, and according to different ethical horizons. To speak of it being 'loosely connected' (Clark, 1983: 23) no longer does justice to the way in which it is decentred, even though in its corporate and bureaucratic forms it would try to restrain its anarchic tendencies. But new interconnections continually open up, both within the university and between it and its external constituencies. Identities merge, if not morph, into each other. Third space managers open up spaces and identities anew (Whitchurch, 2008). 'The centre cannot hold':[2]

> Thus packs, or multiplicities, continually transform themselves into each other . . . becoming and multiplicity are the same thing . . . a multiplicity is continually transforming itself into a string of other multiplicities, according to its thresholds and doors.
>
> (Deleuze and Guattari, 2004: 274–275)

Through the internet, the university's academics move almost instantaneously across the world in 'chronoscopic time' (Hassan, 2003). It moves swiftly across temporal regions of the world, and across cognitive regions of the world. It traverses discursive regimes – of the market, of service, of impact, of therapy – and political regimes. It moves at pace; it daren't be seen to be slow. Contemplative time is outlawed here; when was an academic last seen simply *thinking*?

Is not, then, *a squid* a better metaphor for this kind of university than a rhizome? Despite its anarchic tendencies, still the rhizome is too static an image. Far better, surely, to opt for an image that captures a sense of speed. The amoeba has the fluidity and the flexibility required but it lacks the pace. It also lacks the range and the scope. The squid can insert itself into crevices. It can move with amazing speed and transport itself from one situation to another with ease. There is hardly anywhere that it cannot reach. It can engage with both small and large entities. It has a shell and can withstand would-be predators. Aren't all these features of the liquid university?

'The greater the speed, the greater the control'

The liquid university can go anywhere; well, almost anywhere. At any moment, it is engaged in conversations across the world. And those conversations are both physical and virtual. Its knowledges spread out in unforeseen interminglings of space and time.

Boundaries between disciplines tend to dissolve in this epistemic freneticism. Data explode. Books in the library are not yet defunct but they are being displaced. Paul Virilio is perhaps the most acute observer of these transformations, straddling at once dimensions of science, technology, time, computerisation and communication. The university, we can also note, is bound up in all the dimensions that attract Virilio's attention. The university now races at the speed of light across the globe. It messages, its data streams, multiply, and: 'Given this explosion of data and its required information technology, the gap between the sensible and the intelligible continues to deepen . . . Thus speed becomes the sole vector for electronic representation' (Virilio, [1984] 1991: 33, 35).

In this situation, we are faced with what has been brilliantly termed an 'ignorance explosion' (Lukasiewicz, 1994). The pages of the journals in the libraries of the world and on the internet contain much more than can be assimilated. Most journal papers are largely unread and, in the process, the gap between our 'knowledge' of the world and our possibilities for turning that knowledge into understanding grows. At best, 'knowledge' becomes mere data streams with individuals reduced to being information processors.

Now, borrowing still from Virilio, we can say that the university moves in 'an accidental, discontinuous and heterogeneous space' (Virilio, 1991: 35). And this, we should note, is a space that the university itself has done much to generate, through its research technologies, such that much science is now conducted through the computer and on the computer screen rather than in the laboratory. 'We must at least resolve ourselves to losing our sense of our senses, common sense and certainties, in the material of representation' (ibid.: 48).

More generally still, in this multimedia age (Kress and Leeuwen, 2001), meaning is conveyed through many media, and former hierarchies across media of communication are lessening. Written text – especially text composed with words – gives ground to other forms of representation. Now, in making a claim, the academic has to choose how best to convey the intended meaning – in speech or writing or sound, and then more specifically, whether in symbols, metaphors, words or numbers, and then to what extent the different modes will be adopted and in what combination.

Academic communication and communication within the academy are not what they were; whether they are more than they were or less is another matter. What can be said is that it, too, quickens. The books shorten in length (for academic time no longer permits lengthy and considered close reading), the internet journals – with their shorter timelines for publication – flourish, the emails multiply, and the screen images cascade faster than the eye can accommodate. The conversations of the academy become more heterogeneous and are speeded up.

For Virilio, 'the greater the speed, the greater the control' (2005: 65). Virilio was drawing here on the military analogy: the ability to move faster than the enemy was likely to yield more power and, thereby, victory. That used to be the case. But, now, increasing speed is leading to a situation that is much less under control. 'What will we wait for when we no longer need to wait to arrive?' (ibid.: 120). Instantaneous speed and movement call for more or less instantaneous action. This is not only a world in which the university has its being but it is a world that the university plays its part to bring about. That the university is faced with profound challenges of communication and meaning-making is in part a reflection of an emerging world for which the university is partly culpable.

The gift of the ubiquitous

In this liquid world, the university reaches out beyond itself. No longer sure of the meaning of grand terms such as 'knowledge' and 'truth', it moves through what we might term *the gift of the ubiquitous*. The liquid university recognises no boundaries: it goes geographically and epistemologically where its knowing interests take it.

The university's new ubiquity is a gift in several senses. Its ubiquity is a gift to *itself*. Its interconnectedness with the world – more or less literally the whole world – opens new possibilities for it. Themes of 'service', 'the civic university' and engaging with 'the public sphere' now take on a global aspect. Fulfilling its purposes, whatever they may be, can now be played out in all manner of arenas. Even locally, the university can stretch out its arms to encounter and sense a multitude of organisations, in both the public and the commercial sectors, as well as state agencies, professional bodies and so on. Academic travel, both physical and virtual, now extends the new exploratory capacities of the university across the globe. The reach of the liquid university and its scope to fulfil its own ends multiply.

The university's ubiquity is also a gift to *the wider society*. The university has a presence more or less everywhere and for quite different purposes. Whether, for example, engaging with elderly people for the purposes of oral history, working with an African village to give it an understanding of theatre, or investigating the effect of climate change in the Arctic, the university spreads its possibilities around the globe. And, as remarked, these possibilities are increasingly being accomplished in virtual space. Now, the university is engaged in global conversations in real time, and 24 hours of the day. (The students can gain physical access to the library at any hour but the personal computers of both academics and students allow continuous global travel.) The university's ubiquity, therefore, offers benefits to the world; the liquid university is a university of the world.

The university's ubiquity is a gift in a yet third sense. It is a gift *for the university*. In this ubiquity, the university comes to listen to the world, to take account of the world, in all its differences. It becomes sensitive to the cultures and the languages of the world. In so doing, it becomes strangely a quieter place in a way; a quietness born of understanding that there are evermore understandings that may come its way; a quietness born of a sense of its own limitations; a quietness born of a will to receive as well to offer (services) and to provide (knowledge). Its ubiquity, therefore, allows the university to grow as it becomes a space for the intermingling of languages and cultures (locally, regionally and across the world). In turn, this growth of openness and generosity becomes a gift for *the world* (a fourth sense of gift), for the world itself is helped in its development. 'To recognize the Other is therefore to come to him across the world of possessed things, but at the same time to establish, by gift, community and universality' (Levinas, 1969: 76).

Ubiquity is not a straightforward good. The university's ubiquity may open new spaces for the university to exert its influence in self-serving ways (to advance its 'academic capitalism'). Ubiquity comes with gifts in its arms if and when the university reaches out in a spirit of otherness.

For Levinas, 'to possess the idea of infinity is to have already welcomed the Other' (ibid.: 93). In understanding ourselves in the horizon of infinity, we are already taking account of the Other. And so it is for the university. If it understands itself as in infinite space, it also makes space for otherness. It sees the Other as a space in which it can develop its own understandings. It will shy away from arrogance, tendencies to impose itself, and to extract as much as it can from the world, and seek to live with the world, and with infinity.

Space, therefore, opens possibilities and prompts possibilities for the university. But two sets of distinctions are in order. First, we should distinguish *physical space* from *virtual space*. Virtual space adds to the physical spaces in which the university works. Now, the university can reach out to the world and be in the world, even from within its own campus. However, and second, despite their differences, we can see physical space and virtual space as constituting a single set of empirical spaces; and against *empirical space*, we can place *attitudinal space*. With what attitudes might a university see itself as global? Is it one of dominating the world (the academic world, at least), of rising up the international league tables, and of making its presence felt in consultancy and other income-bearing projects? Or is it one of living in the world, of living in and with infinity, aware of its own finiteness?

Space is not necessary for the presence of grace. We recalled earlier (Chapter 6) how prisoners such as Gramsci and Bonhoeffer were able, in their prison cells, to write their prison notebooks, and to speak of hope and generosity. 'Sit in your cell and your cell will teach you everything' was an oft-quoted saying of Abba Moses (Rowan Williams, 2004a: 82).[3] Ubiquity in the form of empirical space opens opportunities for new and good work for the university only if it is accompanied, indeed propelled, by attitudinal space; by the university embarking on its various academic and commercial travels in a spirit of benevolence, being open to the Other. This will not reduce the university's autonomy but expand it: 'The presence of the Other . . . does not clash with freedom but invests it' (Levinas, 1969: 88).

There is the presence of gifts in the university's ubiquity. But those gifts are not simply there. They will unfold if and only if the university goes forth into the world seeing itself in infinite space. Then, it just may be really aware of its own finiteness and open to the Otherness of the world. Then, the gifts of ubiquity may flourish.

Transient diversity

The term 'university' is in danger of losing substantive meaning, becoming hardly more than a cultural adornment (such that all manner of organisations wish to be called 'university'). University research students in semiotics might turn their hand to working out just what is going on when trans-national companies and other organisations take on – or manifestly aspire to take on – the title of 'university'.[4] What has the term 'university' come to *signify*? There is a liquid aspect to the very term university. It cannot easily be contained, being called upon to serve disparate functions. But yet, in the very calling up of the term, subliminally, such organisations in wishing to associate themselves with the term 'university' presumably are tacitly indicating a wish on their part to be associated with certain kinds of activities and certain kinds of values.

Let us hypothesise that those activities are truth-oriented activities and that value attaches in society to such activities. We may say, then, to draw on Bernard Williams's (2002) term, that universities are associated with 'truthfulness'. That is to say not that every utterance that emanates from a university is a form of truth but that the university is felt to have a dominant interest in truth. Its utterances, by and large, have a degree of reliability to them in that they are the result of inquiries that have integrity and are able to be judged by quite severe standards of proclamation. Students may and will get things wrong but their wrongness is precisely an outcome of their being tested against those standards (whatever those standards may be in different domains) and it is within the horizon of those standards that students are expected to progress. (The quality of work expected of a final year student is more than that of a first year student.) To proclaim – a proposition, an idea, a finding – with any authority or approbation, one must pass muster against severe criteria.

It follows that the liquid university is not at will to roam aimlessly. There are limits to its wanderings: its ventures. Doubtless other onerous conditions apply also to being a university: universities are expected not to be corrupt nor fall deeply into debt.[5] But those conditions are contingent conditions whereas the truthfulness criterion is a necessary condition of what it is to be a university. An institution could not legitimately term itself 'university' if its pronouncements were continually suspected of being false or exaggerated or partial or dogmatic or for show or even simply for impact.

There is, then, as we may put it, an epistemological ethics that accompanies the name of 'university'. No matter how liquid it becomes, no matter how porous its boundaries, no matter in what new ventures it engages, and no matter which new constituencies it reaches out in or in which media it does so, it still has to maintain an epistemological integrity to fulfil the promise of its name 'university'.

The multimedia world beckons the university, it seduces the university. New interactive and iconic technologies open possibilities for virtual experiences; virtual lives and virtual identities indeed. The university can move into multiple worlds, and almost parallel worlds, limited only – it seems – by the limits of imagination. But our reflections show that the university needs to be wary unless it is prepared to prejudice its very title. The test has to be neither 'Might this creation or interaction lead to marketable outcomes?', nor even 'Is this venture opening an interesting experience?' But rather 'Will this venture offer new and significant insights and understandings?'

We live now not amid two modes of knowledge – as some contend – but multiple modes. Personal, creative, interpersonal, experiential, tacit, kinaesthetic and iconic modes are only some of the modes now proliferating. The university knows no epistemological bounds, it seems (cf. Leach, 1998). It is offered and has helped to generate epistemological riches. Riches, though, may be seductive. In its epistemological forays, the university is at risk of losing sight of home. It sees epistemological stars glittering and goes off somewhat blindly in their pursuit. In the process, all manner of epistemological possibilities are encountered and experienced.

'Diversity' is a large theme in higher education policy frameworks; that much is well recognised and understood. In a mass higher education system, between themselves, universities should evince diversity reflecting their different 'missions'. Much less remarked on are the system and institutional capacities for *epistemological diversity* in a liquid age. The knowledges that are opening up allow each university to have its epistemological profile, a profile that recognises that the old categories of hard/soft knowledge and pure/applied knowledge are no longer adequate (cf. Becher, 1989). Epistemological diversity and specificity are signs of a now ever-widening epistemological space in which the liquid university moves.

These epistemological travels are entirely proper, provided that the (liquid) university remembers its calling of truthfulness (to be interpreted generously, as earlier remarked). But the call, the pull even, of the new knowledges – practical, digital and personal and configured in unforeseen and unpredictable patterns across time and space – may help to dissolve the memory. To draw on a term from Zollman (2010), what is needed in this epistemological maelstrom is not diversity as such, but rather *transient diversity*. The liquid university delights in its epistemological journeying and the diversity of experiences that such journeying opens, but it is a transient set of delights in that the liquid university does not forget that it is a university.[6] The 'university' (the idea) calls back the university (the institution). Accordingly, all of its new experiences will be subject to interrogation by the tribunals of its standard bearers, even if its new experiences will be called upon to help to develop those very standards.

Liquid identities

The liquid university leads to liquid identities. As noted (Chapter 6), what it is to be 'an academic' is no longer clear. Other categories – perhaps 'teacher', 'supervisor', 'project leader', 'researcher', 'co-worker' or 'curriculum developer' – are borne more easily as self-descriptions. Characteristically, too, individuals are not identifiable by any single category. Across multiple roles, they take on multiple identities, it seems. They become adept at engaging with particular discourses in different settings: a teaching session, a meeting of Senate chaired by the vice-chancellor, an informal meeting to discuss a 'third-stream' opportunity, a meeting of the editorial board of a journal and an invited visit abroad: each has its own script and encourages a particular role, with its own discourses, deferences and self-projections.

This fluidity of academic identities is mirrored by the assembly of knowledges and understandings to which academics become alert. Formal knowledges intermingle, with their boundaries becoming more open: internet working encourages nomad-like explorations. A concept in one domain is more easily noticed and transported, albeit at the price of some corruption, into another domain. At the same time, as the academic role extends out into the wider society – in interactions with government agencies, private and public sector organisations, and channels of communication – so 'academic knowledge' flows into professional, policy and practical knowledges.

Another source of fluidity lies in the professionalisation and formalisation of academic work. On campus, in developing their activities and projects – in teaching, in research and in more entrepreneurial activities – inter-connectivity develops between professional managers, academic managers and the academics themselves. The distinctiveness of the roles does not quite evaporate but their connecting boundaries become weaker and flexible. The emergence of 'third space' professional managers (Whitchurch, 2008) is one factor in this increasing fluidity of identities on campus. These professional managers are part of the story of the emergence of the corporate university (Chapter 4) and are an independent source of decision-making to which the academic identity has to accommodate.

What is one to make of this empirical story of the development of academic identity? How does it bear on the matter here? In their (2003) book on *Science, Social Theory and Public Knowledge*, Alan Irwin and Mike Michael examine emerging relationships between science, policy-making and the wider society, especially insofar as they affect the public understanding of science. Part of the story developed there is that of the increasing complexity of science and scientific knowledge as it intermingles with understandings in other domains. In forming an understanding of those matters, Irwin and Michael (ibid.: 11–19) coin the term '*ethno-epistemic assemblage*'. For any major matter in the public and policy domain – such as AIDS, energy provision, nuclear power, genetically modified foods, animal welfare and food production – a complex of knowledges merge and inter-relate across several domains (science, technology, politics, public understanding, policy formation). They are not stable knowledge complexes: they are 'epistemic assemblages'. But the prefix – the 'ethno' in 'ethno-epistemic assemblages' – is significant. For the choice of knowledges will be and should be in part influenced by social and even societal considerations and worked out through dialogue and even contestations (for example, over rights, the availability of knowledge in society, access to resources and participation in decision-making).

Given these insights from Irwin and Michael, we can say similarly that the adoption of an academic identity or, rather, academic identities, is in part a matter of choice. Admittedly, this is a complex field. Academic knowledges, academic life, and academic identities are each fluid and form a dynamic region. But there remain ethical choices to be made in the formation of identities. The liquid university has many possibilities. The kinds of academic identity, the knowledges taken up, and the scope and the modes of their deployment, have ethical bases. Is an academic identity essentially one of seizing the main chance as opportunities are opened up within the entrepreneurial university (perhaps in forming 'spin-off' companies, partly for personal gain) or for widening access to knowledge and understanding in society or for furthering the goals of the corporate university? In the liquid university, academic identity presents its possibilities and its ethical challenges.

Conclusion

The liquid university is almost upon us; and its emerging can be readily discerned in many ways. The liquid university is not bound by considerations of time or space, or of presuppositions about valid forms of knowing the world, or of assumptions about the epistemic relationships through which its knowledges engage with the world (its 'stakeholders'). The liquid university slides across the world, aided by the digital revolution. But the liquid university is more than the virtual university (cf. Robins and Webster, 2002).

The liquid university is liquid in more senses than its communications systems, being liquid in its positioning, networks, 'clients', epistemologies and identity structures. It has no centre, neither geographically nor in any other sense.[7] It flows in multiple time zones and engages with no particular community, which is to say that potentially it will engage with any community. The theme of 'public engagement' may spring up, but for the liquid university there are many publics and many languages.

Two sets of questions arise. First, are not some currents in which the liquid university moves not running faster than some others? Is there not more impetus in some directions than others? Are the streams not flowing faster in the direction of money (especially income) *and* also high status research in science and technology? (These – money and status – are two somewhat separate currents.)

Second, the liquid university likes to consider that its currents are ethically neutral but is that the case? The liquid university is a version of the post-modern university (cf. Smith and Webster, 1997), and shies away from declaring itself in favour of a set of values. Its ethical purity allows it to catch and swim with different currents, to turn and turn again, and with some rapidity. Of course, some universities like both to pretend that they are liquid (they declare that they can adapt rapidly to unforeseen situations) *and* to hold to a definite value position (they also have a section on their values in their corporate strategies). But this is pretence or self-deception: the two positions – an entirely liquid nature and a secure value position – cannot be comfortably held at the same time.

The liquid university opens itself to the world: it is of the world and even for the world. But sheer liquid-ness is insufficient to warrant the title of 'university'. It is a naïve position. The waters are both dominated by certain fast-flowing streams and are somewhat muddy, and possibly even polluted. If the university is not to be the creature of already present currents and value structures, it has to identify its own ethical structure. This, in turn, will bring some limit to its liquid-ness. There will be some currents it will not follow; some places into which it will not venture. As a metaphor, the 'liquid university' has its attractions but it also carries with it some difficulties.

10 The therapeutic university

> Let me suggest, then, . . . that the modern university is injured . . . in such a situation the need for therapy is obvious and immediate.
>
> (Timothy Bahti, 'The injured university', 1992: 68–69)

Introduction

The four chapters in this part of this book aim to identify feasible utopias. Such utopias have four significant features. First, they are utopian. They are almost certainly not going fully to be realised. Second, they are *feasible*: that is, in being utopian, they are not fanciful. There are sufficient exemplars *already present* that show that these utopias *could* be reached. Third, they contain both optimism and pessimism: they reveal positive possibilities in our present situation but they are confronted with forces in the world such that their coming into being is extremely unlikely. Lastly, utopias are not necessarily all to the good, even if they were realised. As utopias, they look forward to situations that would be mostly beneficial but, as utopias, they often harbour extreme hopes. Dystopias lurk within utopias.[1] Each of these four conditions of feasible utopias can be observed in the idea of the therapeutic university.

The therapeutic university is a particular example of that last phenomenon connected with utopias, namely that of the possible emergence of dystopias. A dystopia is often a utopia whose elements are pressed unduly. The result is that a potentially virtuous path of development becomes pernicious. The therapeutic university presents just this situation: it contains both virtuous and pernicious elements; at once, the possibilities both of utopia and dystopia.

The therapeutic university is with us already, at least to some extent. The therapeutic university has a *care* for human being as such: it has a care towards all of the members of itself, which is to say *all* of its staff and all of its students, but perhaps especially its students. It may be felt that this is a little strange for students are adults, having in many higher education systems an increasing average age.[2] If, some years ago, there were concerns over the university acting *in loco parentis* to its students, presumably something of that concern might be even more present in relation to 'mature' students. Further, the 'marketisation' of higher education is placing students in a market relationship with their institutions; and the notion of 'care' is hardly characteristic of a market relationship. Why, then, this care 'especially' towards its students?

We will explore these matters in this chapter. Let us note at the outset though that there are critical voices as to any suggestion that universities might have or take on a therapeutic function.[3] These voices need to be heard: they have some right on their side but only some right. In taking my argument forward, I shall distinguish two variants of the idea of therapeutic university, and I shall resist one variant and offer my support to the other one.

Lastly, by way of introduction, I will want here to stretch the idea of the therapeutic to include all of the activities in which the university is involved. We unduly limit the idea of the therapeutic university if we limit the concept to its overtly educational functions. The therapeutic university has a care for more than its pedagogical responsibilities.

Living with uncertainty

For those who feel sympathy towards the idea of the therapeutic university, it is fashionable to link this idea also to the idea of uncertainty. The argument runs that, since this is a world of perpetual change, it becomes a responsibility, if not a duty, of the university to enable students to live with this uncertainty. I agree with this point of view but it is insufficient as it stands. Many students may be perplexed about 'life' and about their place in the world. These perplexities are doubtless exacerbated by a sense that the world is changing and changing quickly at that. We may term this sense of uncertainty on the part of the student an *ontological uncertainty*. In this uncertainty, the student is unsure as who or what they are; he or she is without a clear sense of themselves, of their being. It is right that the university will have a care towards such concerns on the part of the student. For the student who harbours such anxieties is less likely, we may surmise, to find either the energies or the fortitude adequate to sustain them through, say, a three- or four-year course of study. The educator of such a student is likely to be more effective if they are sensitive to such possible difficulties being faced by her students.

But it by no means follows that the educator has a responsibility to attend directly to such an ontological uncertainty. Herein lies the opening to the concerns of some of the critics of the therapeutic university. A key concern of theirs is that the therapeutic university will focus on the student's feelings and emotions and, thereby, be diverted from its 'true' concerns with bounded, disciplined, study, taken forward according to standards intrinsic to each discipline or field. Students will be 'infantilised', with the natural challenges of their personal lives turned into problems not only for them but for the academy, turning its educational function into a grandiose therapeutic service, with the university's counselling services assuming an increasingly prominent role. 'Everyday feelings have become pathologised to the extent that simple nervousness and shyness become problems for which external help [within the university] is available' (Ecclestone and Hayes, 2009: 88).

This may well be the case but, by itself, it is a partial reading of what might be meant by the 'therapeutic university'. The critics' concern with what we have just termed *ontological uncertainty* is insufficiently distinguished from, as we may term it, *epistemological uncertainty*. The latter is that form of uncertainty that universities have long celebrated. It lies in a recognition that our accounts of the world could legitimately be other than they are. The university is an institutional space that recognises this viewpoint. It is a space for the continual playing out, and scrutiny, of differences – in claims, readings, and ideas. A university is an institution that is characterised by epistemological uncertainty. Indeed, the university has a responsibility to generate epistemological uncertainty among its students. And it is, therefore, in relation to the idea of epistemological uncertainty that we can *legitimately* look to the coming of the therapeutic university.

Ontological uncertainty and epistemological uncertainty are intimately related to each other and it is vital that both their intermingling *and* their separateness be understood. The therapeutic university in its fullest form does understand this.

'Uncertainty' is a thick concept (Williams, 2008).[4] It both tells us something about the world – that features of it are uncertain in some ways – *and* points to our sensation of being in such a world. We feel uncertain *in* an uncertain world. Our being is unsettled amid uncertainty; and, in turn, we become, or are liable to become, uncertain. To link such a situation of being, of being-uncertain, to the notion of infantilisation is to invert the status of epistemological uncertainty. The world, it can legitimately be argued, is over-run with certainty – certainty in relation to ideologies, religions, the power of science, and the value of markets. A sense of uncertainty that derives from an understanding that readings and perspectives could be other than they are is a mark of *maturity*, and not of immaturity.

Epistemological uncertainty has warrant written into it. All at once, it indicates that, in regard to a significant issue (say, climate change or *in vitro* fertilisation), there are different plausible readings, that the informed voices and the evidence are mixed, and that a sense of confusion within a reflective person is justified. The task of the therapeutic university is to help to open and address such confusion although the way it does this is to move the confusion to another place. We learn a little more, we see more deeply into key concepts, we become more alert to value considerations; and, in the process, yet more dimensions of the situation are opened that, in their wake, bring yet further confusions. So a tacit task of the therapeutic university is to enable us to live with this (epistemological) uncertainty to which, after all, the university has itself contributed through being a space of creative and dissenting voices.

For Wittgenstein, philosophy possessed a definite therapeutic function. Philosophy was a means of seeing that beneath many sources of difficulty lay a problem with the use of language. Through a dissection of key concepts, problems could often be dissolved. Famously, philosophy could 'show the fly the way out of the fly-bottle' (Wittgenstein, 2009: 110) – and so, we might presume, overcome its buzzing and frenetic confusion at the same time. This view of philosophy was always overdone.[5] Often, conceptual 'confusion' is a reflection of different sets of values, perspectives and favoured methodologies for understanding the world. In these situations, conceptual clarification can at most expose and thereby *heighten* our uncertainty, not diminish it. The university, we may judge, is an institution whose being is bound up not with dissolving uncertainty but for heightening uncertainty and also for making uncertainty intelligible and, in a sense, manageable.

Managing uncertainty

Introducing the notion of management into this discussion will seem heretical to some. 'Management' and 'therapy' hardly seem to sit well together. Management implies an instrumental orientation to matters to hand; 'therapy' implies a concentrated concern directed at a particular person. Management implies an 'it', an it to be managed; 'therapy' implies a 'thou', a thou with whom there has to be some kind of dialogue (Buber, 2002). The concept of management, though, does imply a sense of meeting challenges and of seeing a way forward; and similarly with therapy. But therapy has a sense, too, of seeing a way forward *for oneself*. 'Therein the patient must minister to himself.' The patient comes not merely to see himself in a new way but alters his actions thereupon. He is released, or releases himself, to be other in the world.

To carry over the idea of management into the realm of therapy, therefore is not quite to commit a category mistake but it is to extend the idea of management beyond its natural settings. We can hold open the idea that uncertainty can be managed, providing that we keep in mind the honorific status that we now accord the concept of management.

I suggest – as I have urged before (Barnett, 2000) – that the university has a responsibility both to play its part to add to uncertainty in the world *and* to help to assuage that uncertainty. It will be recalled that we observed a moment ago that 'uncertainty' is Janus-faced. It looks to the world and identifies perplexing and even contradictory features of our accounts of the world – there is uncertainty *about* the world; *and* it looks inwards to ourselves, noticing our feelings of unease faced with this confusing set of stories of the world – there is uncertainty *within* us.

There are three layers here, then: (1) the world; (2) our accounts of the world; and (3) our responses to these accounts.[6] And the idea of uncertainty runs together uncertainty at the levels of both of (2) our accounts of the world and (3) our responses to our accounts of the world. It is the task of the university to help to multiply accounts of the world (level 2). And its accounts of the world should be offered in such a way that they lead to yet more accounts of the world (that is the nature of a seminar, or good teaching session or a conference). Unless a university is doing this, it is not a 'university'. It is the task, therefore, of the university to increase uncertainty at the level of our accounts of the world. In the process, and quite naturally, individuals may experience 'uncertainty'. They may *feel* confused or anxious or both. It is this entire set of conditions that I have termed here *epistemological uncertainty*; this *combination* of a lack of assuredness in our accounts of the world (level 2) and our responses to that state of affairs (level 3).

I am contrasting this epistemological uncertainty with *ontological* uncertainty, that form of uncertainty in which, say, students feel anxious about their place in the world; about their own being. While we should distinguish these two forms of uncertainty, there are links between them. Epistemological uncertainty can deepen any ontological uncertainty a student may have. If a student becomes perplexed about the perspectives of the world opened up by her studies, that may exacerbate any concerns she may have about her own being. She may be further dislodged. Equally, a student may have anxieties about her own personhood in the world, and turn to the university to help her to address that ontological uncertainty. She may wager that deep study in some field or other may just help her, in some way, to a more secure understanding of at least part of herself.

What has this account of uncertainty to do either with therapy or the management of therapy? I believe that the distinction I have been making between epistemological and ontological uncertainty is crucial on both counts.

It is the university's *direct* responsibility to bring students to confront accounts of the world that are new to those students. It is the university's implicit responsibility, therefore, to disturb the students with strangeness. The disturbance and the strangeness are linked in a complex formation. It is *not* simply that the strangeness produces the disturbance – although it may do so. It is more that it is part of the university's teaching function *as such* to disturb its students. For in disturbance, or 'disjuncture' (Jarvis, 1992), students are jolted into a new place.[7] In interviews, students will sometimes use terms such as 'panic' or 'scary' to describe the feelings such an educational disturbance naturally engenders.[8] They are bombarded not only with tasks but with a cascade of ideas, concepts and theories. Their comprehending of such complexity takes them into a new place. This is a rightful disturbance on the part of the university. It is one of the university's tasks to generate this epistemological uncertainty.

If it is a task of the university to promote epistemological uncertainty in its students, it also has a responsibility to assuage that uncertainty. Not, as we saw earlier to dissolve it; for that uncertainty may spring from a valid reading both of the way the world is and our differing accounts of it, but to assuage it in the sense of helping students to live with it. Sinclair Goodlad (1976) depicted higher education as a way of enabling students to come to a place of 'authoritative uncertainty'. 'Authoritative' is perhaps too much to hope for; a more feasible idea might be that of 'contained uncertainty'. The panic can be managed. And 'managed' in two senses. It can be tolerated; accepted. The student can live with his uncertainty. This is 'managing' uncertainty in a somewhat passive sense. But there is a more active sense of managing that is lurking here too. For the student may also come to a place wherein she may be active in her own learning knowing that that very activity will bring yet more disturbance. She keeps notebooks, and makes jottings (in any medium) and reflects on her experiences. The student actively manages her uncertainty.

Where is the therapy here? The therapy lies in the student coming into a place where her confusion can be understood as a natural state of affairs. In any discipline or field worthy of inclusion in a university, there are disputes for they each have a discursive openness. Nothing is ever finally settled. There is always room for further qualifications and sophistications and even downright repudiation. Helping students to live in their minds and their practices amid this incessant openness is one of the tasks of the university. But the living ultimately is not, as intimated, a passive living. The living becomes an active living: the student puts herself forward knowing that there are alternative readings of a situation or perspectives that might be brought to it. Her putting herself forward – in seminars, in the laboratory, in the creative arts studio, in the clinical situation – are gifts that she proffers, for the putting forward in a situation of such openness requires courage on the part of the student.

There are several aspects to this educational process that connect to the idea of therapy. The student's confusion is not dissolved; indeed, it may be heightened, but it is now *contained* within the student's mind and being. It no longer threatens to overcome the student. The student is now able to live with uncertainty. Difficulties remain and even multiply; but they are eased. They are much less troubling.[9] The student grows in confidence in expressing herself, in forming and handling her own ideas and practical actions. The world comes to be seen differently. The student moves into a new place through a kind of *epistemological therapy*, achieved not least through the powers of their own critical self-reflection (encouraged through their programme of studies).

Being in the world

I have just suggested that, in a university education worthy of the name, 'the world comes to be seen differently'. How can this be? How can it be that a course of university study can help the student to see the *world* differently? Students are direct testimony to this point: they themselves may say at the end of a course – at the end of the graduation ceremony, as a tutor is introduced to proud family members – that 'this course has changed my life'. Such a reflection may be entirely legitimate, for her course of study – with its pacing, arduousness, standards, conversation, private study, and intellectual and practical forms of strangeness – will have nurtured certain dispositions and qualities that are potentially life-changing.[10]

We may note, *en passant*, that one of the concerns over the marketisation of higher education is that it may lessen the preparedness of students to put themselves forward into pedagogical settings, instead preferring as customers to receive a 'high quality educational product' in return for their monetary investments. To the extent that this is the case, the potential for life-transformation that lies within universities in their educational function will be diminished. So the formation of the student is connected, or can be connected, with his or her being in the world. I want to dwell on this for a moment.

I would like to start with a personal anecdote. I was once a course leader for a part-time Master's course, the students attending an evening class once a week. Some would travel a very long way, even over 150 miles, and kept going all through the winter months. Occasionally, I asked them why they did this. On more than one occasion, I received the spontaneous answer: 'It's therapeutic.' How might we understand this statement? My sense is that that their course experience was located in the domains of uncertainty – both ontological and epistemological – that we have been distinguishing.

The students were all busy and experienced professional people in the public sector, doubtless with pressing demands in their working lives, many of which they might have caused them unease. Most would have also had many other responsibilities in their lives, having both children and other family responsibilities. Some even faced their own serious health challenges. For such people, the weekly travel to the university allowed them to enter a space outside their pressing challenges. But this very space offered them yet more challenges, so why might the students have termed it therapeutic?

I conjecture that the experience was termed 'therapeutic' by participants because the pedagogical space was one of conviviality, with much conversation and in which they found themselves among others to whom they could relate to some degree. In that sense, the pedagogy, with its relatively relaxed 'frame' (B. Bernstein, 1996) engaged with any 'ontological uncertainty' on the part of the students. They were finding, and being affirmed in, a new identity – that of a Master's student on a particular university course. But the course opened the students to names of great scholars and researchers whose names they had never encountered; it enabled them to enter a space of new concepts and ideas, in the company of the passions of their tutors. It was a stretching experience and so unsettling; but the participants came to live with that unsettling. And so the experience engaged their 'epistemological uncertainty'.

But, as I have been suggesting, while they are separate, these two forms of uncertainty – ontological and epistemological – are intertwined. And to the extent that we can deploy the idea of therapy in this context, the therapeutic qualities of a university education are also intertwined. 'Therapy' is another thick concept (Williams, 2008): it is both fact and value together. 'Therapy' refers to the fact of a change in a person's mental state and it also connotes an improvement in that person's mental state. We can surmise that the course participants came to have a new sense of themselves as they engaged with their experiences: the challenges of that engagement were met in a satisfactory way and so the participants were able to move forward, into a new place. Engaging satisfactorily with her epistemological uncertainty was edifying in itself to the student but that self-development flowed out into the student's wider being such that the student came to have a surer hold on life itself. The epistemological resolution leads to the ontological resolution; but, equally, forming appropriate dispositions and qualities enables a student to undertake the challenge of wrestling with his or her epistemological challenges.

To suggest, as do the critics of higher education having a therapeutic character, that 'therapy' is associated with 'infantilising' students may have some empirical warrant. But philosophically, it inverts the truth. For the philosophical consideration has turned out to be that, here, 'therapy' is connected with maturity, and with increasing maturity at that. To speak of 'the therapeutic university' is to draw attention to the potential of the university as a space in which severe challenges can be presented and met, such that individuals' being may move into an improved place. Not just younger students, but also individuals who are already mature and successful professionals may be assisted in their own development.

What is new here? If such developmental processes are characteristic of the idea of the university, then they have been long with us. What is new is that there is an ever-heightening interest in the pedagogic functioning of universities. Considerable thought is being given across universities all over the world to students' learning and to finding ways of helping that learning to be more effective. This movement – reflected, for example, in the emergence of a world-wide university community interested in the 'scholarship of teaching and learning' – will assuredly grow. The therapeutic university, on our analysis so far, therefore, has the makings of a *feasible utopia*. This pedagogical releasing of students into themselves is already happening and has been happening; but it could become a common feature of university education. It is *feasible*, therefore. But the process is also *utopian* since the marketisation of universities, for the main part, pulls in the opposite direction.[11] The moment when significant improvements are taking place in curricula and pedagogies worldwide, the coming of students as customers threatens to keep such a utopia out of reach on the horizon.

Social therapy

It has perhaps become apparent through this discussion that to bring the concept of 'therapy' in touch with that of the 'university' is to stretch understandings of the therapeutic. Characteristically, 'therapy' has its point in contexts where an individual's mental or physical state is impaired in some way. It is true that in some cultures, members of affluent social classes will see their therapists on a regular basis, irrespective of there being some manifest problem. Therapy is here a continuing process, even amidst a state of wellbeing, but then this meaning of 'therapy' is parasitic on the sense of therapy as 'the treatment of disorders or disease' (*Collins English Dictionary*).

Across the world, with the coming of mass higher education, non-completion (or 'attrition') rates are rising and so we might hypothesise that the level of anxiety among students is rising. The importation of the idea of therapy into the domain of the university might, therefore, herald a concern over this anxiety experienced by some students. But the idea of 'the therapeutic university' has wider applicability, having its point in referring to continuing educational processes and processes that apply – or might apply – to *all* students.

This being so, with the idea of 'therapy' having been stretched in this way, we may try to stretch it yet further. Society itself may be in need of therapy. There are two societal challenges – indeed, world challenges – pertinent to our discussion. There is, first, the sense that matters are out of control; that human destiny is no longer within the power of individuals to shape. This is the world intimated by such idea as those of 'the risk society' (Beck, 1992) and a 'runaway world' (Leach, 1968; Giddens, 2002). Second, that there is a gulf between wants and the capacity of the world to meet those wants. Both situations point to a sense of abiding incompleteness for humanity. And humanity has to deal with this incompleteness. It is in context of this situation that the phrase 'retail therapy' is nicely ironic. The purchases may supply an immediate comfort in dealing with the challenges of the world but precisely because the situation of incompleteness is now a permanent feature of humanity's situation on this earth, the 'therapy' quickly wears off. Its source is still untouched. In turn, the demand comes again for more such 'therapy'. And so the cycle continues without resolution.

We may note that the context here is, to a large extent that in which Philip Rieff set out his case as to *The Triumph of the Therapeutic* back in the mid-1960s ([1966] 1987). In a post-Freudian era, religion loses its power as a community-forming mechanism and there seems to be little available for collective symbols of meaning. Into this void step the counsellors and psycho-therapists and, more recently, we may note, a heightening of concerns with 'wellbeing'[12] and a growing interest in 'the art of living' (Vernon, 2008). Theologians, so Reiff argued, themselves take on a therapeutic function.

The link with our theme of the 'therapeutic university' is this. We have seen how the idea of 'the therapeutic university' has both pernicious and positive senses. It can refer to processes in which students are treated as young children, unable to take responsibility for themselves, and so not presented with challenging experiences. This is a diminished sense of 'therapy' since the idea of the therapeutic implies, as with we have seen, a sense of moving purposively forward, whereas this connotation permits and encourages students to stay where they are. However, therapy *can* point to situations in which students are deliberately challenged and enabled to live with those challenges.

If we put these two sets of considerations together, new possibilities may be glimpsed for the university. The liquid university (Chapter 9) is global, stretching out into communities and organisations across the world. It can engage in these interactions for-itself, extracting out of them what it can to advance its own causes (cf. Chapter 3 on 'the entrepreneurial university') or it can do so in a more generous spirit. Its formidable resources can be used, in part, to help the world to live with its uncertainty. Not in the sense of giving the world simply anxiety-easing stories or ideologies, but in widening understandings and helping the world to live with the greater uncertainties that result from its new understandings.

It is possible to glimpse here a kind of *social therapy*, drawing on the virtuous sense of 'therapy'. The university can put to good effect its new position within the world to enable the world to be better informed about itself. Being 'better informed' is, here, a shorthand for the stories – that the world has available with which to comprehend itself – to multiply; and for the world to understand that there is dispute, that the stories conflict. These are, in effect, societal and even global, learning processes. The university is one (but a highly significant) institution that can assist the world in such universal learning processes. This would constitute the university taking on a role in societal pedagogy.

The 'therapeutic university' would quietly undertake this role in all its interactions with the wider world, and all the possibilities that are presented to it. Its overt interactions with organisations – through its research, developmental and consultancy activities – present such opportunities. So too the internet opens new opportunities and responsibilities. All universities in receipt of public funds could be obliged to make their offerings freely available on the internet (thereby having a positive 'impact' in the public sphere). The role, too, of its academics as 'public intellectuals' could also be widened to look to those academics to engage in conversations and debates via the internet, so opening it – and pedagogising it – as a public educational space.

Virtuousness and perniciousness

The idea of 'the therapeutic university' *is* problematic. It can be understood as giving to students that which they desire. In the marketisation of universities, students are cast – and come to cast themselves as – customers, extracting the object of their desires (a diploma; an acceptable work position) from the university which they are paying. In this situation, universities come to pacify students, meeting their wants. In the process, students are unwittingly affirmed by universities in the identities that the students are constructing for themselves; not only as consumers but in their particular identities within their social origins. Educationally, students fall short of the development that they could otherwise make. They are thereby infantilised.

This is an impoverished interpretation of 'the therapeutic university'. It points up the pernicious dimension of extending the metaphor of 'therapy' into universities. But it is not the only reading of the 'therapeutic university'; a more positive reading is possible. The idea can be seen as standing for the enlightenment that comes through understanding. Far from infantilising students, higher education calls them into a new and demanding place in which they give of themselves even amid contesting ideas and frameworks. It is a 'therapeutic' experience insofar as the university enables students to live with the ensuing uncertainty. If the pernicious interpretation of the therapeutic university 'cools out' students, this more virtuous interpretation warms them up, giving them energies to live with and face new uncertainties.

Such a more positive interpretation of the 'therapeutic university' opens the way for a new imagining of the university. The therapeutic university can play its part in society's learning processes. A fundamental challenge in the world is that of society – the world indeed – understanding itself and living with the uncertainty that that understanding brings. The way in which the world is grappling with the challenges of climate change is but one example. For that process is partly a matter of the way in which the world engages with differences in the academic community. Faced with a realisation that informed opinion within the academy does not exhibit a consensus, there are temptations in the public sphere both to shrink from the academy *and* to fly to dogmatism, so that what could be an informed debate becomes a site of competing ideologies.

At the time of writing, news is breaking both of academic journals in the sciences allegedly restricting opportunities for publication in a particular field (stem cell research) only to particular research groups, and of a global organisation allegedly exaggerating evidence in relation to climate change. If allegations of this kind are true, the development of the public sphere is being restricted, public opinion is made less aware of dispute within the academy. This is tantamount to a pernicious social therapy, the public being infantilised with simple stories. A more virtuous version of social therapy is also dimly visible, of the academic community exposing its inner knowledge conflicts to the public domain and so helping the public sphere to develop its understanding even at the cost of heightening public uncertainty.

Conclusion

'The therapeutic university' turns out to be a nice example of a *feasible utopia*. The idea has its utopian aspects, here of greater self-understanding and purposiveness, and at both the individual and the societal (and even the global) levels. It *is* feasible. It is already happening, albeit intermittently, and not as a result of a systemic determination on the part of the university community. But it is unlikely fully to transpire. The countervailing forces – of self-interested entrepreneurialism and competitiveness in the positioning of universities into the global economy – are such that this more virtuous reading of 'the therapeutic university' is unlikely to be realised.

Herein lie the possibilities of a virtuous situation that could be realised on the part of the university but where the dominant forces are so large as to diminish the likelihood of that happy state of affairs. The 'therapeutic university' is not merely liable to fall short of its possibilities but is liable to fall *back*. This university *can* ratchet back on itself. Not only its students but the university itself can regress. This university can lessen itself in its educational capability. There is no steady state here. Either the university is going forward, moving – doubtlessly hesitantly – in realising its virtuous potential as a 'therapeutic' institution or it is falling back, undermining itself, becoming not merely less than it might be but even less than it may. 'The therapeutic university' has its virtuous *and* its pernicious interpretations, a situation that – as we noted – is a feature of feasible utopias.

The idea of the 'feasible utopia' places three injunctions on the university. First, it asks the university to look forward to see, given its own character and its situation, what positive possibilities lie before it. It encourages it to see itself not only in terms of its 'being-possible' (Heidegger, [1927] 1998) but of its virtuous potential, its becoming more fully itself. The idea looks to the largest possibilities feasibly before the university. But it is a realistic idea. And here lies the second injunction, for in the idea of utopia, the university is reminded that there are large forces – both beyond the university and within it – that threaten to undermine the virtuous potentials that lie within it. The idea of utopia, therefore, is an injunction on the university to identify those forces – again, both beyond and within – that stand as barriers to its own becoming; to its becoming as fully as authentic as it can be. But those two injunctions point to yet a third injunction. If there are virtuous potentials within it and if those potentials are being thwarted, then the university has the responsibility of doing what it can to realise those potentials.

Here, then, we are pointed once more in the direction of the dual themes of 'authenticity' and 'responsibility' and it is to them we should now turn.

11 The authentic university

Introduction

The authentic university offers the prospect of another feasible utopia. But, as with all such ideas of the university, it has its own characteristics and it poses challenges of its own. It is not enough to ask: 'What is it to be an authentic university?', as if there was some Platonic form of authenticity waiting to be discerned. Rather, the authentic university has to be created afresh continually, amid the circumstances of the age. Authenticity is realised through an engagement in and with a particular setting. It is realised through its overcoming difficulties that contemporary circumstances present, whatever they may be. Authenticity is always authenticity in a particular context.

Authenticity has been a theme throughout this inquiry. In working out the challenges to and the possibilities for the authentic university, we have as resources, therefore, the ideas explored in the previous chapters. The key chapter is that of Chapter 8, in which were sketched some preliminary ideas as to the authentic university. I suggested there that, despite any apparent tension between the two concepts of authenticity and responsibility, it might just be possible for a university to be both authentic and responsible; to gain a position of responsible authenticity. My main proposal in developing that proposition lay in the ideas of inquiry and learning being interpreted very broadly and lived out in a global context as a means of enhancing global understanding.

But in taking that suggestion further, we can also bear in mind the discussions of the other central chapters – on space and time, on culture and anarchy, and on being and becoming. Considerations identified in the last two chapters, in advancing 'the liquid university' and 'the therapeutic university' as feasible utopias, are also pertinent here.

Precariousness

In Chapter 8, it was observed that one insight into authenticity lay in the idea of being 'disencumbered'.[1] But we also noted that the idea was somewhat ill-fitted to the context of the university. Today's university is seriously encumbered. The state, the market, quality regimes, professional bodies, and even the parents of students exert their own claims on the university. We went on, however, to note that even amid the pulls and pushes of regulation, evaluation, uncertain income flows and expectations, not only does it remain the case that the university – by and large – still retains pools of autonomy but that those autonomies may even be expanding. The university has some space in which to eke out its authenticity but any such authenticity is bound to be precarious.

There are four regions, consisting of different kinds of conditions, of the precariousness of its authenticity. First, there are the *contingent-and-general* conditions of this precariousness. Being part of a global learning economy, universities are characteristically subject to a similar set of callings and subjugations. These framings do not constitute a Weberian 'iron cage'; the bars are flexible to some extent. But their cross-national presence makes it possible for 'universities' across the globe to recognise each other as being members of the one collective.

Second, each university has its own positioning. Depending on its markets, income flows, reputation, mix of teaching and research and its epistemologies, so each university will be characterised by its own set of influences and possibilities. Here lie the *contingent-and-particular* conditions of the precariousness of its authenticity.

Third, there are specific *value* conditions of the precariousness of its authenticity. The idea of authenticity only has substance against the horizon of a 'value background' of some kind (Taylor, 1969). Each university has the space and so the responsibility to work out its own value position (which will evolve over time). Each university stands against the framing of its *particular value position*. This is a place of precariousness in that any value framework will be precarious in any institution worthy of the name of 'university' since it is part of what it means to be a university that value frameworks are subject to critique. And that value position has to be worked out and sustained amid the swirls of its particular conditions and the general conditions increasingly affecting universities worldwide.

Lastly, there are – at least in principle – *general value conditions* of being a university and these in turn also lend a precariousness to the university's authenticity. Can any university fully live up to the general value conditions that attach to being a member of the global family of universities? Is it not a precarious calling to be a university?

If a university is to win its authenticity, it has to be won in the context of these four regions. A university, accordingly, will be and become authentic through having a sense as to its own practical possibilities and those attending the world-wide community of universities; *and* by getting as clear as possible about the ethical principles of being a university in the twenty-first century, and about the particular values for which it wishes to be known.

A universal calling

This matter – as to the contexts in which a university's authenticity might be won – may seem pedantic, but it is supremely important. It concerns precisely the 'being-possible' of the university. What hopes might we plausibly entertain on the university's behalf? Is authenticity simply a local matter for each university to work out for itself or might there be a sense in which we can talk of a universal authenticity? Is it just a matter of practical possibilities or might there also be universal principles that come into view?

The theme of universality has been a theme that has accompanied us on our journey from the opening pages of this book. The metaphysical university was doubly universal. Practically, it was both open to scholars from wherever they came and it conducted itself through a 'universal' language, that of Latin.[2] But it was universal in an even larger, even philosophical, sense. For its promise was that it gave access to a universal realm of being – variously to God, Spirit, or Truth – which was in principle available to all and in which all could share. Its scholarly enquiries opened a path to universality in this double sense. 'Town and gown' battles (often bloody affairs) marked this kind of university. They symbolised the gulf between the here-and-now-ness of the local citizenry and the universality – in all its modes – of the university. The very term *university* (with corresponding forms in many European languages[3]) came to speak to the theme of universality. Universities were places that connected with universal themes.

Gradually, this connection with universality has eked away. Certainly, the research university had connections with universality: its truths, won through disciplined and systematic inquiry, yielded claims to universal truth; they were not truths of this or that university or this or that town. But the emergence of disciplines began to place boundaries around even those truth claims – they were claims of this or that discipline – and the privileging of science tilted the evaluative landscape. A truth claim had greater or lesser status according to whether it was or was not part of 'science'. With the coming of the entrepreneurial university, this dwindling of the idea of universality has grown apace. Universities are encouraged to be actively engaged with organisations that relate to their disciplines; and preferably private sector businesses at that. Universities are further encouraged to be active in their regions, and so enhance the regional economy. Parochialism is now part of what it means to be a university.

It will be protested that, for many universities, at least, the local and the global can exist alongside each other. Perhaps there might be tensions between these two aspects of their missions but they can readily be found together. The local need not edge out the global. But the objection misses the point. The idea of the universal – universality – is not to be caught purely by reference to the global. For that, in an entrepreneurial age, can be reduced to a series of disconnected local activities even if global in their scope – in this country, or with that group of international students and in furthering particular interests (of an institution's own social and economic capital; of the global economy even). The concepts of the global and the universal are not synonymous.

Slavoj Žižek is helpful on this matter. He contrasts Kant and Rorty. For Rorty (according to Žižek):

[T]he private is the space of irony, while the public is the space of solidarity. For Kant, however, . . . 'private' designates not one's individual as opposed to communal ties, but the very communal-institutional order of one's particular identification; while 'public' refers to the transnational universality of the exercise of one's Reason.

(Žižek, 2009a: 104–105)

Emphasising the point, Žižek contends that here, in pointing to the limitation of communal ties, Kant 'invokes a dimension of emancipatory universality outside the confines of one's social identity, of one's position within the order of (social) being' (ibid.: 105). This is helpful for our understanding of the university. The university is losing its link to the theme of universality, being enveloped by its own projects and the injunction that it should play its part in economic growth, even if those projects are worldwide and even if the economic growth connects with that of the global economy.

In these last two chapters, however, I have begun to suggest that new spaces may be opening for the university. A new universality may be becoming available to it. In examining the possibilities for 'the liquid university' (Chapter 9), we noted how it is now moving through time and space with amazing rapidity. As such, it can be free of an adherence to any particular cause or concern. We pressed that line of thought a little further in our examination of 'the therapeutic university' in opening up the possibility of a form of 'social therapy' in which the university might extend its interests in learning and inquiry to the world and so *help the self-understanding of the world*. This would not be merely a worldwide context against which the university might form its self-image but it would also be a universal context.[4]

Coming to the theme of authenticity, the consideration opens that the university can be fully authentic when it understands its natural interests in learning and inquiry in universal terms. In examining the therapeutic university, we distinguished between pernicious and virtuous senses of the idea. In its pernicious sense, students will have their own self-understandings affirmed; they will be allowed to stay where they are, untroubled. In the virtuous sense, students are challenged and so move themselves on, into a space of greater understanding and self-understanding. The university is a *universal* space of inquiry and learning as such.

Žižek observes that: 'When Paul says that, from a Christian standpoint, "there are no men or women, no Jews or Greeks", he thereby claims that ethnic roots, national identities, etc are not a category of truth' (ibid.: 104).

Students will have their own identities (plural), at once of ethnicity, nationality, gender, discipline, professional field, and university itself (a new identity may be discovered in being captain of a sports team). The university can and should be inclusive of all of these positions. But it gains its authenticity in transcending them, in enabling students to comprehend themselves as part of humanity and as part of a universal inquiry. The rational life has a transcending unity. This, after all, is one of the justifications of universities being international communities for, as communities of reason and conviviality, they transcend particular differences.

Living in the real world

Authenticity is 'critical realism' in action. In its fullest expression, it recognises that there is a world beyond itself, and brings to bear on the world the largest hopes of the university's fulfilment. Just as for critical realism, then, so for the authentic university, the world is layered. The authentic university strives to comprehend its place in that layered world. It understands that the phenomena with which it is presented

– new government policies, sudden changes in funding allocations, innovations in information technologies, and so on – are 'actual' phenomena. It understands further that these phenomena are often but epi-phenomena, reflective of an underlying set of 'real' forces at play.[5] These real forces are both material, reflecting, for example, differences of power (between the state and universities, and among the universities themselves, and across the disciplines) and they are ideological, with narratives – of 'world-classness', of 'excellence', of 'skills' – also representative of particular sets of interests. It is in relation to these levels of the 'real' and the 'actual' that the authentic university brings its own self-images to bear. The authentic university knows that its authenticity is won only in the context of the forces and expectations that press on it. The authentic university, therefore, has no choice but to live in the real world.

We can now begin to see the complexity of what it is to be an authentic university. Its authenticity is realised through:

1   a grasp of the *levels* of the world that presses daily upon it – the real, the actual and the ideological;
2   a sense of the complex *interplay* of the phenomena in the world that are affecting it, at once local and global;
3   a crystallisation of its own *hopes* for itself, its self-image, which again will be particular to the individual university *and* will have a sense of its participating in evolving and universal processes of human inquiry;
4   an *ethical* understanding of itself, which again will reflect its own value position and will reflect its understanding of itself as participating in universal processes of inquiry, reasoning and communication.
5   *time* as such. It is not only that authenticity is realised through time, and that the university's becoming more fully authentic can only take place through time but it is also that, as we have seen (Chapter 6), the university lives amid multiple timeframes (fast and slow, short-term and long-term).

Living in the real world, therefore, compounds the precariousness of the university's authenticity. Its precariousness is empirical: it lives in an unpredictable environment. And its precariousness is ethical. Any set of values that it forms for itself has continually to be revisited.

These two aspects of its precariousness – the empirical (with its different levels) and the ethical – are intertwined. If authenticity is realised in the real world, then changes in the real world have in part to be reflected in changes in the way a university understands the values through which it wants to develop. This is not to cast the university into a post-modern mode of being; or, at least, it need not do so. But it is to set the university the arduous task of reinterpreting its self-image and its hopes for itself in the circumstances of the age, as the university reads those circumstances. And, to repeat, those circumstances are at once assessments of its immediate context and of the university's sense of its future possibilities *in* that context. The authentic university lives in the past, the present and the future all at once, judgements that are all influenced by its discernments of its situation. Living in the real world is far from easy for the authentic university.

Conditions of authenticity

It follows from these observations that authenticity is a project. The authentic university is so in virtue of its continual strivings for authenticity. Doubtless, it will often fall short, but it persists in its endeavours.

Let us enumerate some of the elements of this project, of the university being and becoming authentic, as we have identified them so far:

1   Just as the concept of authenticity looks both inwards and outwards, so too the authentic university gains resources not only from an understanding of itself – its traditions and its main values – but also in taking account of the world in which it finds itself. 'Authenticity is not the enemy of demands that emanate from beyond the self; it supposes such demands' (Taylor, 1991: 41).

2   Authenticity is not frozen in time. The authentic university strives continuously for its authenticity. In so doing, it continuously revisits itself, in the light of the theme of authenticity, to monitor the degree and the extent of its authenticity. And the authentic university resets its aspirations for authenticity, in the light too of the changing circumstances attendant on it.

3   Authenticity is a process of continuing becoming. The authentic university is always anticipating its own authenticity and it is always falling short of the possibilities for its authenticity. The horizon of authenticity recedes before it, which only impels its efforts towards its authenticity.

4   Being a complex institution, full of conflicting debates and even disputes, authenticity requires neither consensus nor harmony. The authentic university is built on reason, but it is a site for dispute over the conditions of reasonableness.

5   As a form of feasible utopia, the authentic university reaches for the highest realisation of its potential authenticity. The authentic university is not withdrawn from the world but is immersed in the world. The issue concerns the grounds of that immersion. Does it swim to some extent under its own direction *and* in a worthwhile direction?

6   No university can be authentic without living out the themes of learning and inquiry to the fullest extent and so helping the growth of world understanding. What this means will be particular for each university, depending on the possibilities available to it. What can be said is that this injunction can – and, therefore, *should* – be interpreted on a global scale, for modern communications technologies open just such a set of possibilities.

7   Implicated in living out the themes of learning and inquiry is not only teaching but also is involved all the academic activities of the university. Through its research, consultancy and developmental possibilities, the university is extraordinarily well placed to take up the themes of learning and inquiry in promoting understanding, reflection and inquiry across society.[6]

These seven elements, in effect, are conditions of being an authentic university. Here, in these seven conditions, we see how authenticity and responsibility (Chapter 8) can be found together; and so how a university can gain a position for itself of *responsible authenticity*. There should be no squeamishness about invoking the idea of responsibility here for 'authenticity opens an age of responsibilization' (Taylor, 1991: 77). Far from it being the case that authenticity and responsibility pull in different directions – inner and outer directed respectively – now, we see that those callings (of authenticity and responsibility) flow together. In striving for its authenticity, the university heeds its own interests in learning and inquiry (its inner responsibilities) while putting them to work in all its activities locally and across the world (so heeding its wider responsibilities). This project of authenticity is not easily brought off; far from it. The university is prey to many opportunities that would divert it from the path of its authenticity.

Bad faith

Most ideas of any substance have both virtuous and pernicious readings. So it is with the idea of authenticity. As a feasible utopia, the authentic university will strive to live out the virtuous senses of authenticity, with its connection to an outer world, to an ethical positioning, and so forth. But inducements lie in wait for the university, which amount to pernicious readings of authenticity. Dystopias are never far away.

Supreme among such pernicious readings of authenticity are those that exemplify bad faith. For Sartre, bad faith is exhibited in the lie to oneself; when one dupes oneself (Sartre, [1943] 2003: 72): 'in bad faith, it is from myself that I am hiding the truth'. I am both the deceiver and the deceived. This condition, we may consider, can be found in institutions – such as universities – just as much as it can be found in individuals.

We can say of a university that it exhibits bad faith when it is characterised by just such a dominant self-deceiving mode of being. For instance, a university exhibits bad faith when it persuades itself that it can do none other than orient itself towards income generation as its dominant mode of being. Or it exhibits bad faith when it proclaims that its research and teaching are complementary and are of equal status when, on even a cursory inspection of its resource allocation and staff promotion procedures, this is far from the existing state of affairs. Or it exhibits bad faith when it considers that all of its activities have to have their place amid tight procedures, routines and risk analyses. Or it exhibits bad faith when the term 'academic community' is blithely used to capture a university's self-image, even though the physicists will have nothing to do with the sociologists, and there is a constant state of tension between the academics and the managers. These are literally examples of 'bad faith': the faith that the university has in itself – as a 'community', as a space in which academic work can flourish, as an open and self-critical environment – is corrupted and, in its self-deception, is corrupted by the university itself.

What might we understand then by the idea of self-deception? Is it that the university misunderstands the truth about itself *or* that it understands the truth about itself but blocks out that truth? For Sartre, there is here a complex of both knowing and not-knowing; of both good faith and bad faith. If I am hiding the truth from myself, I have to be conscious of that truth. 'I must know in my capacity as deceiver the truth which is hidden from me in my capacity as the one deceived' ([1943] 2003: 72).

A university will know, in its collective bones, that research and teaching do not enjoy the same status, even though, at the same time, it believes that they do. A university will know that it is still deserving of the appellation 'university' even if a majority of its academics are not actively engaged in income-generating activities, and even though it proclaims and acts to the contrary. Bad faith is, therefore, as Sartre notes 'very precarious', hovering 'between good faith and cynicism' (ibid.: 73). The university is liable to break out in a recognition that, for example, teaching and research are far from enjoying a similar status and seek to do something to remedy the situation (by introducing new routes to full professorships that provide for those who are passionate about and innovatory in their teaching). But the same university may equally be liable to reassert its claim about the equivalence of research and teaching, even while it widens further the opportunities for research-intensive academics to 'buy themselves out' of their teaching commitments.

In these and other examples of bad faith, the university splits itself asunder. The university not only falls short of what it might be, but runs the risk of diminishing its capacities for self-understanding. It has been long remarked that universities would study everything else in the universe before they study themselves. Their tendency towards bad faith is the beginning of an explanation of this phenomenon. As self-deception, bad faith is a prime form of the reluctance towards critical self-evaluation. This reluctance to critical self-evaluation – or 'blankness' as F. R. Leavis put it (1969: 1, 58) – leads in turn to a much larger problem, however. It is that given these tendencies towards bad faith and a reluctance to engage in critical self-evaluation, the university is liable to miss the possibilities that lie just in front of it. For in its bad faith, the university will not move on. It rests uneasily content with the nostrums of self-deception with which it cloaks itself (that our teaching is 'excellent'). And it fails to see into, to imagine, the possibilities that lie readily to hand.

The jargon of authenticity

The Jargon of Authenticity is the title of a ([1973] 2003) small book by Theodor Adorno. One of the founders of the Frankfurt School of Critical Theory, Adorno was – in that book – critical not merely of the language of authenticity but of the tendencies and processes that went under the name of 'authenticity'. Some today might want to speak critically of the *discourse* of authenticity. Authenticity is not harmless but is dangerous: 'Whoever is versed in the jargon [of authenticity] does not have to say what he thinks, does not even have to think it properly' (ibid.: 6). Worse, because it is so sure of itself, it can be used to stifle free speech. Since it is sure of its own authenticity, it can become 'a metaphysical-moral verdict of annihilation against the man who can speak out' (ibid.: 38) A collective 'authenticity' (for example, that universities should be 'entrepreneurial') may be felt to be – by a maverick rector or vice-chancellor – a horror and, ultimately, a prison. Should we, then, abandon talk of 'the authentic university'? Will its use not always presuppose just what (always) should be on the agenda for debate? That would be a premature judgement.

There is a serious matter here. Ultimately, not just what is to count as 'the authentic university' (important though that question is) but also 'who is to decide what is to count as "the authentic university"?'. In other words, behind a discourse – or 'jargon' – of authenticity lies a *politics* of authenticity. Universities do not move, do not have their being, in a neutral space. It is a space in which its current flows are influenced by the large forces – of the state, of the market, of the corporate sector. So who is to determine what counts as 'authenticity'? Even if there was to be a contemporary discourse of 'the authentic university', it would be a skewed discourse, tilted under the weight of the large forces. Is a neutral space available, undisturbed by partial interests, wherein the terms and conditions of the authentic university can be determined?

To this problematic has to be added a further issue. It may be objected that talk of 'the authentic university' is in itself problematic. It seems to presume, even if we can give substance to the idea of 'authenticity', that a large institution such as the university can be characterised by authenticity. The construction 'the authentic university' raises to the institutional level an attribute that makes sense only in relation to individuals. We can say of x that he is – or is not – authentic, but can we say that of a *university*? Does the construction 'the authentic university' not 'reify' the university? It implies that the university is a single and unified entity such to which we can attribute qualities of persons. The construction – 'the authentic university' – is a category mistake.

I want to deal with these two objections together. We can talk of 'the authentic university' (and, for that matter, 'the liquid university' or the 'therapeutic university') in part because of the politics of the university. These phrases as feasible utopias take their bearings both from the pernicious character of the situations in which universities find themselves and their utopian – but real – possibilities. Universities *are* complex organisations, internally and externally. Part of this complexity is to be understood by the unequal forces that act upon them, of money, positioning and influence. The *habitus* of the university is tilted in certain directions. It is in virtue of this situation that we can inquire into the extent to which a university is authentic – or inauthentic. To the extent that a university is diverted from its true path, to that extent it is inauthentic. To the extent that it has possibilities before it for going along that path even further than it has in its past, to that extent, its authenticity lies before it.

I have suggested that a university is a 'university' through its connections with learning and inquiry. It is to the extent that it is fulfilling its possibilities in promoting learning and inquiry that we can speak of the authentic university. It is when we can see a university being tempted to stray from this path – in pursuing contracts and income for their own sake, in positioning itself for influence and advancement, in becoming a corporate organisation – that the spectre of inauthenticity beckons. The university is a complex of traditions and tendencies but there may be dominant emerging tendencies – susceptible to an assessment of its authenticity. At the same time, this complex is increasingly a managed complex. It is partly in virtue of its now being a managed organisation that we can contemplate the university being steered in the light of utopian ideals. What is before us is the possibility for the university to develop its own 'organised praxis' – to draw on a Sartrean expression (Sartre, [1960] 2004b: 448).

'Authenticity' *can* degenerate into a 'jargon', or an ideological discourse. It can be empty; it can be saturated with special pleading. In turn, 'the authentic university' can stand for the fulfilment of partial interests. But it could just help the university to reflect on its virtuous possibilities and to fulfil them to the fullest extent. The complexity that constitutes the university tends to close spaces but also to open spaces. The university has now possibilities before it to become authentic in a way denied it in the past. Now, it can reach out to the world, it can help the world better to understand itself, it can engage with peoples and communities across the globe, and it can open itself to the realm of the infinite, in becoming a space for universally-oriented learning and inquiry. 'The authentic university' need not be a form of jargon but can act as a spur to collective purposive reflection and action.

Conclusion

The university could be *becoming* authentic. Even if it wished, it could never *be* authentic. The forces pitched against its being authentic are persistent and considerable: a permanent state of assured authenticity is not within the university's reach. Its authenticity would always, will always, be a matter of continuing struggle. The struggle will be with external forces but also internally. For what it is to be authentic will always be a matter of dispute, even within the academy.

The authentic university is another feasible utopia. It can be glimpsed. Even allowing for dispute within and beyond the academy, it will minimally consist of each university working out what its maximum possibilities are for advancing learning and inquiry against a horizon of universality. This means striving all it can to advance students' will to learn and to widen the learning spaces available to them (within their courses; in the wider university; and off campus).[7] It means academics being involved in projects that enable them to promote learning and understanding in civic society. It means that opportunities are seized to engage with the wider world, even in other countries. It means academics communicating with each other across disciplinary boundaries to see how their collective endeavours can advance public interests. And it means the university making itself intelligible to the world in every possible way.

The glimpsing of authenticity and bringing it off are entirely different matters. For the components and the general conditions of authenticity have then to be translated into institutional projects. Authenticity, indeed, is itself a project, always in the making, as the university steers between its own self-interest (which it all too easily parades – in bad faith – *as* its authenticity) and external inducements. The authentic university, then, is utopian: the obstacles in its realisation, including the university's own bad faith, are so considerable that it is unlikely to come about.

Within the authentic university as a utopia lurks, then, the dystopia of *in*authenticity, when the university deludes itself that its self-interests constitute its authenticity. But authenticity is, nevertheless, a *feasible* utopia for the university. We see it acted out every day both in tiny occurrences (as academics act out the (underpaid) role of examiner in other universities), and in large activities (as a 'research' university engages enthusiastically in a community project or with another university in a developing country) or puts on a full programme of well-publicised public lectures (free of charge). The authentic university *is* within our reach.

12 The ecological university

The true utopia is the belief that the existing global system can reproduce itself indefinitely; the only way to be truly realistic is to think what, within the coordinates of this system, cannot but appear impossible.

(Slavoj Žižek, 'In 1968, Structures Walked the Street – Will They Do it Again?',
2009b: 26)

Introduction

The ecological university is a university whose time has come. This timing is a complex of circumstances. The time is such that the ecological university can be glimpsed, both as an idea and in its institutional form. The time is such also that the world needs its universities to be ecological. And the time is such that the world is already encouraging forward, albeit hesitantly, its universities in an ecological spirit.

But how might 'the ecological university' be understood as a feasible utopia? And how might the idea of the ecological university relate to the ideas of the liquid university, the therapeutic university and the authentic university? That 'the ecological university' forms the final chapter to this book implies that it offers a transcendent summation of the previous three utopian visions of the university, but how might that be? All of these matters are in front of us.

The idea of the ecological

On more than one occasion in this inquiry, Bernard Williams's (2008) notion of 'thick concepts' has been helpful. The 'ecological' has become another such thick concept, working in different planes of meaning. The idea of the ecological points us to systems, and to their inter-connectedness. It draws attention to the environment and the dynamic character of the entities in the environment and their relationships. The idea of the ecological has, therefore, several *factual* elements to it. But the idea of the ecological has within it connotations of wellbeing; that there are states of wellbeing in the interconnectedness of the environment. And it also connotes ideas of a care towards the environment. The ecological spirit – as we might put it – is oriented towards bringing about and 'sustaining' not merely the environment as such but a state (or states) of wellbeing in the environment. The idea of the ecological contains, therefore, *ethical* dimensions as well.

This dual account of the ecological – at once factual and ethical – by no means exhausts its complexity. The account we have just given indicates that the ecological works at multiple *levels*. For Félix Guattari, there are three ecological levels, or 'registers': 'the environment, social relations and human subjectivity' (Guattari, 2005: 28). Within each of these registers, questions arise as to the articulation of the internal elements and so, too, questions arise about the articulation of the registers themselves. We can inquire into the functioning and, indeed, the wellbeing of each system at each level; and we can inquire into the functioning and wellbeing of their interconnections, across the levels.

The 'ecological' becomes a metaphor that can be stretched into yet further domains. And so, for instance, we encounter talk of 'knowledge ecologies'. Here, we can inquire into the constituents of knowledge and their inter-relationships, and their relationships with other spheres, including the natural and the social worlds. How are forms of knowledge clustered? How do they connect with the world? And do those connections sustain relationships of reciprocity or relationships of domination and control? There may be natural and, by extension, unnatural relationships here. Knowledge is connected to the environment through understanding, but supposing that that understanding is partial or malign or self-interested? We may want to say that a knowledge ecology is impaired in some way or that it could be improved. In other words, the idea of a knowledge ecology has its place too against an ethical horizon. (We shall return to the matter of a knowledge ecology.) The idea of 'deep ecology' engages with these sentiments, since it is essentially:

> [T]he idea that the human perspective must not be thought as superior to others, but rather as just one of many. We do not 'look down' on empirical reality from an external vantage point. Rather, we are essentially a part of this reality.
>
> (Unwin, 2007: 154–155)

The idea of the ecological takes on increasing complexity and possibility, therefore. With its ethical and global resonances, it begins to be a metaphor for the fullest expression of possibilities for this earth and for the place of humanity on it and in it.

The idea of the ecological university

The ecological university is not merely a networked university but takes its networks seriously. It has – to draw on Heideggerian terminology – a care or concern towards them. It understands that it is interconnected with its wider environment in manifold ways and seeks to develop those interconnections.

But the ecological university goes further. For it comprehends itself as having a responsibility towards those interconnections. Through its interest in promoting understanding through learning and inquiry, it seeks to contribute what it can so as to advance the wellbeing of each aspect of the world upon which it might have an effect.[1] This university adopts an 'ecosophical perspective' (Guattari, 2005: 34), a perspective that works at all of the levels of its being as a university. Becoming ecological is a huge project, taking the university into a new order of being. This university inhabits 'a new ecosophy, at once applied and theoretical, ethico-political and aesthetic' (ibid.: 67).

It might be tempting to think that the ecological university will be concerned about its impact on the environment. So it may; but this way of putting things is doubly problematic. First, 'the environment' is too often – especially in the context of the ecological domain – understood as referring to the natural environment when, as implied, it can and should have a much wider ambit, embracing the personal, social, cultural, institutional and technological environments *and* knowledge of those environments; in short, the world in its fullest senses.

Second, and just as if not more important, the notion of 'having an impact' on the environment, however widely construed, is part of the problematic to which the idea of the ecological is addressed. 'Having an impact' can stand for an instrumental orientation in which the environment is seen as a domain to satisfy human wants and interests; it implies a separation of human beings from their environment (the environment is 'othered', out there); it suggests a predilection in favour of the environment being changed rather than it being left to be as it is; and it places humankind in the centre of things rather than seeing humanity as having no such privileged status. On all of these grounds, the notion of 'having an impact' is problematic. This is not to neglect the points that a university can have beneficial impacts on its environment *and* it is part of the ecological orientation to promote beneficial impacts.

But then a further difficulty arises for the idea of 'having an impact'. What is to count as a beneficial impact and, by extension, what might a deleterious impact look like? Are there criteria that we can call upon to help us sort the beneficial sheep from the deleterious goats? Here, the concept of sustainability is helpful, whichever ecological level or domain we have in mind.

A university can monitor its actions to gauge the extent to which they are, for example, enabling individuals so to develop themselves as to be self-sustaining. Is their learning such that they are developing powers of self-criticality, and powers of imaginative creative thought such that they are likely to be self-sustaining through their lifespan? At the levels of communities and of society, a university can ask itself how much it is helping communities and society to flourish. Is society learning about itself, and its many communities, such that those societal learning processes are not merely sustained but are enhanced? Are its scholarly and third stream activities being conducted against the horizon of such a consideration? Of course, linked to this question stand matters of democracy, freedom and inclusion. At the level of the world, a university can ask itself, are its activities depleting the world of its resources or are they adding to the world's resources? And by 'resources', we have to include the knowledges, languages and understandings in the world, as well as the material resources and the natural resources of physical world.

In the first place, therefore, the ecological university has a care towards its environment, which is to say that it has a care towards the world. It is an actor in and across the world, it is connected with the world and it is concerned about the world. 'Care', as noted earlier, is a fundamental concept in Heidegger's philosophy: indeed, 'Dasein's

Being reveals itself as *care*' (1998: 227, Heidegger's emphasis). In other words, it is through the things that are cared for that our being discloses itself. Correspondingly, the ecological university reveals itself, in the first place, through its care *for* the world and not in its impact *on* the world. The university has both the position and thence the responsibility to care about and care for the world. Through its care for the world, the ecological university even comes to have a 'conscience' about its place in the world.[2]

Just part of its place in the world lies in the university being part of global conversations, through its formal and informal communication processes. All universities are, in this sense, global. Universities are implicated in the global conversations of academe. So questions arise as to the character of its conversations – in books, in papers, in academic settings, in its teachings, in its overt interactions with the wider world, in its public meetings on campus and in its internet exchanges. What are the guiding lights of these communications? To what ends are they oriented? With what ethical considerations? Does it have a care for the character of its communications and their intended recipients?

The ecological university is sensitive also to the totality of its global environment. It not only is engaged with others – for that is common to all universities – but is also and more especially aware of its conversations and activities having a beneficial potential for the world. So the ecological university acts not in its own interests but in collective interests

> that, in the short-term, don't profit anyone, but in the long term are the conduits of a processual enrichment for the whole of humanity. It is the whole future of fundamental research and artistic production that is in question here.
>
> (Guattari, 2005: 65)

The coming of the ecological university

I suggested at the outset of this discussion that the ecological university is a university whose time has come. Why might we think this and to what degree is this feasible utopia – of the ecological university – actually feasible?

We can identify inducements in favour of the emerging of the ecological university at both national and global levels. *Nationally*, the coming of the ecological university is being prompted by factors such as social disorder; the evolution and uses of information and communication technologies, for personal, public and commercial purposes; poverty across and alienation from society; the evolution of democracy; the continuing presence of illiteracy in all societies and (in many) the gross educational under-achievement of sections and parts of societies, marked by gender, ethnic and social class differences. *Globally*, prompts towards its coming include those of the overt ecological challenge – evident in global warming, climate change and degradation of the natural world; global terrorism and crime; world energy crises; world-wide or massive regional economic crises; global diseases; depletion of languages across the world; large-scale famines and population movements; and large-scale disasters and their threats, both technological and 'natural' – such as nuclear explosions and tsunamis.

Doubtless, these lists are far from exhaustive. Together, even as they stand, they constitute a formidable array of circumstances that point to the propitiousness of the ecological university.

But note the argument here. It has two aspects in particular. First, it is not that there are many crises in society and across the world and that the university has a responsibility to respond to them. It is rather that the university, through its activities in learning, inquiry and development, is *already* inter-connected with this world. Its students (many of whom may be 'mature' students) are very often already acting and working in the wider world, either alongside their studies or as part of their studies or even prior to their studies. Its researchers and scholars are already involved in fields and engaging with topics that bear directly on these issues. In its developmental activities – whether overtly for income generation for itself, or for economic generation in, say, the local region or for more public purposes – the university comes up against these issues. And in its communicative processes – in print or via the mass and electronic media – many of these issues come into view too (connected with issues of global literacy, and global understandings). In this sense – that the university is already engaging implicitly with the large issues before us on this planet – the ecological university is simply facing up to the responsibilities that are *already* embedded in its work.

The other crucial aspect of the argument lies in the following step. It is *not* that the grave features of the world (of the kind cited above) are in themselves characteristic of the callings on the ecological university. The grave and incessant features of the world are merely the empirical forms of the summons that comes to the university. They do not constitute an argument in themselves. The argument rests on a more general point. It is that these grave and incessant features of the world are but graphic exemplars – and empirical markers – of the claims of the Other.

The ecological world is aware not only that it is a player in the world but that it has resources and possibilities that can aid the world. The ecological university is prompted ultimately not through the manifest crises in the world but more by its sense of itself in the company of otherness. It understands itself as in-the-world and therefore as responsible to the world. In the end, the ecological university gifts itself to the world. The research university was a university *in-itself*; the entrepreneurial university was a university *for-itself*; but the ecological university is a university *for-the-Other*.

The ecological university is as much a set of ideas as it is an empirical entity. It will take various forms. What it is to be an ecological university will differ as between a major research-intensive university and a university with a more local and teaching intensive role; it will differ as between a large multi-faculty university and a small more specialist institution. But every university has the capacity and now the spaces and, therefore, the responsibility to partake in realising the idea – or rather the cluster of ideas – that constitute the ecological university.

Ecologies of knowing – and the wise university

The idea of the ecological can be turned, as noted, to good effect upon knowledge; or, better still, upon knowing. What are the relationships between different ways of knowing? What are the relationships between different ways of knowing *and* the world? Is knowledge, as it has been constructed especially in universities, imploding? Do the dominant forms of knowledge have suicidal or megalomaniac tendencies? Can they live with themselves and live with each other and help the world to flourish? To ask questions of this kind is to adopt an ecological perspective. It is to call forth the idea of knowledge ecologies.

Although 'ecology' has not been part of the argumentative apparatus employed by Nicholas Maxwell, it is worth returning to his ideas (Chapter 5) for they embody an ecological perspective and they home in on the university. Maxwell believes that, as it was developing in the eighteenth century, the formation and justification of systematic knowledge – for which read 'science' – took a wrong turn. For Maxwell (2008), the form that 'knowledge inquiry' has taken is actually 'grossly irrational'. It is so because it fails to comply with 'four elementary rules of reason':

1   Articulate and seek to improve the specification of the basic problem(s) to be solved.
2   Propose and critically assess alternative possible solutions.
3   When necessary, break up the basic problem to be solved into a number of specialized problems.
4   Inter-connect attempts to solve the basic problem and specialized problems, so that basic problem-solving may guide, and be guided by, specialized problem-solving.

(Maxwell, 2008: 5)

Maxwell believes that knowledge inquiry has failed to put rules (1), (2) and (4) into practice. In particular, it has not identified basic problems of living (1), far less tried to solve them (2). And, while it has undertaken inquiry into specialised problems (3), it has failed to join up those inquiries and their findings (4). Instead, then, of such irrational knowledge-inquiry, Maxwell urges the establishment of '*wisdom inquiry*', 'the primary change [needing] to be made is [that of ensuring] that academic inquiry implements rules (1) and (2)' (ibid.: 7). Such a conception of academic inquiry would allow a much greater role for the social sciences and the humanities for they would play a significant part in the formulation of the basic problems to be solved (1); and, by extension, they would come into play much more in the formulation of the solutions (2).

Maxwell is posing a stark contrast here in the possibilities for academic inquiry. On the one hand, knowledge inquiry is dominated by a conception of science, in which values, emotions, human considerations and philosophies of life are expunged from the approved methods. On the other hand, values, emotions, human considerations and philosophies of life become part of the totality of *wisdom inquiry*. One temptation might be to think that while knowledge inquiry (that is, science as traditionally conceived) is somewhat narrow, at least it is rigorous; wisdom inquiry, in contrast, sounds somewhat ill-disciplined. On the contrary, Maxwell contends that it is wisdom inquiry that has the greater rigour: feelings and desires are not to be taken at their face value but rather, being now part of the inquiry, 'feelings, desires and values need to be subjected to critical scrutiny'.

This is a hugely powerful argument.[3] Here, I want to make a set of observations linked to our present theme of the ecological. What Maxwell is doing, in effect, is counterposing two knowledge ecologies, an allegedly pure and rational form of inquiry, devoid of the messiness of human beliefs and desire, *and* a more inclusive form of inquiry in which human values and wants have their place. And each form of inquiry has a characteristic relationship (or lack thereof) to the world.

An understanding of Maxwell's work as an identification of *rival* ecologies of knowledge has important implications. First, this understanding raises questions about the relationship of different forms of knowledge to each other. Are science and the humanities utterly separate forms of inquiry *or* might they be understood as different aspects of a unified inquiry (for example, that of understanding the universe and humanity's place in it)? Second, an ecologies-of-knowledge perspective places questions against any presumption that some forms of academic inquiry are more important than others. By extension, it helps us to see why it is that science has become so dominant as a form of knowledge in society and why 'the research university' is largely 'the scientific university' (Chapter 2). This is a knowledge ecology that is tilted towards knowledge inquiry rather than wisdom inquiry.

Third, and beyond these matters about the relationships internal to knowledge, an ecology-of-knowledge perspective poses questions about the relationship between academic inquiry and the wider world. For two hundred years or more, that debate has been construed as a stand-off between those who would pursue knowledge as 'its own end' (Newman, 1976: 99 *et seq.*)[4] and those who value knowledge insofar as it has manifest impact on the world. *Both* of these camps counterpose knowledge and the world: they just see the relationship as different (entirely separate on the one hand; much transfer in both directions on the other hand). In contrast, an ecology of knowledge perspective encourages us to see academic inquiry as *part of* the world, bringing in values, sentiments, and hopes of the world, albeit subjecting them to critical scrutiny.

'Wisdom' surely implies a perspective that is: (1) far-reaching; (2) comprehensive; and (3) oriented to moving matters forward into a better place. We see all three elements in Maxwell's idea of 'wisdom inquiry'. Such inquiry (1) addresses matters of profound significance; (2) brings all valid forms of inquiry together, respecting the contribution that each can make; and (3) is oriented towards proposing solutions to the major problems of an age. A university sensitive to such a knowledge policy (Bergendahl, 1984) would itself be a university *of* wisdom *and* a university *for* wisdom.

A university that was guided by such a set of ideas would be tacitly working to develop fundamentally radical knowledge ecologies, oriented towards the promotion of societal and global wellbeing. Such a university would pose for itself large questions: what relationships does it envisage between forms of inquiry, both present and future possible? What relationships does it envisage between itself and the wider world, so far as its knowledge inquiry is concerned? For example, to what extent might an ecological university want itself to engage with the wider world in effecting solutions to problems and to what extent would it see its ecological role more one of relating to and enhancing the public understanding of issues? (This juxtaposition is not to imply that these options are mutually incompatible.) There would no one knowledge ecology for the ecological university; and such matters would be part of its own conversations. That continuing debate would be part of its own wisdom.

This wisdom, it should be noted, would be energised by a kind of faith, a dual faith that it is worth striving for a different world order and that the university can play a part in bringing that new order about. It contains a sense that the dominant forms of knowledge *are* worthwhile but that, by themselves, they are inadequate and that their undue influence has had and is having serious consequences.[5] As Žižek puts it:

> The problem, of course, is that, in a time of crisis and ruptures, sceptical empirical wisdom itself, constrained to the horizon of the dominant form of common sense, cannot provide the answers, so one *must* risk a Leap of Faith.
>
> (2008: 2)

Ecological possibilities

Identifying possibilities for the ecological university includes the identification of current activities as well as future possible activities. A feature of all feasible utopias – of which the ecological university is but the prime example – is that there be examples to hand. Possibilities for the ecological university, therefore, are both present possibilities, already to be observed, and future possibilities combined. They include:

- developing and vigorously pursuing a strategy of civic and community engagement (Watson, 2007b);[6]
- putting academic work on-line (cf. Peters, 2007);
- holding public lectures – and putting podcasts on-line;
- working with local/regional authorities and community and third sector groups in addressing social issues;
- working with groups/communities in the developing world (projects here could include cultural projects as well technological and social projects);
- offering pro bono advice;
- producing materials for public consumption (a university in Colombia produces mini-booklets containing accessible work by its scholars for public consumption at minimal prices);
- research that tackles issues of concern and that might help to alleviate suffering or deprivation (locally and globally);
- academics becoming public intellectuals, imaginatively utilising media so as to communicate to publics and so to enhance the public sphere;
- putting each class of students in touch with another class in another country and so develop a trans-national and trans-cultural learning space and so helping the formation of students as 'global citizens';[7]
- offering to accredit the socially-oriented activities of students off-campus (where, for example, an individual student works in a care home or joins (as it is called in the UK) the St John's Ambulance Service);

- promoting inter-connectedness across disciplines and forging public-oriented pro-grammes of activity (the UK's University of Durham is doing just this, in its Institute of Advanced Study, with a university-wide project led by two senior professors 'to communicate authoritative work on a spectrum of significant matters of being and knowing in a lively, open and accessible manner' (Amin and O'Neill, 2009));
- universities coming together across the world to promote this kind of ecological thinking – of which the Talloires movement is the most prominent;[8]
- universities being funded in part from the public purse in regard to the extent to which such a mission of concern towards the wider world is evident in their life and activities.

Such a listing, it should be noted, does not and cannot begin to amount to a blueprint for the ecological university. The ecological university is being proposed here, it will be recalled, as a feasible utopia. It is necessary, therefore, if the argument is to hold water that *some* exemplifications be provided. The feasibility of the ecological uni-versity needs to be demonstrated. But any set of examples cannot be felt to offer a definite steer in realising the ecological university. Each university has to work out its ecological possibilities for itself and keep them continuously under review.

Pertinently for this inquiry, Russell Jacoby distinguishes between 'blueprint uto-pias' and 'iconoclastic utopias', expressing the difference in this way: 'The blueprints [in their detailed prescriptions] not only appear repressive, they also rapidly become dated' (2005: 32). In contrast, 'the iconoclastic utopians offer little concrete to grab onto . . . [but they] are essential to any effort to escape the spell of the quotidian)' (ibid.: xvi–xvii). These iconoclastic utopians 'offered an imageless utopianism laced with passion and spirit' (ibid.: 33). The ecological university is precisely just such an iconoclastic utopia.

Rival versions of the university?

It may be said – and even objected – that a list of activities of the kind just presented is characteristic of what has been termed 'the service university' or 'the civic univer-sity'. There is overlap, certainly, with those ideas: they all take in each other's washing to some extent. But there are some important distinctions across these ideas. Both the service university and the civic university have a sense of the Other, but it is a bounded sense of the Other in each case. The service university understands itself as serving its society, both locally and possibly nationally. It defines itself in at most national terms and takes its bearings from the overt wants of society. The civic univer-sity largely confines its self-understanding to its locale and again is liable to surrender itself to meeting the – quite legitimate – aspirations of the local community for public advancement.[9] In contrast, the ecological university understands itself in relation to the world as a whole; and here, the 'world' includes but goes well beyond humanity as a whole.[10] The ecological university reflects two of the themes that have run through our discussions in this book, namely those of universality and infinity.

In its universality, the ecological university understands itself in relation to all of humanity and all of its worthwhile forms of understanding. It holds itself open to new knowledges or to sustaining traditional knowledges that might aid mankind's self-understanding. It sees its truth-oriented activities against the horizon of the universal, that is to say it understands its truth-seeking activities as having a universal horizon of significance. A student or a researcher will be interested in the life of an individual poet or the structure of a particular compound or the nature of a small community in a limited historical period or the nature of disease in one social group in one country but, still, those inquiries and those learning processes will have the universal as their horizon of significance. They will take into account understandings across the world and they will have an eye to the universal potential significance of the inquiries to hand. The local, and small-scale, will be pitched on a canvas of the global, and will seek to widen global understandings.

In its relationship to the infinite, the ecological university understands that its ambit is the universe and all that is in it and even beyond it. 'All that is in the universe' includes our knowledge of the universe and so it embraces all forms of knowing. Valid forms of knowing themselves stretch out, and are potentially infinite. The poet, the ballet dancer, the midwife, the Eskimo and the mystic: all are recognised as having valid forms of knowledge. The ecological university is, therefore, faced with the conundrum of determining which forms of knowing have a validity of their own in its embrace of the infinite.

The ecological university, then, is both *without* boundaries and *with* boundaries. It moves – perhaps hesitantly – between these conditions of its being. It is both inclusive and yet demanding, for its activities will be tested against the ecological criterion: does this activity advance wellbeing – of the world, of the universe? *All* of its activities would be at least held up implicitly to the conditions of the ecological spirit. It hears the world, it is receptive to ways of understanding the world, and it reaches out to the world. Universities may be more or less ecological; they may set themselves on an ecological journey, deepening their ecological sensitivities at all levels but the call of the ecological is unconditional in a way. Once its call is heard and *heeded*, a university is bound to bring all of its activities into question and look for ways of allowing its ecological spirit to inspire the whole university.

Conclusion

The ecological university is, therefore, another feasible utopia. It is idea and vision *and* it is action. To pick up the themes of Part II of this book, it is being *and* becoming. It is always becoming. It is always wanting to become itself. It struggles with the circumstances of its age to go on realising itself as an ecological university. It is anarchy *and* culture: it contains and believes in the idea of the ecological: this is its culture. But it is also somewhat anarchic, for the idea of the ecological looks to an absence of governance, in that ultimately it resides in elements of a system living peacefully together. It lives out the idea of the ecological in space *and* time: its activities capture the idea of the ecological in multiple spaces and in the horizon of past, present and future time. And it is both authentic *and* responsible: it lives out its own interests in learning and inquiry (and so is authentically itself) and it does so with an eye to the wellbeing of the world (and so has a sense of its responsibilities to the world). In all these respects, it is a feasible utopia; and in all these respects, it resembles our other three feasible utopias (the liquid university, the therapeutic university and the authentic university).

But the ecological university is different from those other three feasible utopias. The ecological university has its being and its possible becoming *intentionally* against the horizon of the categories of the infinite and the universal. The ecological university is without bounds, operationally, epistemologically and ontologically. It lives in an open-ended way with and for the world. It goes on stretching itself in its interactions with the world. But the ecological university is not without conditions of its being. In particular, it does what it can to help to sustain and enhance the wellbeing of all that it encounters. The ecological university understands itself as living out a sense of the Other in the fullest possible way.

The ecological is none other than the fullest expression of the idea of the university. It is the fullest realisation of the university's *being-possible* (to return to the Heideggerian expression that we encountered at our outset and have encountered at various points since). This is work, though, always in the making. It is utopian in that the ecological university will fall short of its sense of its possible self. Individual acts and policies may well exemplify what it is to be an ecological university, but both the empirical environment and the possibilities for the complexities that constitute the university will cause the ecological university *always* to fall short of those possibilities.

The possibilities – the being-possible – of the ecological university are also dependent on the imaginative powers that are brought to envisaging the ecological university. What it is, and what it might be, to be ecological are always susceptible of further imaginings.[11] The ecological university is a feasible project but it remains always utopian. And it is content with that situation, as it struggles perpetually to do all it can to bring itself to its ecological fullness.

The ecological university is necessary, feasible and desirable. It is always just in reach and always just beyond reach. The ecological university is haunted by its shortcomings and yet will continue to be inspired both by itself and by its possibilities.

Coda

The spirit of the university

From ethos to spirit

Approach any university in the world and a sense of it will begin to form. Outside the grounds of the university, perhaps there are displays about itself and those displays may provide insights about its present and even its past work. Perhaps there are photographs of past and present individuals who are associated with research conducted at the university. Perhaps its grounds turn out to be extensive before one even encounters a building. How old then are the buildings? What is the character of any new buildings? What is the symbolism of the architecture? Do the new buildings have space – perhaps with an atrium – for serendipitous encounters and conviviality? What seems to be the ages of the students as they enter and leave the buildings? What is their ethnic mix? Do their body language and their dress give clues as to their socio-economic class or even their geographical origins? It may be a cosmopolitan university but is this a local university or an international university? (It could be either.) Entering the main reception area, does one enter a welcoming space? Are there indications – perhaps a visual display – of a number of public events that day? Are there interesting and even well-known visiting speakers?

Once, consideration was given to the 'ethos' of a university, a somewhat nebulous sense of an institution, the evidence for which was elusive. Its elusive character was very much a part of an 'ethos'. Now, an age has emerged in which significance is understood through some kind formal assessment that preferably deploys a numbering system and monetary values. Consequently, the idea of ethos recedes: it contains a sense of fuzziness and wooliness and it drops out of the higher education lexicon.[1] And perhaps it connotes, too, a sense of an enduring state of affairs when what is wanted today is perpetual change and movement. 'Ethos' speaks, after all, of abiding collective meanings deep in an institution's collective psyche. As such, ethos is going to hold up efforts to become 'dynamic', open to change and experimentation.

If ethos is in difficulty in today's higher education vocabulary, perhaps a better idea is that of 'spirit'. We may speak of the spirit of a university with fewer qualms, perhaps. After all, a spirit moves and perhaps with some rapidity. So it can do some justice to a sense of the university moving in time and space. But ideas of spirit present their difficulties too. Jacques Derrida – commenting on the absence of the idea of spirit in Heidegger's work[2] – observed that the term 'remains steeped in a sort of ontological obscurity' (Derrida, [1987] 1991: 15). Again, it seems to have qualities of the ineffable, of the mysterious. 'Spirit' is another difficult concept then. But it may yet be a powerful concept for our unfolding times.

This book can be understood as a call for the reawakening of the spirit of the university. But what might be meant by 'the spirit of the university'?[3] The phrase points us to the energy in an institution such as the university and its *possible* energy. Without spirit, a university is no university: it will have had the life taken out of it. 'Spirit is ... never at rest but always engaged in moving forward' (Hegel, [1807] 1999: 50). A task of university leadership, accordingly (and unlike university 'management'), is that of infusing a university with energy, with spirit. With a new leadership, a university may find new spirit; or an already waning spirit may be further dissipated. Spirit has vigour: 'Spirit is flame' (Derrida, 1991: 84). Ideas help to enflame and they can give a university more life. More becoming even.

But spirit-as-flame is only possible amid air. Crowd out the air and the flame dies; and the spirit with it. Increasingly, the air is being sucked out of universities as they become more corporate, more bureaucratic and more managed (Chapter 4). 'Low morale' can be seen as a sign of this reduction of university air; 'high morale' can be seen as a sign of a vigorous university spirit.[4] That these sentiments and reflections are to be heard in a way across the world is indicative of the way in which dominant ideas of the university are now global in character; and of the way in which some of the university's emerging forms have life-*extinguishing* qualities.

'Life' was a favourite category of the former literary critic, F. R. Leavis. I do not think that he ever articulated what he meant by 'life' but surely in his writings – not least on the idea of the university – we can glimpse a sense of intellectual and creative vigour.[5] And so we can ask as to the life of a university, and conjure the sense of what it might be to be part of this university as distinct from that university.[6] Just what is its *life*? With what vigour does it move forward? In what kind of air? Is it a stultifying air? Is it a refreshing air?

Spirit may have direction: it can energise in some direction or other, blown perhaps by the currents of the university. There is considerable energy latent within universities. It is no contradiction for individuals to express enormous enthusiasm for their own projects and professional endeavours and bemoan the nature of the corporate university to which they are subject (Watson, 2009). Are there ideas of the university that can both take account of its situation and help it to move forward so as to realise its full potential, and in ways that open it up, that give it air, that give it a new spirit?[7] The idea of the ecological university may just perhaps help to impart such a new spirit. More than anything, the ecological university is characterised by an ecological *spirit*.

Forward to metaphysics

The university can realise itself by finding a new spirit but, if the university is to realise its fullest possibilities, that spirit will bring with it the largest ideas of the university. Consequently, categories of the infinite and the universal have been visible in much of our explorations. The idea of the ecological university stretches itself over *infinite* space and is sensitive to all readings of the world: its inclusive spirit is *universal* in nature. This is not to say that 'anything goes' for the ecological university. Its capacity for the infinite has its limits. Its universality is granted on conditions. The ecological university *is* a university. It goes on becoming itself against the horizon of the ethical and in safeguarding standards of rational communication. In pressing forward, the ecological university guards its back.

But to place the ecological university in the company of the categories of the infinite and the universal is, in a way, to realise anew the metaphysical university. The metaphysical university promised, it will be recalled, an encounter with a meta-reality. Over time, that idea came in different guises, variously God, Truth, Spirit, and Knowledge (the capital letters are crucial in each case). The promise was that by diligent study, admittedly somewhat removed from this world (in inward-facing clois-ters), the scholar would come into a totally new relationship with the world. Indeed, would soar into a meta-reality. This was surely implied, for instance, in Newman's idea of 'a philosophical perspective', wherein knowledge was 'its own end'.

As we noted in our opening chapter, in a secular, post-metaphysical age, we cannot retreat – as some would wish to do – to the substantive ideas of those former ages. Even the idea of 'a liberal education' has to be declared passé.[8] It has its time and place in a par-ticular socio-historic setting. But we are entitled to observe that the idea of the ecological university invokes the metaphysical in its associations with the infinity and universality.[9]

Perhaps we should not be surprised. For the idea of the university traditionally stood for the highest realisation of human being. Its recent lurch in the directions of the entrepreneurial university and the corporate university would surrender the university to parochialism, the short term and the self-interested. They are, in these senses, corrupt forms of the university. But these reflections should not over-worry us. We do not yet see a university 'in ruins'. In some ways, the university is in good health. That is part of the problem. The sorry nature of its state is largely hidden from view.[10] The university's association with the largest possible categories can be resumed. The ecological university is a utopian project but it is also a feasible project.

Finale

In this book, I have tried to develop a particular argument, namely that the university has a dynamic and always unfolding being and that idea, thereby, poses challenges as to the further becoming of the university. Its becoming places responsibilities on the university for imagining its future. I have contended, further, that we should respond to these challenges in part through the identification of feasible utopias. In addition to that general argument, I have tried to accomplish two additional tasks. The first is to show that our ideas of the university are hopelessly impoverished. Why hope-lessly? Because they are not merely limited but are being driven forward with such determination that it may appear that 'there is no alternative'. But the entrepreneurial university and the corporate university – either in themselves or together – should not be felt to constitute the endpoints of the unfolding of the university. Here lies the second task I have tried to undertake, namely to indicate the significance and poten-tial of the imagination. Our ideas of the university are limited, in the first place, by our imagination. If our thinking about the university is impoverished, then let us dare to imagine new kinds of university.

Notes

Introduction

1 A question that these opening two paragraphs raises is this: 'What is the status of this inquiry?' Is it conducted within the academy or outside the academy? Can the academy inquire into itself? Can it reach an 'extraterritorial standpoint from which to regard or comprehend the university as such?' Wortham (2006: 19), drawing on Derrida, poses precisely this question. I would only say here that the inquiry is one of a choice of university-being (as it might be put) as much as it is a choice of the register in which to reason about the university.

2 Immediately after the sentence in which that phrase 'Being-possible' appears comes this important sentence: 'Dasein [i.e. Being] is the possibility of Being-free for its own most potentiality-for-Being.' This sentence could be said to capture the whole spirit of the present book.

3 Cf. Ernest Gellner's (1970) paper on 'Concepts and Society': 'Nothing is more false than the claim that, for a given assertion, its use is its meaning. On the contrary, its use may depend on its lack of meaning, its ambiguity, its possession of wholly different and incompatible meanings in different contexts.' Here, in this inquiry, 'university' presents with 'wholly different and incompatible meanings' but this very ambiguity opens spaces for new imaginings as to the possible meanings of 'university'.

4 John Daniel is especially associated with the idea of the mega-university through his (1998) book *Mega-Universities and Knowledge Media*; and in that book, Daniel offers (ibid.: 29) a stipulative definition of 'mega-university' as 'a distance-teaching institution'. My recollection, however, is that the term 'mega-university' was in circulation at least in the 1970s, not least to reflect the eruption of mass higher education across the world. (In any event, I am not clear why the idea of 'mega-university' should be restricted in the way Daniel proposes, particularly in regard to the criterion concerning distance-teaching institutions. Are the universities of Buenos Aires and Mexico City, with their largely campus-based – albeit floating – student populations of 200,000 not also 'mega-universities'?)

5 'Indeed, there is a certain 'tension between universities and "higher education"' (Rothblatt and Wittrock, 1993a: 1).

6 On the idea of 'ideological lightness', see Filippakou (2009).

7 Cf. Raymond Williams's (1989) *Resources of Hope*.

8 Inevitably, my key sources have changed somewhat over time but I have drawn especially – I observe – on modern European philosophy (such as Nietzsche but also increasingly on existential philosophy from Heidegger to Sartre), on Critical Theory (especially as expounded by Jürgen Habermas), and on intellectuals who were either wholly European or had most of their formative life in Europe (such as Ernest Gellner, Paul Feyerabend, Jacques Derrida, Luce Irigaray, Gilles Deleuze, Félix Guattari, Paul Virilio and Slavoj Žižek). Other especially formative presences include Charles Taylor and Alasdair MacIntyre and most recently, Critical Realism especially as worked out by Roy Bhaskar.

9 Gilles Deleuze, in his ([1968] 2001: 56) *Difference and Repetition* has advanced an idea of transcendental empiricism, which is surely close to my suggestion of feasible utopia (although certainly more sophisticated).

10 Helpful texts on utopia in ways pertinent to this inquiry include Barbara Goodwin's (2001) collection (especially the Introduction and the first two chapters), David Halpin's *Hope and Education: The Role of the Utopian Imagination* (2003); and Russell Jacoby's *Picture Imperfect: Utopian Thought for an Anti-Utopian Age* (2005). Thomas More's ([1516] 2003) foundational tract, *Utopia*, continues to attract attention, albeit divided attention (was More an early Marxist or not?).

11 On pernicious and virtuous ideologies in higher education, see Barnett (2003).

12 The key text on networks and which inspires some of the thinking here is Castell's (1997) work on *The Rise of the Network Society*.

13 Heidegger hovers in the mention of 'care', it being one of his major categories.

14 According to Kateb:

> If utopia is to survive . . ., it must be possible to conceive of a situation in which free thought, spontaneous life, meaningful choices, the eruption of the unexpected, the presence of the mysterious, are all compatible with a way of life which could still be thought utopian.
>
> ([1971] 2008: 11)

1 The metaphysical university

1 The scholars of the medieval universities were characteristically young men of about 15–25 years of age. However, Scott (2006) suggests that 'there were a few female students . . . in southern Europe'.

2 The title of the relevant chapter in Bourdieu's *Pascalian Meditations* is 'Critique of Scholastic Reason', since 'While the suspension of economic or social necessity is what allows for the emergence of autonomous fields, [it also] threatens to confine scholastic thought within the limits of ignored or repressed presuppositions, implied in the withdrawal from the world' (2000: 15).

3 According to Brown:

> This sermon of Richard Fishacre at Oxford, following the Augustinian model of study, shows the way of investigation in the early medieval universities. The final goal of all study is to come to a greater understanding of God's view of reality, by taking as primary source the sacred Scriptures, which reveal the divine wisdom.
>
> (Marenbon, 1998: 190)

4 On values in universities, see the volume edited by Simon Robinson and Clement Katulushi (2005), especially the essays by the editors themselves and those by Peter Scott, Rowan Williams, Zygmunt Bauman and Chris Megone.

5 According to Dunbabin: 'If you had asked a master of the early schools what the idea of a university was, he would have had to scratch his head . . . before deciding ' (1999: 31).

6 It is not coincidental, we may surmise, that a current national monitoring system in the UK is known as the 'transparency exercise'.

7 'It is an essential element in wonder that we recognize what . . . we cannot fully understand, and acknowledge as containing something greater than ourselves' (Midgley, 1989: 41).

8 For a vision of the university that has affinities with the ideas here, see Sarles (2001).

9 In a survey of mission statements, Chris Duke (1992) found rather little in the way of a 'paradigm shift' despite apparent superficial changes.

10 This idea of universalism has its modern defenders. See Jaspers' ([1959] 1965) *The Idea of the University* (e.g. p. 38) for an exposition of the idea.

11 The medieval curriculum built upon the trivium (logic, grammar and rhetoric) and the quadrivium (arithmetic, music, geometry and astronomy) were educational devices to promote this transcendence. See Cobban (1999: 150, 156).

12 On the relationships between neoliberalism, higher education and the knowledge economy, not least the rise of 'knowledge capitalism', see Olssen and Peters (2005). On globalisation, see Arimoto, Huang and Yokoyama (2005); Currie and Newson (1998); King (2004); and Scott (1997).

13 On the idea of meta-reality, see Roy Bhaskar's (2002a) *From Science to Emancipation: Journeys towards Meta-Reality – a Philosophy for the Present* and (2002b) *Reflections on Meta-Reality*.

14 In a discussion of 'metaphysics after Kant', Habermas (1995: 15) suggests that 'as Europeans, we [cannot] seriously understand concepts like morality and ethical life, person and individuality, or freedom and emancipation, without appropriating the substance of Judeo-Christian understanding of history in terms of salvation'.

2 The scientific university

1 Of course, the stages of the long history of the development of the university can be perceived in many different ways. For example, Wittrock (1993) sees the reformulation of the idea of the university at the turn of the eighteenth and nineteenth centuries (notably in Germany and then in England) as a definite stage in itself whereas here, it is both – in its English variant – the end of the metaphysical idea of the university or – in its German variant – the beginning of the scientific university. However, the sense of the unfolding of the idea of the university is more important than holding to any particular set of stages.

2 'The German term *Wissenschaft* covers study in both the sciences and the humanities', Editor's footnote in Karl Jaspers' *The Idea of the University* ([1959] 1965: 21).

3 'Control' in the empirical sciences works at two levels. First, there is characteristically an experimental situation (though not always, as in astronomy) in which the environment surrounding an entity under investigation is controlled, such that the features of the entity can be isolated and examined in an uncontaminated (or 'objective') way so as to identify the causal law that pertains in that situation. Roy Bhaskar has written extensively on this matter, for example in his *A Realist Theory of Science* ([1975] 2008: 34). Second, there is a 'knowledge-constitutive interest' in 'technical control over objectified processes' (Habermas, 1978: 309).

4 For decades, Ernest Gellner wrote brilliantly and with much wit in part to try to explain just why it is that science comes to attract high marks in modern culture *and* the difficulties that attach to any such attempt. After all, just how does 'reason' reason its own reasonable-ness? See, for example, his (1974) *Legitimation of Belief*; his (1988) *Plough, Sword and Book: The Structure of Human History* and his (1992) *Reason and Culture: New Perspectives on the Past*.

5 Geiger (1993: 253) observes that 'In the decade after Sputnik (1958–1968) federal support [in the USA] for basic research in [American] universities increased by a factor of seven.' In this one instance, we witness the tightening of the relationships between universities, the state (and the military) and industry (especially the high technology industries).

6 See the report by Lynn Meek, Ulrich Teichler and Mary-Louise Kearney (2009) which demonstrates the links between knowledge understood as physical and biological sciences, research policy, innovation, the relative diminution in 'blue-skies research', the rise of 'world-class universities' and the global knowledge divide. This gives rise to a new acronym: 'HERI' – Higher Education, Research and Innovation.

7 According to Cannella and Paetzold:

> There is no doubt that science – particularly physical science – has great authority in our society. The quantification of science has helped to provide legitimacy for this authority. . . . Many authors have noted that it is beginning with the movement toward quantification, and the development of statistical methodologies to accompany and

influence scientific methodologies, that the hegemony of science (as traditionally represented through scientific method and objectivity) in society began to occur . . . In the
early stages, scientists may have assisted decision-makers concerned with social policy
issues; today, scientists have become directly responsible for economic, political, and
social control.

(1994: 335)

8 Now, science is contained neither spatially (there are more scientists in the private sector
   in industry and the military than there are in universities), nor cognitively (as the boundary
   between science and technology dissolves) and nor in its modes (as scientific 'procedures'
   are carried out in cyberspace in company with communication and inquiries in the public
   sphere).
9 See John Gray's *Enlightenment's Wake*, in which he observes that 'the Enlightenment project
   of promoting autonomous human reason and of according to science a privileged status
   in relation to all other forms of understanding . . . has issued in . . . nihilism' ([1995] 2007:
   217).
10 See the paper by Kincheloe and Tobin (2009) on 'The Much Exaggerated Death of
   Positivism'.
11 See also Habermas' (1972) nuanced commentary on Marcuse's depiction of science as
   ideology. See, too, more recently Richardson (2005) on the 'hegemony of the physical
   sciences' and its effect on the 'softer sciences'.
12 A major question that this set of observations raises is this: could science develop a different
   ethical base and pursue its activities within a different kind of horizon? See much of the
   work of Steve Fuller (e.g. 1997, 2000) and Roy Bhaskar's philosophy of critical realism (e.g.,
   2002a, 2002b). Also the essay by Trifonas (2004) which ties the possibility of a new ethics
   for science precisely to a new sense of responsibility for the academy.
13 Here, we should note that Kant (1992) sharply distinguished the status of philosophy and
   theology: theology constituted, along with Medicine and Law, merely one of the higher
   faculties. It was the task of philosophy, as the only lower faculty, to 'control' (ibid.: 45) the
   higher faculties; hence 'the conflict of the faculties'. On theology as such, Stanley Hauerwas
   has attempted 'to understand better' why theology, at least, 'is no longer considered a
   necessary subject in the modern university' (2007: 12).
14 See Finnegan (2005) for explorations as to how different forms of knowledge, including
   scientific knowledge, can be democratic in its mode of production and not simply
   sequestered within the academic community. 'Researchers' can be found increasingly
   'beyond the University walls', even if often working in conjunction with academics.
15 Heidegger observed, however, that reason runs into difficulty when it tries to ground itself:
   how can reason ground reason? 'The principle of reason' is without (much) reason: 'plenty
   of shadows are cast over the principle of reason' (1991: 13). Accordingly, 'the principle of
   reason is . . . not a statement about reason, but about beings' (ibid.: 44). But then, if there
   are beings (plural), and different ways of being in the world, we may surely reflect that there
   open up the possibility of there being legitimately different forms of reason.
16 For Heidegger, there is at work here, in technology, a profound and dangerous way of
   seeing – or 'enframing' – the world, in which the world furnishes resources as a 'standing
   reserve' for exploiting the world. See his essay 'The Question Concerning Technology' (in
   Heidegger, [1978] 2007).
17 See *Modes of Thought* (Horton and Finnegan, 1973), especially the essays by Horton and
   Gellner. Characteristically, the cultures of traditional societies have been associated with a
   sense that mankind is part of nature, and in 'communion with the world' (ibid.: 253) rather
   than apart from it; Gellner, though, injects some major qualifications into this view. See
   also Abram's (1997) *The Spell of the Sensuous*, which is packed with examples of this way of
   being in the world.
18 A related issue is that of the status of science-based knowledge claims. It may be that science
   generates an undue sense of certainty in a fluid world: 'science is incapable of offering

cognitive certainty. [Consequently] scientific discourse is depragmatized . . . [unable to] offer . . . definitive statements for practical purposes' (Stehr, 2001: 59).

19 Fuller (1994: 7) raises the question: is knowledge an outcome of the 'free inquiry' characteristic of universities, or is knowledge the label given to the 'social relations that have endured in those spaces we have called "universities" over the centuries'? – to which Fuller responds that constructivists 'should have no trouble in endorsing the latter of these two options'.

20 Universities are increasingly steered by the state in these directions. See, in the UK, a government policy document, *Higher Ambitions: The Future of Universities in a Knowledge Economy* (BIS, 2009), which unashamedly looks to channel an ever larger proportion of higher education resources in the direction of the 'STEM' disciplines.

21 Cf. Stephen Rowland's (2006) *The Enquiring University*, especially Chapter 6 and the idea of 'critical dialogue' across the disciplines.

22 For an example of at least hints of just such a self-examination, see the Europaeum (2009) report on *The Future of European Universities: can the European universities retain anything of their heritage – in enlightenment and a sense of a collective endeavour – that still enables them to develop their place in and for the world?*

3 The entrepreneurial university

1 On the implications for the discourse of higher education heralded by the entrepreneurial university, see Reid (1996).

2 The influence of the pharmaceutical industry on academic research is the most glaring example, on which there is an extensive literature. For a scholarly paper from within the scientific community see Lexchin *et al.* (2003), which concluded, after a meta-analysis of the literature, that 'systematic bias favours products which are made by the company funding the research'. Bok (see immediately below) presents helpful examples of this and related forms of influence by the pharmaceutical industry leading to 'secrecy' and conflicts of interest for academic scientists.

3 For much fuller and balanced examinations of issues concerning the presence of markets in higher education, see Bok (2003) and Brown (2010).

4 It is worth noting that Peters in his (2003) paper on 'education policy in the age of knowledge capitalism' goes on to offer some nuances on 'knowledge capitalism', including the idea that it accommodate multiple 'knowledge cultures' and that 'there might be a new socialist market economy based on knowledge'. See also Peter Scott, who suggests (2005: 297) that 'The knowledge economy is turning out to be a bit of a disappointment' in which 'a post-industrial utopia . . . has been replaced by a darker vision . . . [including] competitive materialism, and in which solidarity has been eroded by anomie'.

5 For a balanced portrayal and analysis of these trends, see Geiger and Sa (2008).

6 For a brilliant imaginary depiction of a university built on such principles, see Jacob (2000).

7 In such a situation, knowledge would be becoming 'commodified' as a principle by which academic knowledge and science production in particular would be 'steered' by the state. See Jacob (2009).

8 Cf. Hellstrom, T. (2007: 477–488) 'The varieties of university entrepreneurialism: thematic patterns and ambiguities in Swedish university struggles'.

9 In using the term 'archaeology' here, one has to be sensitive to the sense of 'archaeology' intended by Foucault, who sharply distinguished it from the history of ideas. Archaeology is much more alert to discontinuities and ruptures than charting continuities and sequential flows. See Foucault (1974: 135–140).

10 See Peter Scott (1997) on the possible responses of the university to the expansion of the forms of knowledge in the knowledge society.

11 'Hospitality' was a term subject to deconstruction by Derrida, who suggested that while there were in principle different forms of hospitality – namely conditional and unconditional

hospitality – 'unconditional hospitality is impossible' (Derrida, 2001: 99). This view would imply that hospitality may not be terribly hospitable. Surely Derrida himself would have experienced hospitality without conditions? Except that Derrida was Derrida; so unconditional hospitality is dependent on the nature of the visitor; which is to confirm Derrida's thesis as to the conditionality of hospitality?

12 On academic identity, see Henkel (2000), Barnett and Di Napoli (2008) and Fanghanel (2010).

13 See Read (2010) for an examination of the potential for an emergence of fluid 'business-facing' academic identities.

4 The bureaucratic university

1 According to Morris: 'The number of staff engaged in . . . technical, administrative and support activities has increased to the point where they now constitute as much as one half of the staff of a modern UK institution of higher education' (2003: 563). That pattern has continued its trajectory since that time. Actual data are available from the Higher Education Statistics Agency (HESA). Its summary statement for 2008–09 on higher education institutions in the UK, observes that 'On 1 December 2008, there were 382,760 staff employed in the HE sector, of whom 179,040 (46.8%) were academic professionals.'

2 According to Kroeber: 'a moderate estimate puts the increase of university administrators during the past forty years at seven times that of tenured faculty' (2000: 146).

3 Either of the two major university world league tables offer support to this view – those of the *Times Higher Education* magazine in the UK and of the Shanghai Jiao Tong University.

4 On surveillance, see especially Foucault (1991: 200–209) on Bentham's Panopticon: 'Hence the major effect of the Panopticon: to induce in the inmate a state of conscious and permanent visibility that assures the automatic functioning of power' (ibid.: 201). See also the reader edited by Sean Hier and Josh Greenberg (2007), especially Part One.

5 Cf. Graham and Wood (2007) on 'Digitizing Surveillance'.

6 For a nice exposé of this phenomenon, albeit in a pre-computer age, see Sinclair Goodlad's (1985) essay on 'Administrative Reductionism'. In that essay, we see vividly how bureaucratic procedures not merely stand outside *bone fide* academic activities but actually hinder and compress them.

7 See Kreber (2009) for explorations as to the ways in which disciplines exert influence on teaching and learning.

8 See the paper by Graham Lock and Chris Lorenz (2007) which observes a process of 'hyper-bureaucratization' as having taken place in UK universities, a 'logic [that] by its very nature knows no bounds or limits' such that 'the new university will simply *not work*, not even *in its own terms*' See also John Morgan's article on 'Audit Overload' in the UK's magazine, *Times Higher Education*, 4–10 March, 2010, pp. 32–36.

9 As Philips Griffiths once put it, university activities – such as teaching or learning – possess 'reciprocity' (1965). Their objects, being 'universal', may 'bounce back' from uncertain angles. See also Paul Standish's (2005) paper, 'Towards an economy of higher education', which touches the themes of this book at several points, including – in distinguishing an 'economy of exchange' from 'an economy of excess' – its observation that an economy of excess 'points to infinity' (ibid.: 60) and 'an opening up of infinite possibilities' (ibid.: 69).

10 'Such small steps as writing a memo or editing the draft of a regulation, each with seemingly small consequences, gradually foreclose alternative courses of action' (Clark, 1983: 133).

11 The key term in the leadership literature here is that of 'followership'. See Middlehurst, (1993: 9) *et seq.*

12 Cf. Michael Peters, drawing on Derrida, and coming to the view that 'the notion of the subject is something one cannot get along without' (Peters, 2009: 72).

5 Being and becoming

1 See also the volume edited (2007) by Peter Gratton and John Pentelicmon Manoussakis, not least Charles Taylor's own essay where we learn that, for Taylor, 'the term social imaginary [denotes] the specific potential for creative reinterpretation of the past in the light of some new or future project' (ibid.: 30). This book is an offering very much in that spirit.

2 On the interplay between useless and useful knowledge, see Robert Young's (1992) essay on 'The Idea of a Chrestomathic University'. '*Chrestomathia*', a collection of papers by Jeremy Bentham, is the nearest tract, Young explains, to be a philosophical foundation statement for a university, it helping to found what has since come to be known as University College London. 'Chrestomathic', . . . Bentham himself explained, [meant] "conductive to useful learning"' (Young, 1992: 105).

3 A connected term here, in Heidegger's philosophy, is that of 'comportment': 'Dasein [Being] can comport itself towards its possibilities' ([1927] 1998: 237).

4 See Watson and Maddison (2005) for an account of institutional self-study within universities as a way of enhancing organisational self-learning.

5 'Dasein [Being] hears, because it understands' (Heidegger, [1927] 1998: 206).

6 Outlining Deleuze's philosophy, Colebrook comments that Deleuze's approach 'does not just mean valuing becoming over being. It means doing away with the opposition altogether' (2002: 125).

7 Bergson notably deliberately brought together evolution and creativity in his idea of 'creative evolution'. For Bergson, there was a natural creativity in life, a 'vital' force but yet willed, that produced inevitably creativity. But this will to freedom and creativity cannot be assumed: 'Our freedom . . . creates the growing habits that will stifle it if it fails to renew itself by a constant effort: it is dogged by automatism' (1991: 127). There is surely much here to explore on another occasion.

8 Cf. Paul Wildman's (1999) essay, in favour of 'polyphonic multiversities', in which 'multiversity' is taken to be 'a multi voice process endorsing multiple (and sometimes conflicting) ways of knowing', a conception of universities that has much affinity with the proposals here.

9 In a global world, such collective identity is inevitably formally reflected in the regional and indeed global networks of universities that are emerging.

10 In relation to teaching, Macfarlane (2004: 129) specifies the virtues of respectfulness, sensitivity, pride, courage, fairness, openness, restraint and collegiality; and (ibid.: 42), in relation to research, courage, respectfulness, resoluteness, sincerity, humility and reflexivity. Of interest here is the degree of variation between these two lists of virtues, valuable as is each set. Macfarlane himself (ibid.: 43) asks and addresses the question: 'Why, it may be asked, have particular [virtues] been chosen and not others?'

11 The phrase 'Against the self-images of the age' I take from the title of one of Alisdair MacIntyre's books (1971).

6 Space and time

1 Gibbs (2004; 2009) is an exception to this pattern.

2 On 'commodification', see especially the work of Naidoo, e.g. Naidoo (2003).

3 Cf. Luce Irigaray (1999) on *The Forgetting of Air in Martin Heidegger*.

4 For a fascinating account of the way in which academic space has ebbed and flowed over a thousand years – as between being socially exclusive and socially local – an account that much parallels the approach being taken here (not least in its drawing on Heidegger), see Marks (2005).

5 Cf. Rowan Williams in giving an exposition of Aquinas:

[I]t is a matter of the natural *intellectus* having the function of responding to what is there, confronting it; so that it reaches its highest point when it responds to what is most totally, unequivocally, consistently *there*. God. Yet ... that ... understanding can only receive, it reaches its destiny by coming to stillness and silence.

(2004b: 131)

6 See Maggi Savin-Baden's (2008) *Learning Spaces* for a brilliant analysis of its subject matter. There is, of course, a related and larger issue captured in Oakeshott's famous depiction of 'the characteristic gift of a university' as 'the gift of the interval' (1989: 101). This phrase poses the question: in what ways can the university today offer a space separate from society, even as it is immersed within it?

7 On 'being an academic', see Fanghanel (2010).

8 Such a widening of the ontological space of academic life is but an inevitable consequence of what Peter Scott has called 'mission stretch' (Scott, 2009: 75).

9 In the UK, so-called 'transparency exercises' are exquisitely misnamed for part of their whole demeanour is to render *in*visible work that is accomplished outside the time of work. In apportioning work under categories of research and teaching, no account is taken of the sheer number of hours expended on those activities (or any other activity) and so, in turn, the place of the activity is rendered irrelevant and work that has to be undertaken 'at home', far from being transparent, becomes invisible.

10 'The house shelters day-dreaming' (Bachelard, 1994: 6). Perhaps, though, it is the home that shelters day-dreaming and that the university has become more like a house and less like a home constitutes a particular difficulty. Dreaming is certainly not encouraged in the modern university.

11 Although it has not been possible in this inquiry to engage with it, the category of hope has never been far away. On utopian hope, see Rorty (1999). 'We [pragmatists] see both intellectual and moral progress not as a matter of getting closer to the True or the Good or the Right, but as an increase in imaginative power' (ibid.: 87). The present argument is very much in the spirit of that sentiment.

12 In this context, I take the phrase 'the public sphere' from Habermas (1989). (I might just mention that perhaps rather strangely, so far as I can see, Habermas' analysis does not extend to a consideration of the part that the academy might play in advancing the public sphere, whereas – for example – in their different ways, both MacIntyre and Leavis have done just this.)

7 Culture and anarchy

1 Ortega y Gasset was a major exception to this rule: talking of 'the mission of the university', he observed that 'Culture is the vital system of ideas of a period' (1946: 44), and its transmission formed one of the three functions of the university (alongside science and a preparation for the professions).

2 For a positive and comprehensive account of anarchism in the context of education, and one with which the analysis here is, I think, in sympathy, see Judith Suissa (2006).

3 See Chapter 1 (especially pp. 1–6) on 'Knowledge and Nation' in Peter Scott's (1990) book of that title. In a way, *this* book bears witness to Scott's suggestion (ibid.: 4) that 'the suspicion remains that the complicated fabric of modern knowledge rests ultimately on a transcendent reinsurance or, better still, reassurance, which we are reluctant to acknowledge'.

4 As suggested, it may be conjectured that except for systems in heavily centrally regulated countries such as China, any central examination of universities' corporate plans are largely cursory. What seems to be happening is that institutional self-regulation is standing in for central control.

5 On *Bildung*, see especially the collection edited by Løvlie, Mortenson and Nordenbo (2003) but see also Rorty (1980: 359–360), although Rorty prefers the term 'edification' since *Bildung* 'sounds a bit too foreign'; Gadamer (1985: 10–19) for whom '*Bildung* is intimately

associated with the idea of culture'; Rothblatt and Wittrock (1993), especially the chapter by Sven-Eric Liedman; and Readings (1996) who sees *Bildung* – as adumbrated by the German idealists – as an educational process for securing a cultural unity within the nation-state.

6 Kamenou (2008) has recently advanced the thesis that culture in the university might be understood as 'cultures-in-action'.

7 See Cobban (1999: 174–177) where different forms of disputations are identified, one of which was the *'disputatio de quolibet* or *quodlibet* (the disputation on anything). Such disputations [enabled debate] of a contentious and radical nature [and] . . . [were] a seedbed for new and challenging ideas' (ibid.: 175).

8 Malitza makes a helpful distinction between 'culture' and 'civilization', between particularity and universality, a distinction that – in the context of higher education – 'does not mean opposition' (1997: 61).

9 After all, 'the principle of reason' finds difficulty in reasoning its own validity for it is more a principle of being (Heidegger, 1991).

10 'Beyond Culture' was the title of a (1967) book by the American literary critic, Lionel Trilling. As I understand it, the book – a collection of essays – amounts to a exploration of the challenge of an 'adversary' culture that seeks to go 'beyond culture' for ultimately, if it is successful, through that endeavour, a class will form and its views will become ritualised and ideologically frozen. It is in the context of such a stance that Trilling's examination in that book of 'The Two Cultures' debate is worked out.

11 Related here is the large debate on culture, cultural citizenship, identity, and the place of the academy, all of which issued in the so-called 'culture wars' and ascriptions of 'political correctness'. See, for example, Lipset (1993), Readings (1996: Chapter 7, esp. pp. 112–116), Delanty (2001: 144–147, 155–158), and Lea (2009).

8 Authenticity and responsibility

1 An exception here is David Watson (a former UK vice-chancellor) who not only considers that 'universities are expected to behave better than other large organisations' but is also prepared explicitly to set out examples of the 'responsibilities' that bear on universities. See his (2007a) paper, 'Does Higher Education Need a Hippocratic Oath?' and his (2008) QAA Briefing Paper on *Who Owns the University?*

2 On the networked university, see especially the chapters by Nicolas Standaert and Susan Robertson in the UCSIA (2009) volume.

3 'Found already in Aristotle, the tag "entities should not be multiplied beyond necessity" became associated with William Ockam (although he never states that version)' (Audi, 1999: 629).

4 For more sympathetic accounts of and commentaries on Derrida than it might be felt that I am offering here, see Wortham (1999), who dwells precisely on the metaphors Derrida employs, and Peters and Biesta (2009). Both of these works also examine the Derridian theme of a 'university without conditions' which 'does not exist, but . . . presupposes a place of critical resistance, a form of dissidence. This is its strength but also its vulnerability' (Peters, 2009: 117). I'd only comment here that this idea, as it is played out, is much linked to the role of the humanities (which constitute a small part of the university today) and is unduly lacking in content and so offers a rather thin idea of responsibility. I think that we have to try to say something that has more substance but yet does not bind the university unduly.

5 Philosophers have long been fascinated by the relationships between philosophy and poetry: after all, are not both activities efforts to conjure imaginative insights into the world, if not actually to picture new worlds? Are not both activities, too, ways of drawing attention to the contingency of language? Richard Rorty was clear that he saw himself, as a philosopher, 'as auxiliary to the poet rather than to the physicist' (1989: 8). See Chapter 1 in Carl Rapp (1998) for a discussion of these matters.

6 David Watson (2008: 3) points to the collective responsibilities among universities in the UK in upholding universities' 'controlled reputational range' but this idea could surely be extended to universities across the world. Increasingly, in a global age, universities recognise themselves to be members of a world-wide community of universities to which they each bear responsibilities.

7 A closely related issue – and one that is implicit in this book from its outset – is that of the matter of responsibility in an age of complexity. For a considered exploration of this issue and for the possibility of 'an educational vision of responsibility', see Fenwick (2009).

8 'Public goods in higher education are goods that (1) have a significant element of non-rivalry and/or non-excludability, and (2) are goods that are made broadly available across populations. . . . Goods without attributes (1) and (2) are private goods.' Marginson's own chapter, 'The new higher education landscape: Public and private goods, in global/national/local settings' in his edited volume (2007: 34).

9 There is a growing literature on the idea of the public intellectual, recent examples of which are the collections edited by Small (2002) and Cummings (2005).

9 The liquid university

1 For example, Leavis' *Education and the University* (1979: 34): 'the English [university] School . . . trains [as] no other discipline can . . . a delicate integrity of intelligence'.

2 Although the phrase 'the centre cannot hold' was probably created by Yeats, for his poem 'The Second Coming', it has been used on various occasions since and notably, for our purposes here, by Burton Clark in his essay on 'The problem of complexity in modern higher education' (1993: 268), and by Nicholas Maxwell in his essay on wisdom (2008: 1).

3 Rowan Williams in his *Silence and Honey Cakes* (2004a: 69) speaks of the persons of the desert treasuring silence not as a means of cutting themselves off from relationship but of 'restoring a language . . . that is as free as it can be from the little games of control and evasion . . . Gradually – and by the gift of the Spirit – a new language will emerge [for the community].' So one can both flee from the world and simultaneously one can flee *into* the world. Cf. 'For consciousness to imagine, it must be able to escape from the world by its very nature, it must be able to stand back from the world by its own efforts' (Sartre, [1940] 2004a: 184).

4 I am referring here, in the text, to the development of so-called 'corporate universities', namely those 'institutions created for developing and educating employees and the company's constituents in order to meet the company's purposes' (Jarvis, 2001: 111) Jarvis notes (ibid.: 116) that the name 'university' 'is not used by all [such] corporate training institutions': my point here is that the term 'university' *is* used by many such institutions, even though they 'are systems of teaching and learning rather than universities in the traditional sense' (ibid.: 111), many – though not all – being open only to employees of the host company (ibid) and 'not all are actually involved in . . . sophisticated academic programmes' (ibid.: 116).

5 The inherent value basis of universities is a feature remarked upon more than once in his writings by David Watson, e.g., in his (2007a) paper in which he proposes a set of ten commandments for universities so as to approach a 'hippocratic oath'.

6 Cf. Weber: 'the university, perhaps today more than ever, has to be in more places than one. . . . it confirms the existing order by reproducing exploitable knowledge. . . . And yet, . . . it must also strive to be open to the unknowable' (1999: 163–164).

7 This very fluidity and complexity is, for Bauman, a feature of the university's strength in a turbulent age:

> [I]t is precisely the plurality and multi-vocality of the present-day collection of the gatherings 'for the sake of the pursuit of higher learning . . . that offer the universities, old and new and altogether, the chance of emerging successfully from the present challenge.
>
> (Bauman, 1997: 25)

10 The therapeutic university

1 'Utopias have a habit of turning into dystopias', observes Sheldon Rothblatt in his lecture on The *University as Utopia* (2003: 32). Rothblatt's essay contains a classification of utopias both in general *and* in relation to the university, coining such neologisms as 'Ecotopia' (the university as a perfect place), 'Edutopia' (the completely open university) and 'Eutopia' (the university of dreams – and 'yet [it] moves' (ibid.: 32)).

2 In some UK universities, the majority of their students on admission are 'mature', that is, they are over 21 years of age.

3 For a review of the idea of therapy in the context of education that draws out both positive and antipathetic views, see Mintz (2009).

4 Williams introduces the idea of 'thick concept' in order to draw attention to the way in which facts and values are often intertwined in language. For Williams, thick concepts are 'thick ethical concepts' (2008: 200). In the rest of this book, I draw on the idea of 'thick concept' on more than one occasion, perhaps doing some injury to the idea as intended by Williams. It seems to me to be a highly fruitful idea that can be extended to indicate ways in which language performs several functions all at once.

5 I draw the set of points in this paragraph – as to the limitations of conceptual analysis – especially from the work of Ernest Gellner, a thesis advanced in several places in his writings, as for example in *Thought and Change* (1969: 184): 'The terrible thing about Wittgenstein was the supposition that the fact a concept was part of "a form of life" . . . settles or solves anything.' Durkheim, on the other hand, (who was 'immeasurably superior to Wittgenstein'), 'was not for one moment tempted to think that the question concerning the [social] origin and standing of our concepts in any way terminated the discussion. This is the beginning, not the end.'

6 This layered view of the world, and of our accounts in the world, has a strong affinity both with Sir Karl Popper's (1975) 'three world thesis' and with the philosophy of critical realism as expounded by Roy Bhaskar, with its conception of 'the domains of the real, the actual and the empirical' (Bhaskar, [1975] 2008: 13). (I am conscious that Bhaskar may feel uneasy in being placed in the company of Karl Popper, of whose philosophy of science he has been highly critical.) F. R. Leavis, too, developed his own sense of a three-layered view of the world, our private responses and our collaborative understandings in it (1969: 48).

7 'Disjuncture makes learning possible' (Jarvis, 1992: 83). See also the (1999) paper by Paul Standish on 'Centre Without Substance' which – in drawing on Levinas and arguing for infinity rather than totality in orienting higher education – also points up the value of disturbance within a student's learning: 'A vibration between divergent but compelling forms of thought can excite agitation in the learner. Ruptures in patterns of thought can make a whole framework tremble.'

8 See the quotations on page 35 of my *A Will to Learn* (Barnett, 2007).

9 On troublesomeness, see Meyer and Land (2005), who show that some degree of troublesomeness is conducive to the student's development.

10 On dispositions and qualities, see Chapter 8 of *A Will to Learn*.

11 Marketisation in higher education often receives a bad press but it can have its benefits. See Maringe and Gibbs (2009) for a balanced analysis.

12 'Wellbeing', I observe, is a theme running through this book. It could be said that it is becoming an ideology in-itself, with both positive and pernicious overtones. For a positive account of wellbeing and higher education, see the NEF report (2008).

11 The authentic university

1 In fact, we noted that a distinction had been drawn by Cooper (2002) between being 'disencumbered' (free from constraint) and 'discumbenced' (not leaning on or not relying on), the latter being the idea on which Cooper places particular weight.

2 Describing Latin as a 'universal language' is, of course, a honorific title. It was universal in

that it was the language of all of the medieval universities across Europe, Latin being the language of their progenitor, the Catholic Church.

3   In European languages, words equivalent to 'university' include 'universidad', 'universität', 'université', 'università' and 'universitet'. In short, there is a kind of universality attaching to the term itself.

4   Judith Butler suggests that there might be 'competing universalities' and that, in that situation, the challenge 'may be, rather, one of establishing practices of translation among competing notions of universality' (2000: 167). Whether or not my idea of 'universal space' can be seen as a universality that encompasses substantive competing universalities, I am not sure.

5   See Roy Bhaskar (2002a: 8) who argues that 'the domain of the real is greater, more encompassing than the field of the actual, which describes the pattern of events; and that in turn is greater than the field of the empirical, which describes the pattern of events that we actually apprehend.' Authenticity, it seems to me, though points to levels of 'reality' above and beyond even these levels, namely to levels of possibility and the imagination. I hope to be able to develop this set of ideas in a later work.

6   The volume edited by Ruth Finnegan (2005) is full of examples in which the academy enlists the support of large numbers of individuals among the public to assist in its research activities and who actually conduct much of the empirical fieldwork (for example, in observing bird migration patterns).

7   In the UK, among other universities, the University of Surrey is developing awards that recognise the learning achieved by students in their various extra-course activities, which might be achieved either on or off-campus. Through this work is emerging the concept of 'life-wide learning' in which the student's university studies take their place simply as one learning site among many that the student may inhabit.

12 The ecological university

1   For a rare discussion and exposition of such views, see Diez-Hochleitner (1997):

> The university . . . remains the institution that can contribute most, from a global perspective, to preserving and developing the quality of life, within the limits of sustainable human development and of conserving and furthering the material and spiritual future of humanity.

2   See pp. 313–325 of Heidegger's ([1927] 1998) *Being and Time*. For instance, 'potentiality [for Being] is familiar to us as the 'voice of conscience' (ibid.: 313). 'it is revealed as a call' (ibid.: 314). 'Conscience manifests itself as the call of *care*' (ibid.: 322 – Heidegger's emphasis).

3   Maxwell's most significant early statement and exposition was that of *From Knowledge to Wisdom* (1984).

4   'I consider, then, that I am chargeable with no paradox, when I speak of a Knowledge which is its own end, . . . when I educate for it, and make it the scope of a University' (Newman, 1976: 103).

5   For a comprehensive and incisive indictment of the dominant culture of reason, see Val Plumwood's (2002) book, *Environmental Culture: The Ecological Crisis of Reason*.

6   David Watson's book (*Managing Civic and Community Engagement*) is important for the argument here since it contains several case studies of universities around the world which are vigorously pursuing such a strategy of public engagement. It is worthwhile noting, too, that David Watson has been actively involved with the Talloires network – see note 8 below – to which reference is made in *Managing Civic and Community Engagement* (as well as the joint book (2010)).

7   The practice of providing opportunities for international exchanges is often proposed and even put into practice (see Davies *et al.*, 2005) but I suggest that my proposal here is more

effective in that it involves a whole class, becomes a structured part of the curriculum and is more environmentally sustainable.

8 The ten-point Talloires Declaration can be accessed at www.ulsf.org/programs_talloires. html. See also Watson, Stroud and Hollister (2010), for whom the Talloires network of universities is an example of universities engaging with their social purposes and with the communities and societies in which they are located.

9 For parallel cautionary comments on 'over-extending the civic role' of the university, see Waghid (2008).

10 I should mention that as I was finishing this book, I came across *After the Globe, Before the World* by R. B. J. Walker (2010) which while located in another field – that of international relations – nevertheless provides some cautions against my argument here, not least in my implying perhaps 'some future politics of the world' (ibid.: 3), an implication that is 'impossible to sustain' (ibid.: 4). At the very least, the metaphors and ideas of travel, emancipation, and the global need to be interrogated more than I have been able to do here.

11 Our imaginations are not opposed to the real (world) but provide ways of realising the real world: 'the Real is on the side of Fantasy' (Žižek, 2001: 67).

Coda

1 Cf. McLaughlin, 'The Educative Importance of Ethos'. Although 'the concept of "ethos" is notoriously difficult to analyse' (2005: 308) and 'much greater reflection is needed on the kinds of educational achievement with which ethos is concerned' (ibid.: 319), nevertheless there are aspects of ethos which can be identified, namely that 'ethos frequently exerts educative influence in relation to matters which cannot be explicitly articulated', and it 'is . . . a necessary counterpart to more explicit and systematic forms of teaching and learning' (ibid.: 319–320).

2 According to Derrida: 'spirit is not a great word of Heidegger's. It is not his theme. It would seem that he was able, precisely, to avoid it' (1991: 2).

3 'Spirit is the power and potentiality of ideas' (Jaspers, [1959] 1965: 44).

4 Admittedly, the matter of morale is a far from straightforward matter. David Watson (2009) in *The Question of Morale*, observes that morale works at different levels in a university, depending on the frame of reference. Watson quotes Adrian Furnham: 'Morale is both the property of individuals and groups.' An issue that this formulation raises is the relationship between these two levels of morale. Might it be that a high individual morale is necessary but not sufficient for a high group morale but that a high group morale is not necessary for a high individual morale? It seems to me, though, a nice issue as to whether a high group morale could be sufficient for a high individual morale. If so, from the point of view of managing a university, then the group morale surely trumps the individual morale.

5 For a brilliant exposition, and critique of Leavis' thought in relation to the university, see Cranfield (2006).

6 Perhaps the best exposé and examination of academic life remains that of Burton Clark's (1987) *The Academic Life: Small Worlds, Different Worlds*. If it was ever possible for such a large undertaking to be replicated, perhaps a successor might tackle directly the matter of academic *life* itself: just how is 'life' to be understood in academia in the twenty-first century (and even beyond)? For an appreciation of *The Academic Life: Small Worlds, Different Worlds*, see Locke (2010). More recently, see also Enders and de Weert (2009), which contains several important essays, including the concluding chapter by Enders and de Weert on the emergence of a 'T-shaped Profession' which 'encapsulates both depth and disciplinary knowledge and broader transdisciplinary knowledge and skills' (ibid.: 262). The question remains, though: what kind of *life* is this T-shaped academic living?

7 Cf. Luce Irigaray (1999) *The Forgetting of Air in Martin Heidegger*, for example, 'Without air, is place liveable for a mortal?' (ibid.: 20).

8 Attempts to 'recover' Newman as a guide to the university in the contemporary era (cf. Pelikan, 1992; Ker, 1999; Graham, 2002) seem to me, therefore, brave but ultimately misguided, important as Newman is in the history of the idea of the university. We need now a fundamentally different way of imagining the university that is sensitive to the time/space complexities and *possibilities* of the emerging university.

9 I want to make it plain that in drawing, in this book, on such terms as 'metaphysics', 'spirit', 'faith' and 'dialogue', I am not wanting to smuggle in a religious, still less a Christian idea of the university, although there are certainly these and other affinities between my position here and that particular idea of the university (on which topic, see *The Idea of a Christian University*, edited by Astley *et al.* (2004)).

10 This passage was drafted in late December 2009 just before the global financial crisis of 2008–09 began to have its effect on UK universities, as the government began in 2010 to reduce its funding for higher education. But these sentences still seem to me (in early 2010) to be accurate. Universities and higher education are as much in demand as ever – in some ways more – and they remain in good health. In any event, it is not at all clear that many other governments across the world are going to be as severe towards higher education: the UK situation amounts, it may be, to a little local difficulty.

Bibliography

Abram, D. (1997) *The Spell of the Sensuous: Perception and Language in a More-Than-Human-World*. New York: Vintage.

Adorno, T. (1973|2003) *The Jargon of Authenticity*. London: Routledge.

Amin, A. and O'Neill, M. (eds) (2009) *Thinking about Almost Everything: New Ideas to Light up Minds*. London: Profile.

Arendt, H. (1958) *The Human Condition*. Chicago: University of Chicago Press.

Arimoto, A., Huang, F. and Yokoyama, K. (eds) (2005) *Globalization and Higher Education*. Hiroshima: RIHE, Hiroshima University.

Arnold, M. (1969) *Culture and Anarchy*, ed. J. Dover Wilson. Cambridge: Cambridge University Press.

Arthur, J. with Bohlin, K. E. (eds) (2008) *Citizenship and Higher Education: The Role of Universities in Communities and Society*. London: Routledge.

Astley, J., Francis, L., Sullivan, J. and Walker, A. (eds) (2004) *The Idea of a Christian University: Essays on Theology and Higher Education*. Bletchley: Paternoster.

Audi, R. (ed.) (1999) *The Cambridge Dictionary of Philosophy*. Cambridge: Cambridge University Press.

Austin, J. R. (1994) 'Rationality and Realism, What Is at Stake?'in J. R. Cole, E. G. Barber and S. R. Graubard (eds), *The Research University in a Time of Discontent*. Baltimore, MD: Johns Hopkins University Press.

Bachelard, G. (1994) *The Poetics of Space*. Boston: Beacon.

Bachelard, G. (2000) *The Dialectic of Duration*. Manchester: Clinamen.

Bahti, T. (1992) 'The Injured University', in R. Rand (ed.), *Logomachia: The Conflict of the Faculties*. Lincoln, NB: University of Nebraska Press.

Barnett, R. (2000) *Realising the University in an Age of Supercomplexity*. Buckingham: Open University Press.

Barnett, R. (2003) *Beyond All Reason: Living with Ideology in the University*. Maidenhead: McGraw-Hill/Open University Press.

Barnett, R. (2005) 'Convergence in Higher Education: The Strange Case of Entrepreneurialism', *Higher Education Management and Policy*. Special issue on Entrepreneurialism, 17(3): 51–64.

Barnett, R. (2007) *A Will to Learn: Being a Student in an Age of Uncertainty*. Maidenhead: McGraw-Hill/Open University Press.

Barnett, R. and Di Napoli, R. (eds) (2008) *Changing Identities in Higher Education: Voicing Perspectives*. London: Routledge.

Barnett, R. and Phipps, A. (2005) 'Academic Travel: Modes and Directions', *Review of Education, Pedagogy, Cultural Studies*, 27(1): 3–16.

Bauman, Z. (1997) 'Universities: Old, New and Different', in A. Smith and F. Webster (eds),

The Postmodern University? Contested Visions of Higher Education in Society. Buckingham: Open University Press.

Bauman, Z. (2000) *Liquid Modernity*. Cambridge: Polity.

Bayne, S. (2010) 'Academetron, Automaton, Phantom: Uncanny Digital Technologies', *London Review of Education* (in press).

Becher, T. (1989) *Academic Tribes and Territories*. Buckingham: Open University Press.

Beck, U. ([1986]1992) *Risk Society: Towards a New Modernity*. London: Sage.

Bennett, O. (2001) *Cultural Pessimism: Narratives of Decline in the Postmodern World*. Edinburgh: University of Edinburgh Press.

Bergendahl, G. (ed.) (1984) *Knowledge Policies and the Traditions of Higher Education*. Stockholm: Almquist and Wiksell.

Bergson, H. (1991) *Matter and Memory*. New York: Zone.

Bergson, H. (1998) *Creative Evolution*. Mineola, NY: Dover.

Bernstein, B. (1996) *Pedagogy, Symbolic Control and Identity: Theory, Research, Critique*. London: Routledge.

Bernstein, R. J. (1991) *The New Constellation: The Ethical-Political Horizons of Modernity/Postmodernity*. Cambridge: Polity.

Bhaskar, R. ([1975]2008) *A Realist Theory of Science*. London: Verso.

Bhaskar, R. (2002a) *From Science to Emancipation: Journeys towards Meta-Reality – a Philosophy for the Present*. New Delhi: Sage.

Bhaskar, R. (2002b) *Reflections on Meta-Reality: A Philosophy for the Present*. London: Sage.

Bloom, A. (1987) *The Closing of the American Mind: How Higher Education has Failed Democracy and Impoverished the Souls of Today's Students*. London: Penguin.

Bok, D. (2003) *Universities in the Marketplace: The Commercialization of Higher Education*. Princeton, NJ: Princeton University Press.

Bourdieu, P. (1990a) *Homo Academicus*. Cambridge: Polity.

Bourdieu, P. (1990b) *In Other Words*. Cambridge: Polity.

Bourdieu, P. (2000) *Pascalian Meditations*. Cambridge: Polity.

Brennan, J. (2010) 'Burton Clark's The Higher Education System: Academic Organisation in Cross National Perspective', *London Review of Education*, 8(3) *in press*.

Brown, R. (2010) *Higher Education and the Market*. New York: Routledge.

Brown, S. (1988) 'The Intellectual Context of Later Medieval Philosophy: Universities, Aristotle, Arts, Theology', in J. Marenbon (ed.), *Medieval Philosophy*. London: Routledge.

Buber, M. ([1965]2002) *The Way of Man*. London: Routledge.

Bulmer, M. and Ocloo, J. (2009) 'Looking Forward: the Researcher's Perspective', in J. Strain, R. Barnett and P. Jarvis (eds), *Universities, Ethics and Professions: Debate and Scrutiny*. New York: Routledge.

Butler, J. (2000) 'Competing Universalities', in J. Butler, E. Laclau and S. Žižek (eds), *Contingency, Hegemony and Universality*. London: Verso.

Cannella, A. A. and Paetzold, R. L. (1994) 'Pfeffer's Barriers to the Advance of Organizational Science: A Rejoinder', *The Academy of Management Review*, 19(2): 331–341.

Castells, M. (1997) *The Rise of the Network Society*, Vol. 1. Malden, MA: Blackwell.

Chambers, T. (2005) 'The Special Role of Higher Education in Society: As a Public Good for the Public Good', in A. J. Kezar, T. C. Chambers, and J. Burkhardt (eds), *Higher Education for the Public Good: Emerging Voices from a National Movement*. San Francisco: Jossey-Bass.

Clark, B. R. (1983) *The Higher Education System: Academic Organization in Cross-National Perspective*. Berkeley, CA: University of California.

Clark, B. R. (1987) *The Academic Life: Small Worlds, Different Worlds*. Princeton, NJ: Carnegie.

Clark, B. R. (1993) 'The Problem of Complexity in Modern Higher Education', in S. Rothblatt and B. Wittrock (eds), *The European and American University Since 1800*. Cambridge: Cambridge University Press.

Clark, B. R. (1998) *Creating Entrepreneurial Universities: Organizational Pathways of Transformation*. Oxford: Pergamon/IAU.

Clark, B. R. (2004) *Sustaining Change in Universities: Continuities in Case Studies and Concepts*. Maidenhead: McGraw-Hill/Open University Press.

Cobban, A. (1999) *English University Life in the Middle Ages*. London: UCL/Routledge.

Cole, J. R., Barber, E. G., and Graubard, S. R. (eds) (1994) *The Research University in a Time of Discontent*. Baltimore, MD: Johns Hopkins University Press.

Colebrook, C. (2002) *Gilles Deleuze*. London: Routledge.

Coleman, J. S. (1986) 'The Developmental University', *Minerva*, 24(4): 476–494.

Cooper, D. E. (2002) *The Measure of Things: Humanism, Humility, and Mystery*. Oxford: Clarendon.

Cranfield, S. (2006) 'Re-conceiving Creativity: F. R. Leavis and Higher Education', PhD thesis, Institute of Education, London.

Cummings, D. (ed.) (2005) *The Changing Role of the Public Intellectual*. London: Routledge.

Currie, J. and Newson, J. (eds) (1998) *Universities and Globalization: Critical Perspectives*. London: Sage.

Daniel, J. S. (1998) *Mega-Universities and Knowledge Media: Technology Strategies for Higher Education*. London: Kogan Page.

Davies, I., Evans, M., Cunningham, P., Frediksson, G., Pike, G., Rathenow, H.-F., Sears, A., Tesch, F. and Whitty, P. (2005) *Developing Citizenship through International Exchanges* in J. Arthur with K. E. Bohlin (eds) (2008) *Citizenship and Higher Education: The Role of Universities in Communities and Society*. London: Routledge.

Dawkins, R. (2007) *The God Delusion*. London: Transworld/Black Swan.

Delanty, G. (2001) *Challenging Knowledge: The University in the Knowledge Society*. Maidenhead: McGraw-Hill/Open University Press.

Deleuze, G. ([1968]2001) *Difference and Repetition*. London: Continuum.

Deleuze, G. and Guattari, F. (2004) *A Thousand Plateaus*. London: Continuum.

Derrida, J. ([1987]1991) *Of Spirit: Heidegger and the Question*. Chicago: University of Chicago Press.

Derrida, J. (2001) *Deconstruction Engaged: The Sydney Seminars*. Sydney: Power.

Derrida, J. (2004) *Eyes of the University: Right to Philosophy 2*. Stanford, CA: Stanford University Press.

Dickman, H. (ed.) (1993) *The Imperilled Academy*. New Brunswick, NJ: Transaction.

Diez-Hochleitner, R. (1997) 'The Future of Universities', *Higher Education in Europe*, N (1): 51–57.

Duke, C. (1992) *The Learning University: Towards a New Paradigm?* Buckingham: Open University Press.

Dunbabin, J. (1999) 'Universities c.1150–1350', in D. Smith and A. K. Langslow (eds), *The Idea of a University*. London: Jessica Kingsley.

Dyson, F. (2006) *The Scientist as Rebel*. New York: New York Review of Books.

Ecclestone, K. and Hayes, D. (2009) *The Dangerous Rise of Therapeutic Education*. London: Routledge.

Elliott, R. K. (1975) 'Education and Human Being', in S. C. Brown (ed.) *Philosophers Discuss Education*. London: Macmillan.

Enders, J. and De Weert, E. (eds) (2009) *The Changing Face of Academic Life: Analytical and Comparative Perspectives*. Basingstoke: Palgrave Macmillan.

Eraut, M. (1994) *Developing Professional Knowledge and Competence*. London: Falmer.

Etzkowitz, H. and Leydesdorff, L. (2000) 'The Dynamics of Innovation: From National

Systems and Mode 2'to a Triple Helix of University-Industry-Government Relations', *Research Policy*, 29: 109–123.

Fanghanel, J. (2010) *Being an Academic*. London: Routledge.

Fenwick, T. (2009) 'Responsibility, Complexity Science and Education: Dilemmas and Uncertain Responses', *Studies in Philosophy and Education*, 28(2): 101–118.

Feyerabend, P. (1970|1977) 'Consolations for the Specialist', in I. Lakatos and A. Musgrave (eds), *Criticism and the Growth of Knowledge*. Cambridge: Cambridge University Press.

Feyerabend, P. (1978) *Against Method*. London: Verso.

Feyerabend, P. (1978|1982) *Science in a Free Society*. London: Verso.

Feyerabend, P. (1995) *Killing Time: The Autobiography of Paul Feyerabend*. Chicago: University of Chicago Press.

Feyerabend, P. (1999) *Conquest of Abundance: A Tale of Abstraction Versus the Richness of Being*. Chicago: University of Chicago Press.

Filippakou, O. (2009) 'The Legitimation of Quality in Higher Education', PhD dissertation. Institute of Education, London.

Finnegan, R. (ed.) (2005) *Participating in the Knowledge Society: Researchers Beyond the University Walls*. Basingstoke: Palgrave.

Foucault, M. (1974) *The Archaeology of Knowledge*. London: Tavistock.

Foucault, M. (1975|1991) *Discipline and Punish: The Birth of the Prison*. London: Penguin.

Franklin, J. (ed.) (1998) *The Politics of Risk Society*. Cambridge: Polity/IPPR.

Fuller, S. (1994) 'Rethinking the University from a Social Constructivist Standpoint', *Science Studies*, 7(1): 4–16.

Fuller, S. (1997) *Science*. Buckingham: Open University Press.

Fuller, S. (2000) *The Governance of Science*. Buckingham: Open University Press.

Gadamer, H-G. (1965|1985) *Truth and Method*. London: Sheed &Ward.

Geiger, R. (1993) 'Research, Graduate Education, and the Ecology of American Universities: An Interpretative History', in S. Rothblatt and B. Wittrock (eds), *The European and American University Since 1800*. Cambridge: Cambridge University Press.

Geiger, R. and Sa, C. (2008) *Tapping the Riches of Science: Universities and the Promise of Economic Growth*. Cambridge, MA: Harvard University Press.

Gellner, E (1969) *Thought and Change*. London: Weidenfeld &Nicolson.

Gellner, E. (1970) 'Concepts and Society', in B. R. Wilson (ed.), *Rationality*. Oxford: Blackwell.

Gellner, E. (1974) *Legitimation of Belief*. Cambridge: Cambridge University Press.

Gellner, E. (1988) *Plough, Sword and Book: The Structure of Human History*. London: Paladin.

Gellner, E. (1992) *Reason and Culture: New Perspectives on the Past*. Oxford: Blackwell.

Gellner, E. (1998) *Language and Solitude: Wittgenstein, Malinowski and the Habsburg Dilemma*. Cambridge: Cambridge University Press.

Gibbons, M., Limoges, C., Nowotny, H., Schwartzman, S., Scott, P. and Trow, M. (1994) *The New Production of Knowledge: The Dynamics of Science and Research in Contemporary Societies*. London: Sage.

Gibbs, P. T. (2004) *Trusting in the University: The Contribution of Temporality and Trust to a Praxis of Higher Learning*. Dordrecht: Kluwer.

Gibbs, P. T. (2009) 'Adopting Consumer Time: Potential Issues for Higher Education', *London Review of Education*, 7(2): 113–124.

Giddens, A. (2002) *Runaway World: How Globalisation is Reshaping Our Lives*. London: Profile.

Goodlad, S. (1976) *Conflict and Consensus in Higher Education*. London: Heinemann.

Goodlad, S. (1985) 'The Sociology of Reductionism: Administrative Reductionism', in A. Peacock (ed.), *Reductionism in Academic Disciplines*. Guildford: SRHE and NFER-Nelson.

Goodwin, B. (ed.) (2001) *The Philosophy of Utopia*. Ilford: Frank Cass.

Gouldner, A. W. (1979) *The Future of Intellectuals and the Rise of the New Class.* London: Macmillan.

Graham, G. (2002) *Universities: The Recovery of an Idea.* Thorverton: Imprint Press.

Graham, S. and Wood, D. (2007) 'Digitizing Surveillance: Categorization, Space, Inequality', in S. P. Hier and J. Greenberg (eds), *The Surveillance Studies Reader.* Maidenhead: McGraw-Hill/Open University Press.

Gratton, P. and Panteleimon Manoussakis, J. (eds) (2007) *Traversing the Imaginary: Richard Kearney and the Postmodern Challenge.* Evanston, IL.: Northwestern University.

Gray, J. (1995|2007) *Enlightenment's Wake.* London: Routledge.

Guattari, F. (2005) *The Three Ecologies.* London: Continuum.

Guignon, C. (2004) *On Being Authentic: Thinking in Action.* London: Routledge.

Habermas, J. (1968|1978) *Knowledge and Human Interests.* London: Heinemann.

Habermas, J. (1972) *Toward the Rational Society.* London: Heinemann.

Habermas, J. (1987) 'The Idea of the University: Learning Processes', *New German Critique*, 41, Spring–Summer: 3–22.

Habermas, J. (1981/1989) *The Theory of Communicative Reason*, vols 1 and 2. Cambridge: Polity.

Habermas, J. (1989|2005) *The Structural Transformation of the Structural Sphere.* Cambridge: Polity.

Habermas, J. (1995) *Postmetaphysical Thinking.* Cambridge: Polity.

Halpin, D. (2003) *Hope and Education: The Role of the Utopian Imagination.* London: Routledge.

Halsey, A. H. (1992) *Decline of Donnish Dominion: The British Academic Profession in the Twentieth Century.* Oxford: Clarendon.

Hassan, R. (2003) *The Chronoscopic Society: Globalization, Time and Knowledge in the Network Economy.* New York: Peter Lang.

Hauerwas, S. (2007) *The State of the University: Academic Knowledges and the Knowledge of God.* Malden, MA: Blackwell.

Hegel, G. W. F. (1999) *The Hegel Reader*, ed. S. Houlgate. Oxford: Blackwell.

Heidegger, M. (1927|1998) *Being and Time.* Oxford: Blackwell.

Heidegger, M. (1950|2002) *Off the Beaten Track.* Cambridge: Cambridge University Press.

Heidegger, M. (1978|2007) *Basic Writings.* London: Routledge.

Heidegger, M. (1991) *The Principle of Reason.* Bloomington, IN: Indiana University.

Hellstrom, T. (2007) 'The Varieties of University Entrepreneurialism: Thematic Patterns and Ambiguities in Swedish University Struggles', *Policy Futures in Education*, 5(4): 478–488.

Henkel, M. (2000) *Academic Identities and Policy Change in Higher Education.* London: Jessica Kingsley.

Hier, S. P. and Greenberg, J. (eds) (2007) *The Surveillance Studies Reader.* Maidenhead: McGraw-Hill/Open University Press.

Horton, R. and Finnegan, R. (eds) (1973) *Modes of Thought: Essays on Thinking in Western and Non-Western Societies.* London: Faber &Faber.

Irigaray, L. (1999) *The Forgetting of Air in Martin Heidegger.* Austin, TX: University of Texas.

Irwin, A. and Michael, M. (2003) *Science, Social Theory and Public Knowledge.* Maidenhead: McGraw-Hill/Open University Press.

Jacob, M. (2000) 'Imagining the Future University', in M. Jacob and T. Hellstrom (eds) *The Future of Knowledge Production in the Academy.* Buckingham: Open University Press/SRHE.

Jacob, M. (2009) 'On Commodification and the Governance of Academic Research', *Minerva*, 47: 391–405.

Jacoby, R. (2005) *Picture Imperfect: Utopian Thought for an Anti-Utopian Age.* New York: Columbia University Press.

Jarvis, P. (1992) *Paradoxes of Learning: On Becoming an Individual in Society.* San Francisco: Jossey-Bass.

Jarvis, P. (2001) *Corporate Universities*. London: Kogan Page.

Jaspers, K. ([1959]1965)   *The Idea of the University*. London: Peter Owen.

Kamenou, A. (2008) 'Universities and Culture', PhD thesis, Institute of Education, London.

Kant, I. (1992) *The Conflict of the Faculties*. Lincoln, NB: University of Nebraska Press.

Kateb, G. (ed.) ([1971]2008)   *Utopia: The Potential and Prospect of the Human Condition*. New Brunswick, NJ: Aldine Transaction.

Ker, I. (1999) 'Newman's *Idea of a University*: A Guide for the Contemporary University?, in D. Smith and A. K. Langslow (eds), *The Idea of a University*. London: Jessica Kingsley

Kerr, C. ([1963]1995)   *The Uses of the University*, 4th edn. Cambridge, MA: Harvard University Press.

Kincheloe, J. L. and Tobin, K. (2009) 'The Much Exaggerated Death of Positivism', *Critical Studies of Science Education*, 4: 513–528.

King, R. (ed.) (2004) *The University in the Global Age*. Basingstoke: Palgrave Macmillan.

Kreber, C. (ed.) (2009) *The University and Its Disciplines: Teaching and Learning Within and Beyond Disciplinary Boundaries*. New York: Routledge.

Kress, G. and Leeuwen, T. V. (2001) *Multimodal Discourse*. London: Arnold.

Kroeber, K. (2000) 'American Universities: A Personal View', *boundary 2*, 27(1): 135–149.

Kuhn, T. (1970) *The Structure of Scientific Revolutions*. Chicago: University of Chicago Press.

Lea, J. (2009) *Political Correctness and Higher Education*. New York: Routledge.

Leach, E. (1968) *A Runaway World*. London: BBC.

Leach, J. (ed.) (1998) *Sites of Knowledge Production: The University*. Special issue of *Social Epistemology*, 12 (1) January–March.

Leavis, F. R. ([1943]1979)   *Education and the University*. Cambridge: Cambridge University Press.

Leavis, F. R. (1969) *English in Our Time and the University*. London: Chatto and Windus.

Lefebvre, H. (1991) *The Production of Space*. Oxford: Blackwell.

Levinas, E. ([1961]1969)   *Totality and Infinity: An Essay on Exteriority*. Pittsburgh, PA: Duquesne University Press.

Levy, D. M. (2007) 'No Time to Think: Reflections on Information Technology and Contemplative Scholarship', *Ethics and Information Technology*, 9: 237–249.

Lexchin, J., Bero, L. A., Djulbegovic, B., and Clark, O. (2003) 'Pharmaceutical Industry Sponsorship and Research Outcome and Quality: Systematic Review', *British Medical Journal*, 326: 1167–1170.

Lipset, S. M. (1993) 'The Sources of Political Correctness on American Campuses', in H. Dickman (ed.), *The Imperilled Academy*. New Brunswick, NJ: Transaction.

Lock, G. and Lorenz, C. (2007) 'Revisiting the University Front', *Studies in Philosophy and Education*, 26(5): 405–418.

Locke, W. (2010) 'The Academic Life: Small Worlds, Different Worlds', *London Review of Education*, 8(3) *in press*.

Løvlie, L., Mortenson, K. P. and Nordenbo, S. E. (eds) (2003) *Educating Humanity: Bildung in Postmodernity*. Oxford: Blackwell.

Lukasiewicz, J. (1994) *The Ignorance Explosion*. Ottawa: Carleton University Press.

Lyotard, J.-F. ([1979] 1987)   *The Postmodern Condition: A Report on Knowledge*. Manchester: Manchester University Press.

Macfarlane, B. (2004) *Teaching with Integrity: The Ethics of Higher Education Practice*. London: RoutledgeFalmer.

Macfarlane, B. (2009) *Researching with Integrity: The Ethics of Academic Enquiry*. New York: Routledge.

MacIntyre, A. (1971) *Against the Self-Images of the Age*. London: Duckworth.

MacIntyre, A. (1985) *After Virtue: A Study in Moral Theory*. London: Duckworth.

MacIntyre, A. (1990) *Three Rival Versions of Moral Inquiry*. London: Duckworth.

Malatesta, E. ([1891]2001) *Anarchy*. London: Freedom.

Malitza, M. (1997) 'Higher Education for the Twenty-First Century', *Higher Education in Europe*, **N**(1): 59–65.

Marginson, S. (ed.) (2007) *Prospects of Higher Education: Globalization, Market Competition, Public Goods and the Future of the University*. Rotterdam: Sense Publishers.

Marginson, S. and Considine, M. (2000) *The Enterprise University: Power, Governance and Reinvention in Australia*. Cambridge: Cambridge University Press.

Maringe, F. and Gibbs, P. (2009) *Marketing Higher Education: Theory and Practice*. Maidenhead: McGraw-Hill/Open University Press.

Marks, A. (2005) 'Changing Spatial and Synchronous Structures in the History and Culture of Learning', *Higher Education*, 50: 613–630.

Maxwell, N. (1984) *From Knowledge to Wisdom: A Revolution in the Aims and Methods of Science*. Oxford: Blackwell.

Maxwell, N. (2008) 'From Knowledge to Wisdom: The Need for an Academic Revolution', in R. Barnett and N. Maxwell (eds) *Wisdom in the University*. London: Routledge.

McCarthy, E. D. (1996) *Knowledge as Culture*. London: Routledge.

McLaughlin, T. (2005) 'The Educative Importance of Ethos', *British Journal of Educational Studies*, 53(3): 300–325.

Meek, V. L., Teichler, U. and Kearney, M.-L. (eds) (2009) *Higher Education, Research and Innovation: Changing Dynamics*. Kassel: International Centre for Higher Education Research.

Meyer, J. H. F. and Land, R. (2005) 'Threshold Concepts and Troublesome Knowledge: Epistemological Considerations and a Conceptual Framework for Teaching and Learning', *Higher Education*, 49: 373–388.

Middlehurst, R. (1993) *Leading Academics*. Buckingham: Open University Press.

Midgley, M. (1989) *Wisdom, Information and Wonder*. London: Routledge.

Minogue, K. (1973) *The Concept of a University*. London: Weidenfeld & Nicolson.

Mintz, A. (2009) 'Has Therapy Intruded into Education?, review article, *Journal of Philosophy of Education*, 43(4): 633–647.

More, T. ([1516]2003) *Utopia*. London: Penguin.

Morgan, J. (2010) 'Audit Overload', *Times Higher Education*, 1: 937, 4–10 March.

Morris, H. (2003) 'Changing Communities at Work in Academia', *Work, Employment and Society*, 17(3): 557–568.

Murphy, P. (2009) 'Defining Knowledge Capitalism', in M. Peters, S. Marginson and P. Murphy, *Creativity and the Global Knowledge Economy*. New York: Peter Lang.

Naidoo, R. (2003) 'Repositioning Higher Education as a Global Commodity: Opportunities and Challenges for Future Sociology of Education Work', *British Journal of Sociology of Education*, 24(2): 249–259.

Neave, G. (1988) 'The Evaluative State', *European Journal of Education*, 33(1): 265–284.

Newman, J. H. (1976) *The Idea of a University*, ed. I. T. Ker. Oxford: Oxford University Press.

Nietzsche, F. ([1889]2003) *Twilight of the Idols*. London: Penguin.

Nisbet, R. (1971) *The Degradation of the Academic Dogma: The University in America, 1945–1970*. London: Heinemann.

Nixon, J. (2008) *Towards the Virtuous University: The Moral Bases of Academic Practice*. London: Routledge.

Nowotny, H. (1996) *Time: The Modern and the Postmodern Experience*. Cambridge: Polity.

Nowotny, H., Scott, P. and Gibbons, M. (2001) *Re-Thinking Science: Knowledge and the Public in an Age of Uncertainty*. Cambridge: Polity.

Oakeshott, M. (1989) *The Voice of Liberal Learning*, ed. Timothy Fuller. New Haven, CT: Yale University Press.

Olssen, M. and Peters, M. A. (2005) 'Neoliberalism, Higher Education and the Knowledge Economy: From the Free Market to Knowledge Capitalism', *Journal of Educational Policy*, 20(3): 313–345.

Ortega y Gassett, J. (1946) *Mission of the University*. London: Kegan Paul, Trench, Trubner.

Peacocke, A. (ed.) (1985) *Reductionism in Academic Disciplines*. Guildford: SRHE and NFER-Nelson.

Pelikan, J. (1992) *The Idea of the University: A Reexamination*. New Haven, CT: Yale University.

Peters, M. A. (2003) 'Education Policy in the Age of Knowledge Capitalism', *Policy Futures in Education*, 1(2): 361–380.

Peters, M. A. (2007) 'Opening the Book: (From the Closed to the Open Text)', *The International Journal of the Book*, 5(1): 77–84.

Peters, M. A. (2009) 'Derrida, Nietzsche, and the Return of the Subject' and 'The University and the Future of the Humanities', in M. A. Peters and G. Biesta, *Derrida, Deconstruction, and the Politics of Pedagogy*. New York: Peter Lang.

Peters, M. A. and Biesta, G. (2009) *Derrida, Deconstruction, and the Politics of Pedagogy*. New York: Peter Lang.

Peters, M. A., Marginson, S. and Murphy, P. (2009) *Creativity and the Global Knowledge Economy*. New York: Peter Lang.

Philipps Griffiths, A. (1965) 'A Deduction of Universities', in R. A. Archambault (ed.), *Philosophical Analysis and Education*. London: Routledge &Kegan Paul.

Piaget, J. (1972) *Psychology and Epistemology: Towards a Theory of Knowledge*. Harmondsworth: Penguin.

Plumwood, V. (2002) *Environmental Culture: The Ecological Crisis of Reason*. London: Routledge.

Popper, K. (1975) *Objective Knowledge: An Evolutionary Approach*. Oxford: Oxford University Press.

Rand, R. (ed.) (1992) *Logomachia: The Conflict of the Faculties*. Lincoln, NB: University of Nebraska Press.

Rapp, C. (1998) *Fleeing the Universal: The Critique of Post-Rational Criticism*. Albany, NY: State University of New York Press.

Read, M. E. (2010) 'Reconfiguring Academic Identities: The Experience of Business Facing Academics in a UK University', EdD thesis, Hatfield, University of Hertfordshire.

Readings, B. (1996) *The University in Ruins*. Cambridge, MA: Harvard University Press.

Reid, I. (1996) *Higher Education or Education for Hire: Language and Values in Australian Universities*. Rockhampton, Queensland: Central Queensland University.

Richardson, K. (2005) 'The Hegemony of the Physical Sciences: An Exploration in Complexity thinking', *Futures*, 37: 615–653.

Ricoeur, P. (1984]1990) *Time and Narrative*, vol. 1. Chicago: University of Chicago Press.

Rieff, P. (1966]1987) *The Triumph of the Therapeutic: Uses of Faith after Freud*. Chicago: University of Chicago Press.

Robbins, J. (2008) 'Towards a Theory of the University: Mapping the American Research University in Space and Time', *American Journal of Education*, 114(February): 243–272.

Robertson, S. (2009) 'Metaphoric Imaginings?'Re-/Visions on the Idea of a University', in UCSIA, *Rethinking the University after Bologna: New Concepts and Practices beyond Tradition and the Market*. Antwerp: UCSIA.

Robins, K. and Webster, F. (eds) (2002) *The Virtual University? Knowledge, Markets, and Management*. Oxford: Oxford University Press.

Robinson, S .and Katulushi, C. (eds) (2005) *Values in Higher Education*. Glamorgan: Aureus/ University of Leeds.

Rogers, B. (ed.) (2004) *Is Nothing Sacred?* London: Routledge.

Rorty, R. (1980) *Philosophy and the Mirror of Nature*. Oxford: Blackwell.

Rorty, R. (1989) *Contingency, Irony and Solidarity*. Cambridge: Cambridge University Press.

Rorty, R. (1999) *Philosophy and Social Hope*. London: Penguin.

Roszak, T. (1992]2001) *The Voice of the Earth: An Exploration of Ecopsychology*. Grand Rapids, MI: Phanes Press.

Roth, K. and Gur-Ze'ev, I. (eds) (2007) *Education in the Era of Globalization*. Dordrecht: Springer.

Rothblatt, S. (1997) *The Modern University and its Discontents: The Fate of Newman's Legacies in Britain and America*. Cambridge: Cambridge University Press.

Rothblatt, S. (2003) *The University of Utopia*. The Hans Rausing Lecture, 2002. Salvia Smaskrifta, no. 2. Uppsala: Tryck Wikstroms.

Rothblatt, S. and Wittrock, B. (1993a) 'Introduction: Universities and Higher Education', in S. Rothblatt and B. Wittrock (eds) *The European and American University since 1800*. Cambridge: Cambridge University Press.

Rothblatt, S. and Wittrock, B. (eds) (1993b) *The European and American University since 1800*. Cambridge: Cambridge University Press.

Rouse, J. (1987]1994) *Knowledge and Power: Towards a Political Philosophy of Science*. Ithaca, NY: Cornell University Press.

Rowland, S. (2006) *The Enquiring University: Compliance and Contestation in Higher Education*. Maidenhead: McGraw-Hill/Open University Press.

Sarles, H. (2001) 'A Vision: The Idea of a University in the Present Age', *Organization*. 8(2): 407–419.

Sartre, J.-P. (1940]2004a) *The Imaginary*. London: Routledge.

Sartre, J.-P. (1943]2003) *Being and Nothingness*. London: Routledge.

Sartre, J.-P. (1960]2004b) *Critique of Dialectical Reason*, vol. 1. London: Verso.

Satterthwaite, J., Piper, H., and Sikes, P. (eds) (2009) *Power in the Academy*. Stoke-on-Trent: Trentham.

Savin-Baden, M. (2008) *Learning Spaces: Creating Opportunities for Knowledge Creation in Academic Life*. Maidenhead: McGraw-Hill/Open University Press.

Schö, D. (1983) *The Reflective Practitioner: How Professionals Think in Action*. New York: Basic Books.

Scott, J. (2006) 'The Mission of the University: Medieval to Postmodern Transformations', *The Journal of Higher Education*, 77(1): 1–39.

Scott, P. (1990) *Knowledge and Nation*. Edinburgh: University of Edinburgh Press.

Scott, P. (1997) 'The Changing Role of the University in the Production of New Knowledge', *Tertiary Education and Management*, 3(1): 5–14.

Scott, P. (ed.) (1998) *The Globalization of Higher Education*. Buckingham: Open University Press.

Scott, P. (2005) 'Universities and the Knowledge Economy', *Minerva*, 43: 297–309.

Scott, P. (2009) 'Markets and New Modes of Knowledge Production', in J. Enders and E. D. Weert (eds), *The Changing Face of Academic Life: Analytical and Comparative Perspectives*. Basingstoke: Palgrave Macmillan.

Searle, J. R. (1994) 'Rationality and Realism, What Is at Stake?, in J. R. Cole, E. G. Barber and S. R. Graubard (eds), *The Research University in a Time of Discontent*. Baltimore, MD: Johns Hopkins University Press.

Shattock, M. (ed.) (2009) *Entrepreneurialism in Universities and the Knowledge Economy: Diversification and Organizational Change in European Higher Education*. Maidenhead: McGraw-Hill/Open University Press.

Slaughter, S. and Leslie, L. L. (1997) *Academic Capitalism: Politics, Policies and the Entrepreneurial University*. Baltimore, MD: Johns Hopkins University Press.

Small, H. (ed.) (2002) *The Public Intellectual*. Oxford: Blackwell.

Smith, A. and Webster, F. (eds) (1997) *The Postmodern University? Contested Visions of Higher Education in Society*. Buckingham: Open University Press.

Smith, D. and Langslow, A. K. (eds) (1999) *The Idea of a University*. London: Jessica Kingsley.

Standaert, N. (2009) 'Towards a Networked University' and 'Pyramid, Pillar and Web: Questions for Academic Life Raised by the Network Society', in UCSIA, *Rethinking the University after Bologna: New Concepts and Practices beyond Tradition and the Market*. Antwerp: UCSIA.

Standish, P. (1999) 'Centre without Substance: Cultural Capital and *The University in Ruins*'. Special issue on globalisation. *Jahrbuch für Erziehung und Wissenschaft*, 83–104.

Standish, P. (2005) 'Towards an Economy of Higher Education', *Critical Quarterly*, 47(1–2): 53–71.

Stehr, N. (1994) *Knowledge Societies*. London: Sage.

Stehr, N. (2001) *The Fragility of Modern Societies: Knowledge and Risk in the Information Age*. London: Sage.

Strathern, M. (2004) *Commons and Borderlands: Working Papers on Interdisciplinarity, Accountability and the Flow of Knowledge*. Wantage: Sean Kingston.

Suissa, J. (2006) *Anarchism and Education: A Philosophical Perspective*. New York: Routledge.

Tanner, M. ([1987] 2000) *Nietzsche: A Very Short Introduction*. Oxford: Oxford University Press.

Taylor, C. (1969) 'Neutrality in Political Science', in P. Laslett and W. G. Runciman (eds), *Philosophy, Politics and Society*, 3rd series. Oxford: Blackwell.

Taylor, C. (1991) *The Ethics of Authenticity*. Cambridge, MA: Harvard University Press.

Taylor, C. (2004) *Modern Social Imaginaries*. Durham, NC: Public Planet Books, Duke University.

Taylor, C. (2007) 'On Social Imaginaries', in P. Gratton and J. Panteleimon Manoussakis (eds), *Traversing the Imaginary: Richard Kearney and the Postmodern Challenge*. Evanston, IL: Northwestern University.

Thorne, M. (ed.) (1999) *Universities in the Future*. London: Department of Trade and Industry.

Trifonas, P. P. (2004) 'The Ethics of Science and/as Research: Deconstruction and the Orientations of a New Academic Responsibility', in P. P. Trifonas and M. A. Peters (eds), *Derrida, Deconstruction and Education*. Malden, MA: Blackwell.

Trifonas, P. P .and Peters, M. A. (eds) (2004) *Derrida, Deconstruction and Education*. Malden, MA: Blackwell.

Trilling, L. ([1963] 1967) *Beyond Culture: Essays on Literature and Learning*. Harmondsworth: Penguin.

Trowler, P. (2008) *Cultures and Change in Higher Education*. Basingstoke: Palgrave.

UCSIA (2009) *Rethinking the University after Bologna: New Concepts and Practices beyond Tradition and the Market*. Antwerp: UCSIA.

Unwin, N. (2007) *Aiming at Truth*. Basingstoke: Palgrave.

Urry, J. (2003) *Global Complexity*. Cambridge: Polity.

Vernon, M. (2008) *Wellbeing*. Stocksfield: Acumen.

Virilio, P. (1991) *Lost Dimension*. Brooklyn: Semiotext(e).

Virilio, P. (2005) *Negative Horizon*. London: Continuum.

Virilio. P. (2010) *The University of Disaster*. Cambridge: Polity.

Waghid, Y. (2008) 'The Public Role of the University Reconsidered', *Perspectives in Education*, 26(1): 19–23.

Walker, R. B. J. (2010) *After the Globe, Before the World*. London: Routledge.

Watson, D. (2007a) 'Does Higher Education Need a Hippocratic Oath?', *Higher Education Quarterly*, 61(3): 362–374.

Watson, D. (2007b) *Managing Civic and Community Engagement*. Maidenhead: McGraw-Hill/Open University Press.

Watson, D. (2008) *Who Owns the University?* QA briefing paper. Gloucester: QA.

Watson, D. (2009) *The Question of Morale: Managing Happiness and Unhappiness in University Life*. Maidenhead: McGraw-Hill/Open University Press.

Watson, D. and Maddison, E. (2005) *Managing Institutional Self Study*. Maidenhead: McGraw-Hill/Open University Press.

Watson, D., Stroud, S. and Hollister, R. (in press 2010) *The Engaged University: An International Comparative Study*. London: Routledge.

Weber, S. (1999) 'The Future Campus: Destiny in a Virtual World', *Journal of Higher Education Policy and Management*, 21(2): 151–164.

Whitchurch, C. (2008) 'Shifting Identities and Blurring Boundaries: The Emergence of Third Space Professionals in UK Higher Education', *Higher Education Quarterly*, 62(4): 377–396.

Wildman, P. (1999) 'From the Monophonic University to Polyphonic Multiversities', in M. Thorne (ed.), *Universities in the Future*. London: Department of Trade and Industry.

Williams, B. (2002) *Truth and Truthfulness*. Princeton, NJ: Princeton University Press.

Williams, B. (1985|2008) *Ethics and the Limits of Philosophy*. London: Routledge.

Williams, Raymond (1989) *Resources of Hope: Culture, Democracy, Socialism*. London: Verso.

Williams, Rowan (2004a) *Silence and Honey Cakes: The Wisdom of the Desert*. Oxford: Lion Hudson.

Williams, Rowan (1979|2004b) *The Wound of Knowledge*. London: Darton, Longman &Todd.

Wittgenstein, L. (2009) *Philosophical Investigations*. Oxford: Blackwell.

Wittrock, B. (1993) 'The Modern University: The Three Transformations', in S. Rothblatt and B. Wittrock (eds), *The European and American University Since 1800*. Cambridge: Cambridge University Press.

Woolgar, S. (ed.) (2002) *Technology, Cyberbole, Reality*. Oxford: Oxford University Press.

Wortham, S. M. (1999) *Rethinking the University: Leverage and Deconstruction*. Manchester: Manchester University Press.

Wortham, S. M. (2006) *Counter-Institutions: Jacques Derrida and the Question of the University*. New York: Fordham University.

Wyatt, J. (1990) *Commitment to Higher Education*. Buckingham: Open University Press.

Young, R. (1992) 'The Idea of a Chrestomathic University', in R. Rand (ed.), *Logomachia: The Conflict of the Faculties*. Lincoln, NB: University of Nebraska Press.

Žižek, S. (2001) *The Fragile Absolute – Or Why Is the Christian Legacy Worth Fighting For?* London: Verso.

Žižek, S (2003) *The Puppet and the Dwarf: The Perverse Core of Christianity*. Cambridge, MA: MIT.

Žižek, S (2008) *In Defense of Lost Causes*. London: Verso.

Žižek, S (2009a) *First as Tragedy, Then as Farce*. London: Verso.

Žižek, S (2009b) 'In 1968, Structures Walked the Street – Will They Do it Again?', in J. Satterthwaite, H. Piper and P. Sikes (eds), *Power in the Academy*. Stoke-on-Trent: Trentham.

Zollman, K. J. S. (2010) 'The Epistemic Benefit of Transient Diversity', *Erkenntnis*, 72(1): 17–35.

Reports

BIS (2009) *Higher Ambitions: The Future of Universities in a Knowledge Economy*. London: Department for Business Innovation and Skills.

Europaeum (2009) *The Future of European Universities*. Oxford: The Europaeum.

NEF (2008) *University Challenge: Towards a Well-being Approach to Quality in Higher Education*. London: New Economics Foundation.

Websites

http://www.tsrc.ac.uk – Britain in 2010–2020.

http://www.ulsf.org/programstalloires.html – the Talloires international network of universities.

Subject index

NB:

1 *This index picks out just the main appearances of central terms (such as authenticity, being, knowledge, mystery, research, space, teaching, time, university, utopia, and values).*
2 *Main references are emboldened.*
3 *Page numbers referring to the Notes are italicised.*
4 *Quotation marks are placed around entries that are either concepts particularly associated with other scholars or are concepts that are critiqued here or are concepts created for this occasion.*

Name index